Alex Kemp was born in London and worked in the Houses of Parliament and as a journalist before becoming a teacher of English as a foreign language. He first went to Greece in 2013. It is now very much his home.

HERE IS GREECE

Alex Kemp

Copyright © 2020 Alex Kemp

All rights reserved. No part of this publication may be reproduced, distributed, or transmitted in any form or by any means, including photocopying, recording, or other electronic or mechanical methods, without the prior written permission of the publisher, except in the case of brief quotations embodied in critical reviews and certain other noncommercial uses permitted by copyright law.

Names, characters, businesses, places, events and incidents in this book are either the products of the author's imagination or used in a fictitious manner. Any resemblance to actual persons, living or dead, other than those clearly in the public domain, and actual events is purely coincidental.

Cover art: David Harrison

Photography: Regina Saltari

Στη Ρεγγίνα

Contents

Chapter 1. My Family and Other Hellenes — 9
Chapter 2. On The Greek Election Trail — 24
Chapter 3. Corfu Quartet — 39
    i.   Paradise Found? — 40
    ii. Lessons in Greek — 53
    iii. Karagiozis and the Musical Island — 62
    iv. Paradise Forgone! — 72
Chapter 4. Travels in Northern Greece — 93
    i.   Epirus — 94
    ii. Western Macedonia — 105
    iii. Central Macedonia — 118
    iv. North By Northwest Greece — 129
Chapter 5. Thrace — 139
Chapter 6. Athens — 165
Chapter 7. Crete — 192
Chapter 8. Travels in Southern Greece — 227
    i.   Under The Ditch — 228
    ii. In Arcadia — 238
    iii. Messenia, Mani & Maleas — 249
Chapter 9. Belogiannis and the Greek Village — 262
Chapter 10. Here is Greece — 273

Chapter 1
My Family and Other Hellenes

I had never really thought of Greece before. If I had been asked to close my eyes and picture the country, I suppose blue skies and seas and a blazing sun would have come to mind. Package-holiday makers roasting like greased pigs on the beach; moussaka and Heineken bottles shimmering somewhere on a plastic table like a grim mirage. Nothing deeper than that really. All this changed though, quite suddenly and irrevocably, when I met an unhappy-looking beautiful Greek girl who had come all the way to teach in an old boarding school in the English countryside for the summer. Within a year I was heaving my way with her to the top of Mount Olympus, a ring in my pocket, and Greece, the real Greece – its people, its places, its spirit – indelibly fixed in my mind.

My introduction began in Athens. I crept into the city in the dead of night. The only souls to be seen were the comic Evzone guards in their tasselled hats, pleated skirts and pompommed slippers, changing the guard in front of the parliament building at 4am. A pantomimic routine of slow-motioned raising of the legs, a twirl of the feet, a hoist of the rifle, a slap of the arms. I was in that drugged-like state from the travel, and with the thick blanket of heat that was wrapped around me even this early in the morning, I felt I was viewing Greece as if from the centre of a dream. I dropped my bags, stood and watched for a while. Just me and the two white-stocking-ed guards, their slippers slapping and squeaking on the marble stones in the centre of Greece's capital.

Next day I woke to find a completely different city. The late-morning heat mixing with the city noise and traffic. The skips were piled up with rubbish, carrier bags of used toilet paper thrown on top – no flushing of paper down the drains in Greece – marinating in the hot sun. A cat working on one to tear it clean open. My skin was prickled and stung by the bright sun, flaming down through the dark-edged streets.

I was staying in the area of Exarchia, a world away from the taverna scenes of moustachioed men I had previously pictured. Exarchia is the area of anarchy. Every wall graffitied over, and then graffitied over again. Everyone clothed in black. Arguments ringing out from the cafés as people drank their bitter Greek coffees, heads thrown backwards, jaws pushed forwards, smacked "tut"s coming through puckered lips to emphasise disagreement with their companion's views. Hands going round and round in the air in small contemptuous windmill movements.

We met a friend of the Greek I'd fallen in love with and had come all this way to Greece for. She was a sweet funny girl who, a year on, would become one of our *'koubaras'* – bridesmaid in Greek, but meaning so much more than that here: once you're koubara-ed, it's a life-long relationship, a mafia pact. We sat and talked for hours, over just the one coffee on the table, not being rushed or moved on by the waiters. When the friend finally got up to go to her job teaching in an under-5s playgroup, almost as an after-thought she turned to say.

"Oh. I forgot… I'm to go on trial next month. For making Molotov cocktails, upstairs in our anarchist coffee bar."

She bunched her shoulders and held up her hands, tilting her head and smiling as if to say what a silly triviality it all was. This small demure girl in her flowery dress skipped away down the street, and I was left the bewildered Englishman. *San tin miga mes sto gala*, as they say – the fly in the milk. Over all the years I would live in Greece, I would often find myself left like this. Lost and bemused. I'd try to be polite and express some mild surprise and mutter something bland like "Oh, how strange... things like that don't really happen in Britain you know," as some misdeed took place in front of me. The response would always be the same: a shrug of the shoulders, a droop of the mouth, a snort through the nose. "Well... *Here is Greece.*"

While I was caught by the level of political interest and the debates that seemed to go on, just as they did 2000 years ago high on the hill of Pnyka still hanging over the city today, the roots of this modern day dissatisfaction were pretty clear. High unemployment, habitual accusations of corruption, failing services, and always the sight of large numbers of policemen gathering together, lounging on motorbikes, insouciantly eyeing the public with a sort of slumbering menace. The tension could be felt everywhere. As I climbed the Acropolis, on the unavoidable tourist trail, winding my way up the path to the Parthenon with the famous pediments and columns above looking the colour of smoker's old brown teeth, I noted how at every turn a policeman appeared to be looming over or aggressively moving on shrinking figures. Men who appeared to be doing no harm, as far as I could see.

The strain on the city was clear. As we later skirted round the large Omonoia Square – Unity Square – now stripped of its centre-piece monuments, looking run-down and bare, just a hang-out for depressed migrants and slinking drug dealers, I passed neighbouring streets where poverty was clearly visible. Well-dressed men and women rifling deep in litter bins. Distress flowing out into the streets. The flags of the Golden Dawn far right-wing political party flowing above.

The atmosphere felt clearer in many ways as I was taken out of the city, past the gnarled olive trees that line Greek roads like lampposts back home, and down towards that wonder of the *modern* world, the Corinth Canal. Slow fat ships squeezed through the eye-of-a-needle channel, leaving a rip of white behind them, as we passed over into the Peloponnese and down the long route to my future family's home. The journey hugged the blue Ionian Sea to our right. And it really *was* blue. I was told the Greeks even have a word just for the blue of their seas and skies: *galano*. Mountains rose up on our left, parched high ground, and a donkey travelled impassively for hours in front on the back of a heroically unroadworthy, falling-apart, pick-up truck. Nose in the air, ears flying in the wind. Our car bounced along the road on the potholes behind, like a boat out on a rough sea.

The journey was long and I arrived tired and apprehensive at the family home. The house was shaded and cool and decorated in stone and dark wood against the white light of the Greek sun outside, as many Greek homes seemed to be. The parents, loud and chaotic, clasped me warmly with hugs and kisses, and I had little time to consider any nerves at the first meeting as, within the first five minutes, they were removing their clothes, bundling me into a car, and taking me out to the beach. I found myself half-naked, wimpily frolicking in the surf with the prospective in-laws on our very first evening together, as the sun set into the sea with an explosion of reds and blues and pinks and greens. But this seemed right and completely in keeping with what I'd felt so far in the country. Greek life appeared to be a life with its clothes off. A life unencumbered. Life with the doors and windows left hanging wide open.

We drove back for a dinner of rabbit, caught by the father, Thanasis. Gruff, bald as a shiny dark pebble, Thanasis had hardly a word of English.

"*Troye!*" – eat! – he commanded, flinging his open hand out to the table.

The murmur of simmering food came from vast iron pans in the background, a piece of feta the size of a house brick was placed on the side of my plate. I asked for an ouzo with my dinner, but the shake of the head with closed eyes and the bottom lip bitten as if in pain showed I'd made an error.

"*Tsipouro*," I was told. "This is what you should drink. Ouzo is for old people and tourists..."

"*Ochi, ochi!*" – No, no! – said another "*Raki*. We drink raki in the south. Tsipouro in the north."

So a glug of raki was handed to me and my back thumped as my grinning host nodded at me to drain my glass. It was strong, it took my breath and my eyes bulged as I swallowed it down, but I couldn't really tell what elevated it above all other drinks. But everyone seemed to hold very strong views on these sorts of subjects. Even water appeared to have some reverential aspect for the Greeks. Because of the heat? The salted food? Whatever the reason, I noted the Greeks seemed to cherish their water. Old men savour and smack their lips in the cafés over the glass served up with every meal and every coffee. Everyone is a connoisseur of water, able to talk at length on the qualities of the local *nero*. Closing eyes and appreciating all the flavours they can detect. Directing visitors to the best places on their island to find water and anxiously asking if the water is good when visiting somewhere new. I would see them every day, sat on old chairs outside the cafés in the sun, raising their glasses up to the sky with the angled light congregating, as if offering some sort of benediction.

I was once sent out in the late afternoon with orders to get bread. I found the baker had left warm fresh bread on the sill of his dilapidated shop for those stupid enough to be up and still wandering around town. A hand written card had been left next to the bread on the window: leave whatever coins you want. The *ora kinis isihias* – the 'time of common quietness' – had fallen. Work stops, shutters are closed on the windows, the background din of Greece dies away, the towns fall into one huge siesta. Greeks can get very intense about this quiet time. For a country which likes to give the impression that everyone is free, and also quite at liberty to make as much noise as possible, it is a surprise to find that if you have your radio sometime between 3pm and 5pm you could find the neighbours have called the police on you. It is understandable though. The Greek afternoon sleep is truly one of the greatest experiences you can have in life: falling deep under the dark surface of consciousness as the intense white glare outside gets too much, waking later to find that, while you were out of it, the afternoon has rearranged itself into a pattern of rich deep colours and the heat tamed itself into something more manageable. Life begins again.

Having been force-fed at the family home, I was taken off to another beach by my soon-to-be sister-in-law, who wanted me to meet her boyfriend. We set off for her car, my eyebrows briefly rising at the sight of the family's next door neighbour, a giant elderly priest with huge flowing beard, black robes, *kalimavkion* hat and colossal jewel-studded gold cross round his neck, as he glided silently along the path as if on wheels. "*Skortho*," the superstitious Greeks mutter to themselves when they see a priest out of church, in the street or browsing in the supermarket. Skortho meaning garlic, and garlic being hung everywhere in Greece to ward off the bad spirits.

We met the boyfriend, Dimitris, on a beautiful stretch of sea and sand. This beach is one of the few breeding homes for turtles in Europe and it was Dimitris's job to make sure they hatched and made it to the sea. Greece has resisted too much commercial exploitation of its beaches. Hotels and mega-resorts are quite rare and the coast is protected against privatisation. Despite tourism providing one of the few vital incomes into the country, the beach is a preserved utopia. Miles and miles of beach left for sleeping, for gossiping, for nude bathing, for couples making love – not stopping as I walked past, the apologising Englishman. Except here. A huge bar had been built right on the turtle beach: lights flashing and a disco pumping late into the night, with shrieking guests tumbling and spilling down to the sea. Dimitris, who had been a lone figure patrolling this beach for years, now wore a haggard look as his peaceful life with his slow-moving friends had changed sadly and forever.

'*Ta bania tou laou*' – the swims of The People. It's almost a sacred thing. "We can't have an election in the summer," I heard politicians on TV say. "We couldn't possibly disturb the bania tou laou..."

My Greek and I, however, were to take off in a different direction, away from the sea. A road-trip. Heading *inland*.

First, we took care to make sure we were not setting off on a Tuesday. Tuesdays are considered a day of bad luck in Greece. Constantinople fell to the Ottomans on a Tuesday in 1453, Greeks have been wary of Tuesdays ever since. Then we hit the road.

The route we took sent us past many roadside churches, from the regal and grand to the broken-down and squat. I watched all the elderly drivers coming the other way crossing themselves furiously as they drove past each church, like scratching chimpanzees sat in their seats. The cicadas in the fields were all in full voice. We passed through villages with old men outside cafés sweating freely and happily. The pavements being hosed down and smelling of wet dust and jasmine and citrus all mixed up.

The site of the ancient games at Olympia, where the very ideal of the physical and moral potential of man was first laid out, is now a tacky affair. The tourists crowd out the restaurants and knick-knack shops in the modern town. But the arena of the games still lies beyond, composed and secure. We parked up and ran the ancient track, contemplated the stones and plinths with the blue sky sweeping through the columns. I then stood in the museum, eye-level with Hermes's gloriously sculptured, but unthreateningly proportioned, marble cock and balls. The ancient Greeks made their statues with small penises as big ones were seen as the sign of a fool, more beast than man. The rough satyrs and the scenes of drinking and gluttony were shown on painted vases with images of tremendous erections, but even Zeus amongst the gods was depicted with a small appendage. A small penis meant intellect and control in the ancient world. I thought of this as I idly watched the modern-day sweating hirsute Greek man arguing about something at the door of the museum. "*Se grafo sta arhithia mou!*" – I'm writing you on my balls! – he shouted as he mimed a chopping motion with his two hands down to his shoved-forward crotch at the uninterested lady guard on duty.

We carried on past the port city of Patra and, after crossing the long glistening road bridge, we were back over the Gulf of Corinth once more and onto the northern Greek mainland again, this time heading north. We stopped and consulted the oracles at Delphi. I quietly asked the old hidden Pythia high priestess of ancient lore if I was doing the right thing being here and the plans I had in my mind. No sign came back that I wasn't. No smoke rose from the cracks in the earth. So we carried on through the ancient mythical area of the Roumeli, now known as the states of Sterea Ellada and Thessaly. And it was in Thessaly that we finally arrived at our destination. The home of the immortals.

We stared up from the valley at the immense rising mound of Mount Olympus. Initially the lower reaches of the mountain were an easy stroll in hot thick sunshine, full of woods with birdsong and butterflies and deserted pools where we could swim in the water alongside breast-stroking frogs. The smell of open flowers and thyme and oregano hung in the air. But we climbed higher and the paths got harder and started to rise vertically. Rocky landscape slipping down the slopes beside us.

As we climbed higher, the vegetation thinned out. Paths of clouded rocks, scraggy grass and thin trees clinging to the mountainside with roots like vulturous claws. I started to notice several stone circles had been made along our path. As they became more elaborate, some even accompanied by offerings and small pyres, I asked about their significance and was amused to hear they were shrines made by those climbing this route to give honour to Zeus and the other 11 Gods of this parish. There are Greeks today who still believe and pray to the ancient Olympian gods. People who live their lives by the antediluvian traditions of the old gods and call their religion Dodekatheism or Olympianism. Still believing bearded, vengeful, lusty Zeus is here, hiding himself as a bull, or a swan, or morphing into a ray of sunlight, destining and guiding their lives.

The climb was long. Limbs ached, progress slowed. Light falls fast in Greece. So fast you can even see it. You can time the sun as it falls down the sky, like a drop of orange paint running down a blue wall.

We were in real danger of being stranded here in the high uplands as daylight started to give out. This part of Olympus was the area back in the 1920s that Giagoulas and his infamous gang of bandits hid out while preying on hikers, robbing the rich to give to the poor. So much did they terrorise the country that mothers today still tell miscreant children "Eat your vegetables or Giagoulas will get you..." Well I certainly didn't want him to get *me*, so we strained and sprinted and scrambled our final push to the top: 10 hours, 3,000 metres and 20 degrees Celsius lower from when we had set off from the sun-drenched small town of Litochoro below us.

The wind was hard at the top. Snow lay in patches on the loose rocky ground. The highest peak, Zeus's Throne, was a wall of slate grey in front of us as we stood on a high ledge. It was here, enervated and exhausted, that I fumbled for an engagement ring. I tried to look the valiant romantic hero but, utterly tired, I more resembled an old Grecian statue kicked in the privates as I made my proposal to join this Greek life forever and turn this new Greek family into mine. For reasons best known to herself, this free-spirited girl from this other world agreed and we raced, hugging and grinning, to the refuge for climbers at the mountain's top.

"I've just got engaged!" I announced loudly as we burst through the door, to all the climbers in their climbing gear, eating their *fasolatha* heavy bean soup, lamps strapped on their heads. They turned to look at me, slowly contemplating my words, and went back to their chewing. "*Perastika*," one muttered to his plate – get well soon. Clearly they thought the over-excited Englishman hadn't brought a Greek speaker to the top of Olympus with his odd intention of proposing marriage. But they were wrong. My fiancé of five minutes launched into a heated Greek attack on their rudeness. Shouts and gestures rang from all sides of the room, chairs thrown backwards, hands waved in faces. I started to regret the turn of events racing out of control in front of me, as I saw us not being taken in for the night, left to fend for ourselves outside. But then suddenly bottles of retsina and tsipouro were brought out of a cupboard. Laughter, backs slapped, congratulations given. "*Vion anthosparton*!" – have a life covered with flowers! "Marrying a Greek girl! Are you some sort of crazy man?" the men cackled as we spent the night with this crowd, drinking and toasting under a million stars. The clearest sky I had ever seen in my life, on the very roof of Greece.

Next morning, the cold air, sharp as a blade, cleared the lingering hangovers as we headed down the slopes. Far, far below us the Aegean Sea could be seen, brilliant in the sun, and beyond, Greece's second city, Thessaloniki.

The Avenue Nikis on the front at Thessaloniki, lined with tall buildings of apartments, stretches by the sea along to the White Tower – the emblem of the city, though, of course, not actually white – where Thessalonikians go to be seen, to drink coffee, to watch old Greek tragedies in the new modern theatre. Above the centre of the city, perching on Eptapyrgio Hill – Thessaloniki's own Acropolis, meaning 'seven towers', though, of course, there are actually ten – is Ano Poli, the old town. A different feel in this part of the city. This is the remaining bit of Thessaloniki that survived the Great Fire of 1917 and the later, equally ruinous, council planners' butchery. Traditional architecture, mazy small streets opening into classic old squares.

Old friends of my now newly engaged girl, my *kopela*, had arranged an evening for us to celebrate in an old bar in Papafi Street. Musicians living around the city, they arrived with bouzoukis, baglamas, guitars and violins. Endless glasses of tsipouro were drained. I shared my lamb chops, with one of the bearded friends and fastidious English manners were trounced by typical Greek straightforwardness... "You're not eating this are you?" I gestured to my final piece hoping, expecting, a no, my fork hovering ready to take it. The man didn't even look up, the ambiguity of trivial English politeness passing him by. "Eh? Oh... yes..." The food swallowed in a flash. Sharing food is, of course, the mandatory way of eating in Greece, but this man obviously didn't feel the *dropi* – the shame that Greeks feel of eating the final piece. Often this shame will bring attendant bad luck too, so many times you will see just one lone hunk of meat sat on every plate at the end of the night. However, drink the last drop from the bottle and there is no shame; in fact, you will find *tha se agapai i pethera sou* – your mother-in-law will love you. A rare occurrence in Greece, apparently.

The music started. Rebetiko. Music from the dark hearts of the Greeks. The Greek blues. This is as far away from the cheap plate-smashing music as you can get. Originating around the time of the Population Exchange in the 1920s, in the port areas of Piraeus and Thessaloniki, the centres of huge immigration from Turkey and the

East. The sounds were mixed with Greek, Balkan, Jewish cultures to create this extraordinary outsider music. Coming from the downtown hash cafés, with tales of love, lost love, pain, poverty, intoxication. These were songs from the edges of society.

We stayed late. My final woozy view of Greece before my flight home later that morning was this local tavern, hidden in the back streets of Thessaloniki, filled with smoke and song, the locals plaintively singing the sad but inspiriting numbers from Greece's past.

*

One year later, I was standing outside a barber's shop in a quiet shaded square on the heat-baked island of Samos in my wedding suit. The sun dripping down on me like thick honey. The barber was nowhere to be seen. I was due to be married in the town hall in a little less than an hour. I called out to the stout old lady arranging flowers on her stall in the centre of the square *"Pou ine..."* The word for 'barber' deserted me. I mimed a pair of scissors above my head. The old woman looked vaguely concerned but offered only a shrug, jutted out her chin and then, having shouted something indeterminate, disappeared. I found myself all alone, aside for a sleeping stray dog lying next to me looking stone-dead in a patch of midday sun. I was feeling increasingly uncomfortable and aware of my rumpled state in the rising summer heat. Suddenly, from nowhere a moped appeared, haring fast round the corner with the fat old flower seller on the back, beaming and clutching her arms tight round the young driver, the barber, in front. She had gone to his house and woken him up for me. *"Natos!"* she shouted, pointing happily at him *"Natos o barberis!"*

We had chosen to marry on the island of Samos as this was where a young man – my soon-to-be father-in-law – whilst carrying out part of his compulsory national service in the army, had fallen in love with a girl studying the traditional Greek style of ceramics – my soon-to-be mother-in-law. It was a good choice. Zeus married Hera on this island, with a wedding night that lasted 300 years. Samos is far from the mainland, like a rock flung miles over the Aegean Sea. Turkey is clearly visible off its eastern shore, almost even a swimmable distance away. Life seemed slower here, sweeter, easier. People going about their lives moving at a perpetual summer pace, fat with unspent time. In ancient history,

Samos was considered so richly fertile and blessed that they said that even the birds here produced milk. '*Keh tou pouliou to gala...*' The old proverb now only crops up as a slogan on the gaudy signs of Greece's biggest supermarket chain.

The registrar of marriages in Karlovasi in Samos worked from an office straight out of the 1950s. No computers, papers flapping under old desk fans, desperate to be set free, wedged down tight under paperweights. The old clerk had never faced the problem of a foreigner wanting to marry here on the island before. He scratched his head under his huge picture of Kolokotronis, the Greek general who drove out the Ottoman Empire, and hit on a plan. "We'll make you a Samosian..." he decided and I watched as he set about creating some fabricated documents that somehow showed that I had been born and bred in Samos. The clerk looked inordinately pleased with his schemes.

A few days later and I – now a Samosian, despite having only been on this island for the briefest time – found myself in a large aureate hall, on my new home island, in front of the Mayor of Samos, waiting for my bride. My mother-in-law was standing behind me, spitting lightly on my head. "*Ftou ftou ftou...*" This was for good luck. To keep 'The Eye' away from me. The Eye – To Mati – is the malevolent effect that comes from people staring at you because you're too beautiful, or too clever, or too aggravating, or too annoying. Or maybe just because you're standing like a fool in front of a large wedding crowd of jabbering Greeks, not really having much of a clue what's going on. Symptoms are headaches and fatigue. The prevention is to wear a brightly painted eye around your neck or, as I was now experiencing, to have someone close to you rain down a shower spit. There is also a spell that must be said three times with a glass of water and a glass of oil. After each recital the spell-sayer places a finger in the oil and then lets the drops fall into the water. If the oil disperses, so will your headache. This sorcery was once told to my wife by her grandmother. But this is no good, she can't do it herself, it only works if the spell has been passed down from a woman to a man.

My bride-to-be finally arrived at the town hall. Her father, who must have planned this moment since she was a child in his arms, though probably not with an uncomprehending Englishman involved, still sweetly went through with the long traditional Greek declaration: "*Sou parathitho tin kori mou...*" – I am delivering you my daughter... Even though I could only nod, bovine-dumb, and try and look suitably thoughtful. Friends who had come from England mixed, a little stiffly at first, with the Greek family and friends. One friend of my new Greek family, with a house on Samos, was the daughter of the great historical poet, Giannis Ritsos. Ritsos's poetry is full of politics and identity and struggle, banned at first but now celebrated throughout Greece. His daughter was here keeping the English contingency happy, trying light-hearted conversation – *tipikotites* – that the Greeks believe the Brits are so keen on: chit-chatting about the weather.

"What do you call the English?" I once asked my wife.
"Ugly"
"Yes, ok, we don't have the olive sun-kissed beauty of the Greeks and all that sort of thing, but what's the name for us?"
"*Ugly*. That's it. That's the name for the English. In plural. One *Uglos*, a country of *Ugly*."

As we sat on the boat taking us from the wedding in Samos to the party on the next island along the chain, Ikaria, I looked at my English friends: suits off, shorts on, white legs out. I felt the Greeks had perhaps got it about right.

We were soon disembarking on the wild and weird island of Ikaria, where that famous, shortest, one-manned flight took place. I had vague misgivings about being on the land of Icarus and my just launched marriage, Greeks can be very superstitious. But then, of course, everyone forgets that Icarus also flew. Even if my life here in Greece did start to fail and fall at some point, it would surely only mean the end of what had still been, however briefly, a triumph.

Ikaria has a crazed feel about it. Away from the handsome crescent harbour with its cramped clutter of old buildings, watching with inscrutable faces as the incomers step onto their island, the interior landscape turns red and rocky. The roads beyond are fringed with spiky arrowed plants. The residents all supposedly live well into their hundreds, with their longevity secrets desperately sought out by emulous visitors to the island. Ikarians are winningly odd. Eccentric. Time seems to be of absolutely no concept at all. Not a single Ikarian ever wears a watch, many shops don't open up until well after midnight. The island also regularly bursts with flashes of light as Ikarians like to stand at upper windows of their houses holding mirrors as ferries pass by the coast, tilting them to reflect the sun so as to send their friends on the boat a goodbye message as they sail away.

We had just arrived though, the island still a mystery to be discovered. Giorgos, the brother of one of our two koubaras met us to help take us from the harbourside. Some of us were loaded into cars for the drive on towards the wedding party, the *gledi*, but the English group were nervously piled into the back of Giorgos's beaten-up old van. The convoy made its way through rolling hills with a cacophony of blaring horns, as the 'Ugly' were thrown from side to side in the van as each corner was taken by Giorgos in happily reckless fashion. Every car horn in the procession was repeatedly blasted, and old lady Ikarians leaned from their windows as we passed each tiny stone village to shout and wave handkerchiefs for good luck at the newly-weds. "*Keh kalous apogonous!*" – Have good descendants! Kids ran up behind the cars, slapping at the windows. Men in the fields looked up from their animals for a moment, noted the newly married strangers and raised tools in salute. Ears ringing, disoriented, we arrived at Yaliskari, the location of the wedding party, as a red ball of sun gently flopped down into the sea.

We had chosen to be here on Ikaria as, again, there was a family history associated with this island. It was on Ikaria that my wife's grandfather was exiled after fighting with the communists during the Greek resistance to the German Nazi occupation of the country. Visits to the prison camp by my mother-in-law, whose father had been taken from the family for many years, were for later though. The party got underway. Wine flowed – we were, after all, on the island where Dionysus, the God of drink and bacchanalia was born, and the island which has the most famous *paniyiri* in all the country: festivals where whole villages are out drinking, eating and dancing for nights without end.

There was a band in the taverna where we set up the wedding party playing traditional Ikarian folk music and the Greeks and the English formed a large circle attempting Ikariotikos dancing: arms clamped on shoulders, steps and kicks, swirling up the dust from the taverna's old stone floor. A goat and a pig had been freshly slaughtered just for us, making me feel squeamish and guilty. The long-bearded owner of this stone tavern on the rocks tumbling down to the sea where we were holding the gledi only remembered the animals needed to be dealt with when he heard the pandemonium of car horns and shrieks coming over the hills an hour earlier. By a certain point in the evening, the owner was the drunkest of anyone at the party, genially indicating his support with a smiling, closed-eyed, thumbs-up as the English stepped over him to help themselves to more drinks from his cellar.

My mother-in-law had moulded me a special *Pythagorean* cup for the occasion, and presented it to me during a drinking routine at the gledi, where everyone was made to dance with their drained glass on their head. Invented by Pythagoras of Samos, the cup allows the drinker to fill up with wine only to a certain point. If you try to fill the cup with any more wine, everything pours out of a hole at the bottom. Created to ensure workers 2000 years ago stayed sober, I'm afraid it was all rather too late for me. As the gledi and the dancing and the music continued, and the sun slowly climbed itself out of the sea again and my very first day married into this Greek world began, I took a walk away from the party on my own. I looked out over the water, stupid-faced with a new happiness. I thought of the country I'd joined, rolling away in the sun-bleached land behind me. I thought of the mountains, the ancient cities, the baked roads, the people... And as I stood and stared, part of a poem about Greece by Ritsos that I had once been told came flitting into my mind.

A small bird that flies in the sun
If you look at it once, you will smile
But if you look at it twice or three times... you will start singing

Chapter 2
On The Greek Election Trail

Amongst the mother-in-law jokes so popular in the '70s and '80s, I don't recall many about the wife's mother being the returning parliamentary candidate for the coalition of the radical left in Greece. Nevertheless, this was the situation I now found myself in. Greece was facing a time of extreme political upheaval – and my mother-in-law was at the very centre of it.

The Prime Minister had resigned. His leftist party, Syriza, elected in a surrounding spirit of hope and optimism barely nine months earlier, had called a general election. The resignation came after endless negotiations had failed to avoid what many considered a miserable capitulation to the country's creditors and the request of another bailout from the European Union, forcing a split in Syriza's party. My mother-in-law – my *pethera* – had stood and won as an MP for Syriza in her home town in the county of Ilia down in the Peloponnese in the Greek general election of June 2012. This came as a great surprise to her as much as to anyone else. Now she was seeking re-election, having won more comfortably again in Syriza's sweep to power in January of 2015. But she knew it wouldn't be easy.

Back when her profession was just a simple potter, my mother-in-law had become politicised during the monstrosities of the Greek dictatorship in the early 1970s. Along with many of her generation she had fought against the regime, becoming active in the community and in the feminist unions and then finally, years later, she stood for parliament. Her hometown seat was a mix of urban areas and some of the largest farmlands in the country. It's an area which had been badly affected by the Greek crisis but, as a whole, not in as deep poverty as experienced elsewhere in the country. Since her first tentative steps to stand as an MP back in 1982 though, my mother-in-law, and the country, had seen Greek politics grow to become a much larger and far more dramatic entity.

I was just starting my new life here. But, like everyone, I was preoccupied by this election. Finding out more about Greece, finding my place, would just have to wait until the country had decided on its direction too. Passions were running high and this election was all anyone was talking about. After Greece's catastrophic economic plunge – a crash worse than the Weimar Republics in the '30s and on a par even with the Great Depression – the country was on its back. Unemployment was at 35% in some places. I was introduced to young people, university educated people, who hadn't worked for over five years. 30-year-olds, 40-year-olds who had been forced to move back to their families' small apartments and were having to live off their parents, or their grandparents' pensions, with there being no real unemployment welfare benefits in Greece. Living off the very pensions that the European Union were trying to slash. Begging and homelessness was rife in Athens. Normal life had been altered dramatically. I had seen a wedding reception being held in a disused old petrol station out in the countryside beyond the city. The family told me they had no money to pay for a real venue. People were still determined to try and lead a life as before the crash, but it was hard. I stood and watched as the bride and groom danced together slowly under the yellow lights, next to the broken petrol pumps.

In saving Greece, as they saw it, the EU had insisted on an austerity programme that instead seemed to devastate the Greek economy further. They continued to stick with it, with a crazed fundamental zeal, even when all analysis showed these ideas were doing more harm than good. Riots in the streets ensued. General strikes. A friend of my newly married-into family had been working in a bank on Stadiou Street in Athens when a bomb had been thrown through the window. Anarchist friends of my koubara in Exarchia clashed daily with the police. Protesting pensioners, my father-in-law included, were wrestled to the ground in front of the parliament in Syntagma Square. There were capital controls forced by the EU on the banks and people were unable to get access to their money to buy food or medicines.

The Greek people were desperate for an alternative. Any alternative. They elected the Syriza government and Prime Minister Alexis Tspiras to stand up to the EU, to fight against the imposed pain. It hadn't quite worked out like that. After the failed negotiations, there was real anger and a split in the country. This election was going to be hard fought and polemic, and I was going to accompany my mother-in-law on it.

First, I attended a rally for Tsipras in a large square in the Egaleo district in western Athens. I took my place, wondering how different this election campaign would be from those I was used to back home. There was a large crowd here. It flowed a long way back, past the Byzantine church, over the wide busy roads, stopping traffic trying to get in and out of Athens's centre. In this world of multi-media coverage, the politician making open-air rallying speeches in front of a large massed crowd in a town square seemed a real throwback to a very different age. People came in a receptive mood. The anarchists of Exarchia not to be seen today. Many took the opportunity instead to conduct debates amongst themselves, and more still had brought chairs and elaborate picnics and bottles of ouzo and treated the occasion as a chance to socialise. Politics is, after all, the social glue of the country.

Tsipras talked for over an hour. The crowd seemed appreciative, but one man, a man who had been applauding loudly next to me all evening, told me

"Yes he was impressive today."

He flicked an olive into his mouth, rolled it round with his tongue, thought for a while.

"Ah... he can be impressive *every* day if he likes. But will I vote for him this time? I'm not sure, I'm not sure. I'm still thinking... *Tin ipografi sou keh to pouli sou na prosehis pou ta vazis...*"

It took me a while to work out the saying in my head – your signature and your penis, you have to be careful where you put both. I looked back at the man standing there with his dirty grin. He winked and jutted out his arm, offering me an olive. Spitting his stone high into the thick Athens air.

Down in the Peloponnese, south of the country, it was sweltering, even in the September late evening. I was accompanying my mother-in-law on one of her first campaign outings. A drive of an hour or so, up in the hills high above her home town of Amaliada. We arrived at a small old village and took root in a characterful old *kafeneo* – the local gathering place for older generation Greeks, where coffee and rakis are sunk and debates rumble on between slow games of backgammon. Obligatory hospitality was offered. It was insisted that everyone in our visiting campaign team who had descended unasked on these villagers must have drinks and *mezes*. Then my mother-in-law stood to make a brief speech to the assorted workers, farmers, small shop owners, old women in traditional headscarves, an old priest surrounded by bottles: the odd crowd which had gathered here to listen. There was always at least one Syriza voter in towns like this who would be tasked with rounding up locals from the area, out on the farms, high up with herds on the mountain ridges, to come and listen to the constituency MP.

As the sound of Tsipras addressing the nation on an unwatched tv set floated down from an open window above, my mother-in-law talked to the villagers and, surprisingly, concentrated on Syriza's fraught European endeavours rather than any of her own local successes. Any lingering optimism that the pro-Syriza feelings of January may still exist here soon vanished as the meeting opened out to questions from the crowd.

"You stood there nine months ago and promised us all sorts of things. Syriza has done nothing!"

"Even if you want to help us farmers, you can't. Germany, the Troika, they decide everything. You can do nothing. Nothing! Why do you even pretend?"

The mood appeared angry. Everything said at high volume, with aggressive body language, or so it seemed to my fey British senses anyway. The locals even turned on each other. When one claimed he has lost more than 40,000 euros over the last six years, his friend gave him short shrift.

"Well that's before Syriza then, isn't it? Why do you even talk? *Malaka*..." He threw a *muja* – the open-handed symbol of derision – in his friend's face, dramatically turning his wooden seat away to complete his point.

I saw that Syriza's historic victory at the beginning of 2015 perhaps wasn't a rising of the concerned voice for the underprivileged, those struggling at the bottom. Perhaps it was just a vote just to get rid of the European-organised austerity, which had affected them personally and, now that fight has been frustrated, the feelings had dissolved back into the same old self-serving concerns. Whether I was right or not, I noted the arguments all centred resolutely on Europe and the measures and the memorandums. Any social or local issues failed to get any air time in these old cafés. It felt like a campaign forced into a very narrow, but overheated, area.

The loudest opposing voice came from a man I remembered well from last January, when I flew in from England to visit my mother-in-law on the day of her victory. The man had bought me raki after raki, making toasts, slapping at my face with joy, hugging me vigorously in the main square in Amaliada on the night of the election results, so happy was he with Syriza's victory. Nine months, it appeared, was a very long time in Greek politics.

There were more angry complaints made in the village square on this thick, hot, heavy evening.

"This country is flawed," said the villagers. "Too many cheats…"

"Well, who's best to try and change all that?" my mother-in-law replied. "The old parties of corruption?"

PASOK and New Democracy had squatted on Greece for over 40 years. The country *was* these parties, these parties *were* the country. Since the fall of the dictator, the country had alternated between one of these parties in government. They had done much to modernise Greece, it's true. Greece wasn't a European state when either of these parties were born. PASOK brought in free education and health care. Both parties steered the country to wealthier, more prosperous times. But both did so much to ruinously mismanage the country too. The nepotism flowing through the ruling dynasties of both parties – the Papandreou family in PASOK, the Mitsotakis and Karamanlis families in New Democracy. Premierships just handed down like an inheritance. The bloated state, with civil service jobs created solely to be given out to party faithfuls. The corruption and bribery and pocket lining. Concentration on sweeping away the old corrupt party politics had become Tsipras's mantra in this election, now his battle with Europe had been lost.

Greek elections are *especially* renowned for their corruption: votes often swapped for favours done, jobs given. Candidates told that they will get a vote, or not, depending on what they or their rival will offer. It had been long in the blood of many Greeks, and it seemed almost impossible to change. I learned this to be true myself when I was sent to the corner mini-market.

"Ah, so you're the *gabros* eh? The son-in-law..." the owner of the shop said to me. She tapped at her chin. "You've just reminded me..."

Before I'd even reached home again the shop owner had phoned my mother-in-law to ask for a job for her son. Hinting that the New Democracy rival had already offered her something.

"So you'll do this little thing for me then, yes..?"

Rousfeti – the granting of favours for something in return. *Lathoma* – the nefarious backstairs payment of money in the brown paper bag for special political treatment. The Greeks even have their own specific words for these malpractices.

"*Ksemperdevoume me to palio!*" Syriza now had as their rallying cry – done with the old. It was to be printed on all the leaflets and campaigning materials. Though, in that common Greek dilatory way, the manifestos hadn't been printed or delivered yet, so there was nothing to actually hand out on the campaign trail. And even when they were ready – a few days *after* the vote – there were no pictures of Tsipras, no winning images. This was the Greek Left: collectivism, no individualism.

It felt a little bizarre to be following this political campaign of a party of ex-Trotskyist leftists, here in Greece, outdoors, in the heat with the cicadas and the smell of jasmine in the air. The Syriza lot themselves, though, appeared to me to look down on the Greek Communist Party that exists in the country, the KKE, with their hardline views and militant campaigning skills. I had watched a KKE rally myself on tv and had been struck by the crowds chanting out their slogans in unison. I was also plagued daily outside my window by KKE vans touring the local streets relaying their hard messages through loud speakers with snatches of blasted Soviet-style music. s.

The Communists seemed a little dated and impracticable to me. They have a heroic history in the country, this is true: fighting bravely side-by-side with the British during the Second World War and then being despicably treated by the Allies afterwards, leading to four years of ruinous civil war in the country, but they didn't really fit into today's world. They were unapologetically unreconstructed: opposing gay rights, strident on Greece's on-going naming negotiations with Macedonia. Their mission today, as it seemed to me, just to oppose *anything* put forward by any other party.

There are, of course, two other off-shoot parties of the KKE who passionately hate each other: the Marxist-Leninist KKE and – whatever you do, don't muddle them up – the KKE Marxist-Leninist

However, if Syriza believed themselves as a competent pragmatic Left, the snapshot of feeling here in this typical Peloponnese village where we had started the campaign showed they certainly had their work cut out to convince the people of it this time round.

Quite ridiculously, in this small village, there were three kafeneo all within a few steps from each other. In the past a village would have a kafeneo for those with right wing views and a kafeneo for those left wing views. As my mother-in-law moved between each one to chat to the patrons, sitting and despite the shouted conversations, sharing ashtrays with them, the debates continued in the kafeneo she had just left behind, like secondary explosions.

"Why did they come here? Just to drink our coffee?"

"Well what can she say anyway? Syriza: five months, 50 lies."

"Why don't we vote for – newly formed centrist party – Potami? They haven't had the chance to lie to us yet..."

Like the prosaicism of those able to start an argument in an empty room, these views were all heated and pugnacious, despite each of the men seemingly agreeing with each other. I didn't hear anyone with a kind word for Syriza. And yet, despite all this, as we left the village the campaign team felt it had gone well and were confident that most here would vote Syriza in two weeks' time.

Another campaign day, another long journey into the countryside. This time six of us, including the squashed MP, piled into a small clapped-out car, the undercarriage sagging down deep on its springs. We were to tour a selection of tiny villages, again high in the remote hills.

"This is a good village for us," someone said in the back. "Last time we took five votes here..."

We stopped at a grocery, but the shop owner didn't want to talk. His daughter had, that very day, emigrated to Australia. One of the flood of young people who were leaving Greece. The brain-drain that was another fatal concern for the future of the country. The man seemed very down and, unusually for a Greek, told us, as if confessing an illness, he didn't feel like talking politics today.

"If you lose your parents," he said, "They call you an orphan. What do they call you when you lose your child, eh?"

He moved between each one of us, looking into our faces.

"Eh?... Eh?..." He stopped in front of me. I had no answer.

Expressing the key feeling amongst the people that my mother-in-law somehow had to address, the man told her "Nothing will ever change. It's the system. The system is broken..."

He said this patting at her arm, with a sad, knowing air. As if *everyone* understands she was wasting her time on this fool's errand as an MP and he felt bad to be the one to have to break it to her.

We visited another kafeneo. Another group of old men, dressed in old clothes, worry beads swinging from their fingers, unwavering views thrown out into the air.

"Give me 24 hours," said one. "That's all I ask. Just 24 hours in a room with the government and I could sort out this whole mess."

The man had a strong, lined face that had been worked over by the sun and wind of these Peloponnese lands for 70 years or more. He talked of his lack of money, the hopelessness of his circumstances.

"I will survive this though," he said, standing up from his chair, rising to his full height. "I will survive. Because..." he paused for effect, looked around him to check everyone was listening "Because I am Greek!"

He thumped his fist hard on his chest. The other old men of the café all nodded their white heads, like bobbing dandelion clocks, in agreement.

A younger villager appeared down the road, swearing and gesticulating, he ran up to my mother-in-law and, nose-to-nose, started shouting at her how Tsipras had let the country down.

"He could have been the Chavez of Europe!" he said, swinging his arms in circles, round and round.

The man continued like this and I felt worried for my mother-in-law's safety, when it was translated to me that actually he was offering his support. He would be one of the men in the villages organising future help in the run-up to the election.

So we carried on. Travelling to more villages. More views. More bellicose aggrandising. We stopped at a taverna. A group of 20 men with, as always, just a small smattering of women sat outside. As my mother-in-law talked to them, drinks and hospitality were offered again. I sat next to an old couple with their headscarfed ancient mother. I asked how many elections they'd seen in their time, how many candidates had called into this village. The old woman didn't know her age and her son was very distrustful. "Watch him," he told her "He wants to *know* things..." The old woman ignored this and talked to me for a while. She said that the other traditional parties used to come, years ago, but don't now.

"They only come and show their faces when they want something. Otherwise you never see them. They just hide away with our money."

A local shepherd sat down at the taverna table and talked of how he was unable to even afford new shoes, placing his decrepit, more hole than shoe, pair on the table. He started working himself up.

"We should get guns!" he shouted. "We should have a revolution! But no, you're not brave enough..." he spat, slapping at the shoulder of the slight, bespectacled Syriza helper sat to his right, knocking him off his seat.

The shepherd stood up and kicked his chair out into the street and lent over and pushed the drinks on our table to smash down on the floor. It was a disconcerting moment...even though he then stood with his arms by his side, stooped in a slightly sheepish silence afterwards, as the large lady owner of the bar came and flapped him out of the way and angrily swept up the shards of glass. But it was a shock to me and it showed just how high passions were running in this election.

Tsipras had baffled many people by calling a referendum on whether to accept the European Union's measures, and then ignoring the result. There was anger and confusion. However, I often also heard weary Greek people asking 'Why, exactly, are we having another election?' Having had Euro election, a general election, and the referendum in the space of less than 18 months, voters were exhausted of elections. Many were concerned that these endless elections, five in the last six years, made Greece look a failed country. My mother-in-law had a double challenge: convince people why they should vote in the first place, and then get them to vote for her.

"How dare you come here and talk to us?"

We were in the square of Zacharo – Sugar Town. A town to the south of the constituency with a murky election history. The mayor of this town, in a bid for votes for his campaign, had once laid on 'love buses' for the menfolk, so it was reported, taking them over the northern border of the country to enjoy the pleasures of Bulgarian ladies of the night. He swept in with an impressive majority. There were further scandals attached to this town and I was told how, like other towns all over Greece, the campaigning posters of MPs from rival parties would be pulled down. The mayors of some of these towns are often spotted hanging from trees and lampposts in the middle of the night, hacking at their rivals' banners. The fight is not always a fair one in Greece.

"How dare you come and try and talk to these people!" one man shouted from a café at the campaign team.

It seemed odd that he was so offended at the sitting MP coming to field questions from the electorate with just over a week to go before the election. But the presence of a politician, if they're not doing you a favour that is, is not often well received. A slanging match evolved around the square, with others outside the café all taking sides. I heard support for Chrysi Avgi – Golden Dawn. It was a troubling reminder that the dangerous far-right party were third in the polls, and a further warning of what was at stake in these elections.

Golden Dawn had risen in popularity dramatically in the country, particularly since the start of the economic crisis. Campaigning on anti-immigration, anti-Muslim, pro-ultra Hellenic ideals. Many Golden Dawn voters supported a return of the military Junta. Many even openly identified themselves as Nazis. Many more wished to expand Greek territory into Bulgaria and Turkey, even up to olden day Constantinople. Two years earlier an anti-fascist rapper had been murdered by Golden Dawn supporters in a café in Athens. Months of violent rioting in the capital and in Thessaloniki followed. The leader of Golden Dawn and several of its MPs were arrested in connection to the murder. All were released.

My mother-in-law's campaign team moved out along the coast to meet more potential voters.

In some of the small fishing ports I was told there should be a bit more support for the Syriza cause. A man raced out of his house, only in his underwear, shouting. His face full of anger.

"Ah, it's you," he stopped suddenly and backtracked to his door. "I thought it was PASOK or New Democracy. I was hoping for a fight! I'll be voting for you next Sunday," he said grinning now, happily showing his missing front teeth. "Don't worry. I will vote!"

Despite the considerable differences I had observed on the campaign out here, my mother-in-law was still roped into the typical antics that I associated with electioneering back home. Although it was not kissing babies in Greece. A few days before the vote, she was asked to judge a brutal Greco wrestling competition, held on white-hot sands on a beach near Ancient Olympia, handing out the prizes alongside the Greek Olympic silver medal holder, stood next to her with his carved naked body poured into his trunks. I was also roped-in myself, stuffing envelopes, and spent hours at the Syriza office in Amaliada town which was hardly a hotbed of political intrigue: two old men permanently stationed outside, one usually my father-in-law, smoking and drinking Greek coffees. I was employed to remind people who wanted to vote for my mother-in-law which party she was standing for. This was not the ridiculous task that I first thought, when I was told that, at the last count, there had been over 90 different political parties in modern-era Greece.

One evening, a man walked by the office. He was pointed out as a teacher who had lost his job in the austerity cuts. This man had turned up often at my new family house at night shouting that he just wanted his job back, he only wanted the chance to work, it was every man's right to earn a living. So, taking up his cause, my mother-in-law had fought tirelessly for him to be reinstated. She was successful and the man was given his job back. A few days later, my mother-in-law later walked through the town square and saw him sat drinking coffee.

"Why aren't you at school?" she asked.

"Ah," he tapped at his temple to indicate his smart thinking. "I've applied for my paternity leave now..."

I followed my mother-in-law on a few tv and radio interviews. One descended into a slanging match after it was revealed that the radio station had asked for 1,000 euros from my mother-in-law if she wanted to appear on their station. She had refused and so had not appeared since January. Instead of any shamefaced embarrassment, the DJs wanted to know exactly what she *did* do with her money, if not paying journalists to appear on their shows. Then after the interview they castigated her in a wounded manner about how she had asked them to tone down the shouting.

"What? She tells us not to shout at her? MPs tell *us* what to do? We can't shout at who we like on *our own* show, is that what she's telling us? *Ai sto thiaolo!*"

I thought this might appear unprofessional to listening voters, but at a bar in the main square in Amaliada where I often sat and watched the news on the main national tv channels, I'd already been struck by the low level of political broadcasting. One of the popular current affairs programmes that always seemed to be on had a multiple split-screen show with different politicians, journalists and presenters. All the guests on the show hurled abuse, spoke over each other, shouted, banged desks, threw papers in the air. No viewer could understand a word of what was going on. And this was Greece's main source for tv news and debate. The lady owner of the bar, idly watching this ridiculous scene played out on the tv whilst running a cloth over a glass, turned to me, nodded at the screen. With an exasperated sigh, she said.. "*Ellada, eh?*" – Greece, eh? – and shook her head sadly. Like many Greeks I met, the woman was one of those who looked on their country as if it were something completely foreign to them, inhabited by people with ways they just couldn't fathom.

The televised debate of the leaders of the parties went out late one evening and was a long, ponderous affair. Lasting over four hours it finishing sometime in the early morning. My mother-in-law appeared on a similar tv debate with her rival local candidates on the slightly less grand 'Olympic' channel beamed from somewhere out in the Ionian Sea. It was still a closely watched event though, even as her debate rumbled on past midnight, by a nation of television, as well as political, addicts.

"Politics for us... It's like the weather for you British," one fellow campaigner said to me. "It's all we ever care about..."

This seemed very true. I saw one man outside a *periptero* – the old style Greek kiosks on every street that are essential to life in Greece and sell pretty much anything you could ever think of. He took down a newspaper from one of the hanging racks and read through the latest political developments. I could see him getting more angry, breathing heavily through his nose. Eventually the old man, unable to contain himself any longer, slung the paper to the ground. After looking down at it, thinking for a while, he leapt in the air and stamped on the paper for good measure. Graffiti is on walls all over Greece with a scrawled, simple, 'PASOK' or 'KKE' on it, like the tribal support of a local football team, or the drawing of a sweetheart's name. It impressed me. I couldn't imagine anyone bothering to waste the paint to spray a tribute to the Liberal Democrats back home.

During this election, Greece had found itself at the very centre of the world's interest. Tsipras and Syriza might even have been holding the fate of the European Dream in their hands. The Greek people also had the very real feeling that Tsipras might also throw their own dreams away too. But this election and the campaign for my mother-in-law I had followed had been very simple, very open. Perhaps a little amateurish, but all the less cynical for it. The Greeks I had seen all held their views to be true, their distrust of politicians was absolute. They all had the unerring belief that, if only they were given the chance, they could personally fix all the country's problems. And I admired each one's incontestable, unshakable, certainty in their complete suitability to be prime minister. Democracy was born here, of course, and perhaps political engagement still exists in its purest form.

So we gathered in Amaliada Square to await the outcome, as we had done in January. We moved to a restaurant for the results. The place was bustling with anticipation and I gazed around at the figures arguing with hands waving in faces. Although, of course, the discussions could have been about the future of the country or it could have been whether they should have calamari for a starter, everything is conducted at about the same volume and intensity. I noticed a few of the customers were smoking. Surely this was a non-smoking restaurant? It is the law after all... Didn't I see a sign…? I turned to the prospective MPs, three of them sat round the table nervously waiting to hear their results. The rule-setters and standard bearers for the town. Two of them next to my mother-in-law were contentedly puffing away directly under the large 'Strictly No Smoking Allowed' sign. The owner happily carried over ashtrays for all of them.

I wondered if Greece would ever really change. If even the MPs believe, as many Greek people seem to, that the interference in personal freedoms is an insult to democracy, perhaps there really is a truth to it when I heard said that Greece is ultimately ungovernable? However, at least in this election, unlike last time, my wife hadn't been apprehended by one of the officials at the count and told that, due to lack of numbers she must join the counting of the vote.

"Well, you have a degree don't you? You can't be stupid. You can count..."

She had actually spent time herself, back in her student days, on the streets protesting and disrupting with the Athens and Thessaloniki anarchists. Civil disobedience and anarchism is a big and just as important faction of Greek politics as voting and traditional parties. Although her group was always more bookish theorists rather than Baader-Meinhof type terrorists. But still, I watched the daughter of one of the prospective candidates for the ward, someone who had previously run with the anti-democracy crowd, with no training or supervision, assiduously counting votes for her mother and the other candidates on an old table in a broken-down school hall. It didn't seem right to me. But then, as the lady of the old bar in Amaliada Square had it: *Ellada, eh..?*

Chapter 3
Corfu Quartet

So now I was really married into this Greek world. Already England had been blown out like a candle in my mind. Me and my new wife, my travelling companion – my *Giristroula* as they say here for a girl who likes to wander – had been touring around and around Greece looking for somewhere to settle. We landed one day in late summer in Corfu. The Garden of Greece. Surely this could be the right place for us to put down some roots..?

Part 1
Paradise Found?

We threaded our way out of the noise and confusion of the airport into the brilliant sunshine of Corfu. There they were: the tiers of multi-coloured houses, green shuttered and piled haphazardly. There was the bay beyond, blue and smooth as a plate. Here was our new life on the island, laid out before us like a feast. Or so it seemed.

Word had been sent a few days earlier that someone would be able to help us and there would be a place for us to stay somewhere in Corfu Town. What we had to do now was to find it… We found a dark damp basement, smelling of mould, and fusty with a crack of dirt and dust that fell into our eyes as I shunted the door open with my shoulder. But it was a dark damp basement on Spianada. Spianada is the largest square in Greece. The largest in the whole of the Balkans, so people say. Built by the French when they controlled Corfu, as compared to when the British did, or the Venetians, all of whom left their marks on the architecture of the city. Here was Liston, a long handsome columned esplanade running down one side. On the other side, a grand rose-coloured ash-walled old fortress towered above. Our dank couple of rooms were next door to the Ionian Academy, a pink birthday cake of a building and the first educational institution in modern Greece. It was now part of the university where Giristroula had managed to wrangle a job teaching music. Standing on tiptoe we could see out of the grimy windows of our rooms at pavement level as the socked and sandaled feet of tourists flowed past. The flood of people rolled on past the statue of the first prime minster of Greece, Kapodistrias, stood saluting across the narrow channel of 20 miles of sea back towards the mainland.

There were bugs in the bed and fleas in the room which left us with big red bloody sores wherever we sat down. We couldn't stay here. And besides, Corfu was shining too brilliantly outside to ignore.

We took a walk into the old town. Past the church of the saint of this island, Saint Spiridon, with his ikons and holy relics gripped and fussed over and protected and kissed by tiny, dark headscarfed, old Corfiot women. The architecture here was unlike anything I'd seen so far in Greece. Collapsing rows of houses above the old port, still lived in, not just window dressing for the tourists. Pastel shades of yellow and pink, blurred and not re-painted in centuries. Hanging laundry criss-crossing on lines above the paved passageways. The narrow alleyways and colonnades of the old Jewish Quarter with flaking damp-ruined walls. Balconies and details on every building.

We met up with Anthi, one of the student teachers at the university, in a bar just off grassy Spianada square with its games of cricket left over from the British reign, and over a *tzitzibeera*, a ginger beer, another peculiarity popular in Corfu introduced by the British, she told us what to expect on this island.

"They'll cheat you."

The crisis that had suffocated the rest of Greece had bypassed Corfu. The tourists had kept the island in the money. Every summer, middle-aged couples with rucksacks, maps, sun-cream and spectacles clogged the streets of Corfu Town, while young singles, topless and tattooed, clutching hedonism to their lobster-red chests crammed in the beach bars in the south of the island. Everyone who owned a business here knew they didn't need to appeal to the customer. They knew who ran this island. And they knew they didn't need *you*.

"*16 evro?*" I would hear angered old local women shout, coming out of greengrocers with their bags. "Oh yes, you've got tourism *now*. You're making money *today*. In the winter though, don't forget it, you'll be back trying to take it from us..." they would caterwaul over their shoulders. "*Ama me ksanadeis na me vrasees!*" – If you see me in your shop again, boil me!

The large moustached greengrocer in his white apron overall would give a pleased-with-himself uncaring wave of the hand, flapping them away, shutting the door on their backsides.

"I feel bad saying it," said Anthi quietly "But some of them... they're... well, they're quite stupid."

As a teacher she'd seen, first hand, the children of the island.

"Their parents all have hotels and tavernas. They make so much money in the summer and the kids are just going to work in, then eventually inherit, these tavernas. They don't need education. They often just don't come to school. Many of my students leave unable to read."

It was my first surprise on the island.

Giristroula and I walked out of town, through the area of Kanoni, past the palace of Mon Repos and out onto a rock headland to watch the sun draping itself in pinks and golds into the sea behind Pontikonisi – Mouse Island – the icon of Corfu, with its 16th century church set on its little islet out on the sea: white walls, red roof and frescoes. Green hills with groves of olives and myrtle trees climbing away behind. How could anything unattractive or asinine or unappealing ever exist here, I thought to myself, on this island that seemed to have materialised for us like something straight out of a dream. The shadow of a huge aeroplane grew larger, darker, rippling over the hillsides. It roared straight over Mouse Island, shaking us as it landed metres from Corfu's famous symbol with a shriek of breaks and a howl of engines. I clamped my hands over my ears. What kind of a place puts their airport right in the middle of town?

On the hills looking down over concentrated Corfu Town, the houses spreading out thinner past Kanoni and Lake Halikiopoulou becoming rolling green and yellow patchwork fields, we walked in the dusty roads in the scorching heat. The only things seemingly awake on the whole island were us and the cicadas. And then we came across it. A battered old village. A crumbling church standing above, the still bell in the arch of the old bell tower suspended in the heat. Ruined ancient houses below with heavy blistered wooden shutters hanging off hinges. Tiny paths ran off into the dark down the sides of skewed old crooked buildings and rough-cut rocky steps led up to God-knows-where. Giristroula and I walked around in silence gazing at this dilapidated but beautiful village, set like a hot yellow stone half way up the cleavage of two tree-thick hills.

"*Psahneteh kati?*" – Are you looking for something?

I peered into the dark where the voice had come from. Sat on a rickety chair outside the one shop of the village, the bakery, was a white haired old man. Pickled-walnut faced, as old looking as the village itself. He heaved himself up on to his stick.

"Are you looking for a house? I know a house that's empty…"

Giristroula and I hadn't said anything to the other about living here. It hadn't even crossed my mind until this creaking venerable old man, so totally Greek and aged and utterly in keeping with his surroundings, mentioned it. We both looked at each other.

"Yes," we replied at the same time.

The old man was Orestis. The self-appointed *arhontas* – the president – of the village. The ancient bakery he now sat outside every day had once been his. It had been taken over in recent years by a harassed woman who had to deal daily with Orestis still coming in to prod the breads and sniff the pittas. Orestis liked to sit outside in his small pool of dark in the otherwise intense bright light that smothered everything else in the village, watching all that went on and knowing everyone's business. He was often accompanied by a few also greatly aged, ladies who all seemed to be hopelessly in love with him. Orestis walked us slowly and unsteadily down the lanes and introduced us to Dionysis.

Dionysis was standing outside the house he had to rent. It was, perfectly, a strawberry-pink villa. Small and square and standing with determination in a tiny garden. In the arch of the stone gateway to the garden a flower emblem and carving told us that it had been built in 1804. There was a dirty old outside toilet in the garden which was overhung by twisting vines of deep-purple grapes thick with wasps. Sprawling squares of thick olive tree fields ran behind, rolling away with the hills as far as you could see. And hiding in this grey-green carpet, hundreds of loud endlessly barking, seemingly convulsed, Greek dogs.

Dionysis told us he had been born in this house almost 80 years ago and had lived with his family of five in the three rooms. He was a large, sprightly man, with a moustache that danced as he talked and eyes that were both laughing and cunning. As he limped and clumped down the path, it was clear he was also the owner a wooden leg.

"I'm a communist", he told us. "I fought out there," he waved a vague arm to the hills. "You can rely on me. I won't cheat you."

We took the keys.

A man on the barest skeleton of an old moped, with a bald head and a long badger-like black and grey beard appeared and stopped outside the house. Without introduction, he got off the moped and in silence connected the wires of the house to a tall telegraph pole outside to syphon off, for free so it seemed, the electricity. He did this wordlessly, with no explanation, without even looking at us, before driving off again with a double toot on his horn and his hand to his brow in salute.

We called in at the local kafeneo. The hub of any Greek village or town. This one was old, solid sand-coloured brick and the higher levels a faded rose colour. Shutters ancient and warped. We entered, blinking into the dark, and met Manolis, the owner. Manolis would open his bar at 5am for coffee. He liked to drink his with ouzo in it. He would be drunk by 7am and slowly grow drunker as the day wore on. Closing at midday, he would then return, Lazarus-like after his siesta to steadily drink again until midnight. Sometimes Manolis would be all alone beside the broken wicker chairs, faded portraits and trinkets. Sometimes the bar would be full with card-playing characters from the surrounding countryside all wreathed in smoke and arguments and laughter. The old men in their thick suits, even in the roasting temperatures, nibbling at sunflower or pumpkin seeds. Cracking the small shells between their front teeth, spitting out the bits, scattering them on the floor between their feet. *Passatempo* I was told these seeds are called, but also the action is to passatempo too. It's a hobby, a past time. The old men passatempo-ing their days away, nibbling and spitting, killing the summer-slow hours. Embalmed in their pleasures and staring into space.

A drunken Manolis told us cock-and-bull stories about his past: being a drug runner in South America, a gigolo on the French Riviera. My guess was he had never been out of Corfu in his life, but he was a good story teller, while he kept himself upright.

As all good kafeneo owners should, Manolis knew everyone in Corfu. Our possessions lay in storage in a warehouse near Athens on the Piraeus harbourside, having been shipped over from London. We needed someone to get them to us here in Corfu.

"*Kanena provlima,*" – no problem – said Manolis, rocking slightly, his knee dropping in a little drunken lurch. "I know people…"

The owner of the shipping company was a woman barely four-foot-tall. She shouted, threatened, gesticulated, smoked three cigarettes at once as we stood in her office arranging the transfer of our stuff. She spat on the floor and took the cash, counting it carefully. Our possessions would be shipped over from Athens in three days' time she told us.

Three days later we received a call.

"I have your things here… I want more money for them now…"

What could we do? All of our world was there, in her warehouse.

She grinned with her brown teeth and gums bared as we entered her grim office again. Giristroula and the woman argued back and forth in heated Greek. Despicable words were thrown into the air. The woman cackled as we left, clutching at her money.

This wasn't the warm welcome to Corfu I'd hoped for. But in her way this woman *had* given us a good introduction to the island. Just as accurate to life in Corfu as the dying sunsets; or those views over the gangs of turtle-back hills; or the cliffs eaten into each day by the swaying curtain of peacock-blue sea with the clattering pebbles in the surf below.

Better to be served badly in heaven than reign in hell, I suppose.

When we opened the crates we found some pictures were missing. Musical instruments too.

"Don't worry," slurred Manolis in the cocoon of his bar, seeing four of us and focusing on none. "Just a mistake. I'll get them back…"

True to his word, the next day we walked up to Manolis's café in the early morning sunshine and there was this large, unsteady on his feet, thickset Greek man, cigarette dead in the corner of his mouth, sheepishly waving the instrument cases in his big fists.

"It... er... it didn't cost me much."

The summer stayed for ever. A happy reveller refusing to leave the party. Each morning I woke up thinking that the covers of the night would now be pulled back to reveal a grey autumnal day, but every day emerged as the last: heat-scorched, luminously-bright, eucalyptus-smelling, cicada-orchestrated.

A little further down from our house on the winding path was the village church, squeezed into the small alleyways like a fat man bursting out of his suit. This yellow painted church, 300 years old at least and very cracked at the seams, had a priest who enjoyed cranking the old church tannoy and delivering his endless *"Kyrie eleison! Kyrie eleison! Kyrie eleison!"*'s at varied times. Favouring early Sundays or late nights, and setting off a thousand villagers' dogs.

The priest in his heavy black robes, stove-pipe hat, jewelled necklaces and flowing beard, would regularly sweep down the ginnelled paths of the village, knocking on doors and, as soon as they opened, waving his smoking handbag – his *thymiato* – into the newly opened doorway, whether asked or not, to ward off any lurking evil spirits inside. Just the once he made a perfunctory glance at our house, and then slid soundlessly by, uninterested. His robes held up by the eager young boys of the church.

Sometimes I entered the old church building to look around. The church chapel lay at the bottom of its bell-tower, like an old dog asleep at its owner's feet: silver vessels, candle holders and ikons inside; the faded gold painted Christ and his saints looking down on me from the ceiling. The priest in his ornate vestments would give me a stare as he looked up from his fiddling in his crypt, growling as he bent back down again to continue his work. I would apologise and leave the vestibule as quickly as possible.

There was a tiny man who lived in the village. Rodent-faced, deep-tanned skin like a battered old brown leather boot and, quite obviously, simple. I never saw anyone happier than this man when, after being mocked as the figure of fun in the kafeneo, drinks were finally bought for him and a chair was brought out and he was allowed to sit down for a while with the men of the village, grinning like a fool.

Most bright mornings, out of my window, I would see this man, having been ratted out from behind the church where the old priest kept his moped, scurrying away fast, guiltily, his arms over his head. He would be pursued by the corpulent old priest who was raining blows down on him with his rolled up papers. The man would salute the greetings from the old ladies outside the bakery as he ran, cowering from the blows.

Late summer was spent lounging outside the house watching mournful-faced men pass, taking clanging-belled goats down the road out onto the hills. Followed by the sad sound of a gunshot ringing through the village lanes. Giristroula and I would walk down the hills, cutting through the fields, passing the long fingers of cypress trees pointing upwards as if alerting us to deep blue skies above. Birds would fly out of the trees in an explosion of colours, like a flare going off in the branches. Enormous green and red lizards, a foot long, bearded, mohicaned with a spiky frills, licked their eyeballs at us, winking morning greetings. Down by the sea, the warm waters, turquoise blue, were clear deep down to the sandy floor. Slow black schools of fish would pass and then turn in a sudden flash of silver and green as they rounded to head off on a different course.

Our landlord's brother was Stavros. He lived in the village, in a large house next to the very small primary school.

"I'm glad you two are living in my family's house," Stavros told us. "I like you two..." He gave us a long hard stare that didn't necessarily show much congeniality. Staring deep into our souls, looking for something, God knows what. Stavros had good English though, unlike his brother who couldn't speak a word.

"*Ach*. He couldn't be bothered to learn English. He was always chasing money from the moment he could walk."

I thought of enquiringly about the validity of his brothers' communist claims, but decided better of it. It was clear the brothers didn't get on.

"I am an artist," said Stavros, rising himself up, puffing out his chest, straightening the small blue cap on his head and handkerchief round his neck.

While Dionysis had made a quiet fortune as the boss of a company tinning tomatoes, Stavros had spent his life as an actor here on Corfu. He had recently been approached to appear in a film of the story of the Durrells – who he, and many Corfiots, had never actually heard of but which had excited the locals as rumour of its filming filtered through the island. He coaxed me into coming along too to volunteer as an English extra.

As we travelled into town in his car he would not talk to me about his brother.

"*Ehoumeh yini apo dyo horia horiates*" – we have become two villagers from different villages. Meaning, I guessed, that they were chalk and cheese.

"He has his life, I have mine," Stavros said. There was then a silence. It seemed Stavros had made his point so I opened my mouth to speak...

"My life is better," Stavros added with a final snap, nodding to himself.

Dionysis would hobble around to our villa at all times of the day unannounced. His cackling face appearing at the small open window. He would tell Giristroula that his workmen wanted to come and fix jobs in the house they'd already fixed as they'd all fallen in love with her, nudging me violently in the ribs as he told his stories. Stories always with Dionysis heroic. Stories that always ended with Dionysis triumphant. Stories that would last forever, going on until the sun had slipped well behind one of the mountain tops high behind the village. If Stavros passed the house, however, Dionysis would fall into muted silence and the two brothers would barely look at each other as Stavros walked by wishing Giristroula and I, in his deep low actorly voice, "*Kalimera.*"

Village life continued like this as summer, finally, imperceptibly, changed into autumn; and as autumn changed just as carefully and deliberately, with tiny movements, into winter. New Year arrived, and on the sixth day of January the priest woke everyone at dawn with his proclamations from his tinny speakers. A full philharmonic brass band then passed down the narrow paths directly underneath our windows. Corfu is a strangely musical island and many of the towns and even small villages like this one have their own philharmonic orchestras. Our village's band played in a hall further up on the twisting road that eventually led down the hill, the only route away from the village, out onto the main road pointing towards Corfu Town. They were close enough so that we would still regularly hear the timpani section's practices riding over the heavy evening air: setting off a million stray dogs hiding out in the fields.

The band today though, in their navies and purples, tassels, epilates and polished helmets with plumped-up plumes, carried on past our house. We clambered out of bed to follow behind the train of people as it led us past the church and the crumbling houses, out into vineyards of overgrown trees, up moss coated steps. Then onto a small road where a stone fountain stood, around a natural spring, that had been built hundreds of years ago. We were very happy to have found this fountain, it was where we had been getting our drinking water for the last few months.

The priest was waiting for all of us up here. He embarked on a long ritual, blessing the water for the coming year. He ended the performance by throwing his ornate jewelled cross through the open grill gate into the dark blue natatorium of water. The cross was quickly followed in by the shirtless, shoeless young men of the village. They swam and scrapped with each other in the dark agitated waters to retrieve this trinketed little ikon. One eventually held it up aloft out of the water and handed it over to receive an extra blessing from the priest stood on a plinth, regal and haughty in his ridiculous hat. This was the Greek tradition of *Fota*, happening in every town and village in the country on this day.

I turned to remark to one of the members of the crowd standing next to me – and *everyone* was here: all the gargoyle characters from the kafeneo; the old ladies from outside the bakery; Dionysis and Stavros, stood at opposite ends from each other; Orestis, sat in prime position; the musicians; the teachers and the students from the village school; the farmers and their goats. I said how it didn't seem particularly hygienic to be doing all this in our drinking water.

"Oh, we don't drink this water anymore. Haven't you seen all the worms floating in there? We haven't drunk this water for years..."

I didn't feel so well that New Year.

I took a trip into Corfu Town one bright morning and stood for 20 minutes outside the bank just to draw some money out of the machine. With nothing else to do, I listened in on the old men stood around chatting as they watched life going past. It would be good to practise my Greek I thought. My smile faded though as I slowly worked out the conversation that was going on.

"Look, there's an Albanian... And there's another one... God damn Albanians. They get everywhere."

"See him..?" one old man said, summoning over a small boy playing by the road, and pointing at a man walking along the other side of the street. "He's a God damn Albanian... *Palio Alvanos...*"

I turned to the men and asked if they really needed to talk like this.

"I'm sorry..." said one, "*Se kseroume?*" – Do we *know* you? They continued, unaffected.

Another old man who had come out of the bank dropped his bank book. I called out and went over and handed it back to him. He smiled, but then looked confused by this random act of insignificant help.

"I'm sorry... but tell me... why did you come over and give this back to me?" he said. "*Se ksero?*" – Do I *know* you?"

Surrounded by Corfiot beauty, I wondered if I would ever fathom Corfiot ways.

The nature had got me, of course it had: the paintbrush heads of the trees seemingly coating the sky a new deep blue every day; the sea flat as a meadow with the hands of both Greece and Albania cupping it at either end; the green folded mountains of the island's central range... Corfu's nature was very special. The people had got *to* me though. Some of them anyway. The mores and manners of the islanders; the sly incursions; the creeping money-obsessed ways. The restaurant owners plying only for the tourist trade.

"Oh you live here?" one taverna owner said to me having served me a terrible Sofrito, the meaty Corfiot signature dish. "I thought you were on holiday and I would never see you again!" he giggled. Impressive honesty I thought, as I poked at the shoe-leather meal, but not quite the Greek conviviality I'd been so happy to have found elsewhere in the country.

Hotel owners prostituting the beauty of their home island for the wealthy Germans and Russians, standing on the balconies of their hideous blots on the landscapes drawing in deep lungfuls of the monied air and exhaling with eyes closed in ecstasy. Men who sat smugly, bathing like walruses in largesse in Manolis's desperate kafeneo, snapping their fingers for another drink.

Back in our village, still halfway up those old green hills, still flooded by sunlight, life in the village seemed to have changed. There was a turn in the air. A dark feeling had fallen over the place like a heavy cloak. I noticed everyone was dressed in black, all faces were unsmiling. The ancient old ladies were gathered, milling about slowly like sombre pigeons outside Orestis's old bakery. One of them told me what had happened. Stavros's son had been killed in a car accident on the mainland, somewhere north of Athens. One of the old ladies, overcome with emotion, hugged me as this news was passed on. The priest of the village appeared at my side too and even he, this grim man of God, placed a hand on my shoulder and gave a brief conciliatory smile.

Stavros's son hadn't visited the village since he was a boy. He was a stranger to most of these people, but I saw here how the Corfiot character – that same Corfiot character that so frequently needled me – now exploded into one of care and concern. Everybody's house was open. Manolis wouldn't think of you paying for a drink. Food was brought out for everyone to eat and everyone wanted to sit and talk. Neighbours went from house to house to check all was ok. And then the sight that really moved me, that made me feel that, just as with all the nature on offer on this island, maybe a paradise amongst the Corfiots *could* still be found here after all... Along the paths of our small village, a desolate broken-looking Stavros came, walking slowly. He was supported all along the way by a fixed, unfaltering, Dionysis. His arms were close around his brother as they made their way down towards the rough-cut steps behind the church and out towards the fields of overgrown olive trees beyond. The dogs stayed silent for once.

Part 2
Lessons in Greek

"*M' opion thaskalo kathisis, tetia grammata tha mathis,*" they say in Greece. Whichever teacher you learn with, such lessons you learn.

The teacher *I* learnt with was a tiny, excitable, slightly mad, retired primary school teacher with a weather-beaten face like an old tree trunk, who came from one of the villages in the middle of deepest Corfu. She gave free Greek lessons every Friday in a dark deserted-for-the-evening school in the centre of Corfu town.

I had been on the island for a several months now, but my Greek had remained wretched and wasn't getting any better. I was in need of help. I learnt, from talk around town, that there was a co-operative group in Corfu who organised all manner of lessons for free. They had set up in the 1st Gymnasium school of Corfu, in the late afternoons and evenings. I put my name down for both sets of the 'Greek For Immigrants' lessons they offered.

The first lesson was a class on Thursday evenings. This class was taught by Trifonas. A huge bear of a man who never talked, only shouted. Trifonas would go through a whole box of chalks in the first 10 minutes of every lesson, snapping them in his paw-like hand as he tried to write on the board and hurling each one to the ground in frustration, elaborately swearing as he slung. Sketchy on the language we may have been, but there was no confusion over these bellowed streams of Greek profanities. Trifonas was an unsmiling man. Each lesson would see him stood at the front of the class, a bellicose man-mountain figure, his teaching method just to *glower* us into learning.

"You," he would point to one of the two identical young blonde girls, overly made-up, sat wearing their bikini tops: Brit holiday reps for the summer who had thought it might be a good idea to learn a bit of the language while they were here, now turning to look at each other with spreading regret and nervous twittering laughter.

"Yes, you," Trifonas would continue as he stalked closer, on the attack. "What's the third conjugated form for the verb 'to speak'?"

Flashed panicked looks between them, and then a pair of simpering giggles that would send Trifonas's eyes up into his skull, cheeks puffing, the biro bending in two between his fingers. Everyone in the room prayed he wouldn't turn to them for the answer. We were only on our second lesson.

What sort of people, aside from myself, had signed up to these classes anyway? I looked around the small, crumbling, grey concrete classroom – cold, with Corfu's brilliantly lit, sun-drugged life going on outside, just beyond the shuttered windows and the playground. We were a queer, disparate bunch.

There was Lyudmila, a painfully shy girl from Ukraine who seemed to know no one in Corfu, refused to make eye contact with any of us, or ever try to use any of her Greek. Sat deep in her anorak even in the height of summer, forever diligently lining up pens on the desk in front of her and arranging her notebooks.

Alexandra was a friendly, loud, stoutly-built Serbian who had met a Greek on the beach on holiday in Kavos, married him within a matter of weeks and never returned home. Alexandra's Greek was better than most of ours, though still pretty patchy. She took a no-nonsense approach to Trifonas, the only one of us who ever dared cross him. Sometimes blazing rows would flare up over the exact meaning of a word, the two of them nose-to-nose. Alexandra actually enjoyed Trifonas's lessons.

"I like his style," she said, shrugging. "He's... direct."

There was Chester, an American with curly hair, moustache and extravagant deck shoes who lived on a boat he had been sailing around the world which was now docked in Corfu's Gouvia harbour. "I've still got half the world to see," he told me. "But what can I do? I've fallen in love with this god-damn island!" Chester's Greek was awful. I made a point of talking as quickly as I could after him during the lessons in the hope that it made my Greek sound slightly better somehow.

A handsome middle-aged German lady, Erica, always well made-up and elegantly dressed with a classy shawl thrown over her shoulder. She sat squeezed into the small kid's desk in front of me. Erica had attended these lessons last year. And the year before. "I want to get it *perfect*."

At the back was Keith. A small, round, dirty-looking Australian in his late 50s. Always in the same bright yellow t-shirt. Always staring at his notes, lost, pulling at his raggedy white beard, making the sound of a goat chewing at a carpet.

"Er... Can we go through that alphabet thing one more time?"

Hopeless.

Next to Keith was a prim, camp, bespectacled man from Yorkshire who worked on the cruise ships – ships which appeared in Corfu from nowhere, like giant floating white summer birds, suddenly, along with the good weather. He would twist and turn this way and that in his seat, pulling the most outrageously offended and affronted faces as he suffered Trifonas's verbal assaults.

A gargantuan, gouty, red-faced Swiss and young, smooth, hipster Belgian sat side-by-side looking as incongruous as possible, and then two girls at the front, one from Albania, one from Bulgaria, who, could actually speak good Greek having grown up bordering the country. They were the ones in the class most amused at my own Greek, nudging each other and putting their heads together, laughing like a pair of seagulls as I spoke. I couldn't work out what they were doing here as I watched them chatting in Greek incessantly to an uninterested, irritated, impatient Trifonas. Then I was told, they could speak but couldn't read Greek. As the lessons wore on, it became clear that despite their advantage, they were faring no better than most of us at learning to read the language.

Learning to read at an advanced age is an unsettling and a faintly humiliating experience. Tracing unfamiliar letters, moving your mouth to spell the words out loud with a slow low sound as you read. Brightening with a vivified flash when the word suddenly becomes apparent. Or, more often, continuing to stare at the jumbled collection of characters. It's like being a small child again. Learning afresh everything you once thought you knew. Except no one teaches you with parent-like patience, repeating over and over again, mouthing the words as you speak. And no one grips your cheeks and gives them a joyful rub when you get the words right as a 40-year-old.

Or so I thought.

"Bravo Alex!"

Friday's lesson was with Voula. A retired teacher used to dealing with tiny primary school kids.

"Bravo Alex!"

I'd given some innocuous details about myself roughly right in my clumsy Greek.

"B*rrr*-avo Alex!" Voula clapped her hands together rapidly under her chin in delight.

Voula was, I realised, slightly crazy. Sweet, fun, caring, dedicated to her students' learning, but crazy. And she seemed to think that I was seven years old.

Voula could also speak no English. To translate for her she had enrolled a young man named Tasos to help. Tasos – awkward, sullen, stood at the front of the class with his drooping shoulders and junior moustache – had not much English himself. Most lessons would be spent with us as mute spectators as Voula and Tasos rowed heatedly at the front, disagreeing, gesticulating, hands shoved in each other's faces before Voula would double-up in cackling laughter and wave Tasos her approval to translate something to us. Something that, even with my rudimentary grasp of Greek, I knew he was translating pretty much completely wrong.

Voula's lessons were livelier and far less threatening than Trifonas's. But still, there was no conversational practice. No using of any of the language we were picking up. Just as in real Greek schools, so I was told, the lessons were solely lectures by the teachers. Learning by rote. And everything solemnly chalked up, over and over, on the old lustreless blackboard.

Voula used her primary school background to good effect though, and she did make you feel she cared about your learning.

"Alex...*Aaa*lex..." she would sing-song say to me. "*Katalavenees?*" – do you understand? – as she knelt by my desk and stroked my arm. I would look up from my book and beam back at her my understanding, or pout my confusion.

One by one the students stopped turning up for Trifonas's weekly persecutions.

"Weak students..." grumbled Trifonas at each new empty chair. "Don't they know you can never learn anything by just giving up?"

Then there was denial, "Well it's not my fault my lessons are on Thursday. I should have been given the Friday evenings..."

At the end it was just me and Alexandra the Serb turning up. Trifonas cornered me after the lesson, outside in the long dark school corridor. He seemed a different man.

"Why are they leaving me?" he asked, wounded eyes searching my face.

I told him I didn't know.

"Never mind." he said pulling himself upright, towering above me, blocking out the light from the old blinking school lamp hanging behind his head. "But you," his heavy fingers jabbed at my chest, "You must stay loyal." He fixed me a stare. "You must stay *loyal...*"

I promised I would.

I lasted one more lesson.

The very last I saw of Trifonas was his exorbitantly large head looking sadly through the open window from the kids' playground into Voula's class, as we grinned at her clowning one Friday evening. My laughter froze on my lips as I saw him. I wanted to reach out and tell him we really weren't enjoying this other lesson as much it looked. He met my smile with a cutthroat glare and lurched away towards town, into one of Corfu's dying, ball of blood, sunsets.

I had been an English language teacher myself for a long time before moving to Greece. Although never a particularly good teacher, I was sure that the Greek lessons here would improve considerably with just a few of the methods I had been taught to use: group conversation practice would have been good, or even just getting us to talk to the student we were sat next to. But this wasn't the Greek way. The Greek way was: listen to the teacher, write it down, hope it sticks.

But then, as the months wore on with Voula, I *did* feel I was learning. I was now the dumb-eyed slack-jawed student I so despised during my teaching days but slowly, I was sure, things *were* sticking.

Obviously Greek is a difficult language – it has its own adage to prove that – and especially for an Englishman like me with no other languages in my armory and no concept of grammar aside from how I picked it up back when I gurgled and crawled.

What troubled me most, I think, was that concept that each noun has a corresponding sex. How could I remember whether the blackboard I stared at was male or female (it was male) or what sex the chair I sat on was (female)? And then there were the neutral nouns. Why were both 'boy' and 'girl' neutral? How could that make sense? Why was a moustache neutral? Surely it couldn't be as cruel as to reflect the unfortunately familiar downy growth on the upper lip of a Greek girl?

And then there was the alphabet, and those sounds... What could the difference be between the cowboy bow-legs of the Greek letter *omega* which makes the sound 'o', and the perfectly round 'o' of *omecron*? An English 'n' with a dripping-down second leg makes an 'e' sound in Greece, as, of course, does the Y or a lower case u. The Ps are Rs, the Bs are Vs and the Hs are Es. And the question mark is a semi-colon.

Words. Words that were utterly identical in sound, but so different in meaning to each other that they were clearly only designed to trip us foreigners up: tax office and euphoria (*eforia*), rent and victory (*niki*) etc etc... There were completely identical words with slightly different accents on different syllables which also meant totally different things – *poteh*: when and never; *yeros*: old and strong; *pothia*: your legs or an apron. Impossible Greek words all around me. Wind-beaten words; sun-baked words; words shouted and exclaimed by the fat men in the markets, landing like flung barrels; or words skimmed softly, like a pebble, by the laughing women outside their homes peeling beans and gossiping on their steps in the evenings.

To complicate things further, ancient Greek, the lexicon of Alexander and further back still – the language from Homer's shores – rears its head today in the modern language and modern day conversations... "You and your *prasin aloga*..." I heard people say when someone did something ridiculous. 'Prasin aloga' meaning, in the ancient language, doing insensible, illogical things. But as it sounds similar to 'green' and 'horses' in modern Greek, most of the natives don't even understand what they're really saying either, thinking they're lampooning the object of their scorn by suggesting they perhaps owned some kind of oddly coloured animal.

Language from Turkey creeps in too. '*Babas*' for father; '*kojam*' for something big. When the Greeks swear heavily they often use the Turkish '*siktir*' instead of the usual Greek "*adeh gamisou*" as they can pretend they don't really know what they're saying and any offence given is simply a mere misunderstanding.

I had it easier than Giristroula's parents though. There used to be two forms of the modern language: *Demotic,* which is the language of everyday folk, and *Katharevousa*, a 'pure' Greek language, which had been devised by some intellectuals in the early nineteenth century to try and connect the modern language to its glorious ancient Greek past. Until the 1970s, Katharevousa was the official language of Greece, used in legal documents and news reporting, although people rarely spoke it. But everyone had to learn both.

I found myself there was actually a *third* form of communication in Greece. The communication formed just by bare sounds. Guttural noises. Greek conversations were littered with them, and could often sound just like the chattering in a zoo. I would twist my head anxiously. Were these sounds alarm calls? Mating signals?

'*Ach!*' and '*Vach!*' Greeks would exclaim when life is full of problems.

'*Adeh!*' or *Aman!*' – when someone has been annoyed.

'*Och!*' for a deep pain in the soul (a mimed stab of the fist into the heart usually needed to accompany this particular sound)

'*Po po po...*' – when someone is lost for words.

'*Re!*' and '*Vre!*' used pretty much constantly, at the beginning or end of any sentence. Just because.

And always, *always*, when speaking, the theatrical sigh that has to empty the whole lungs with a long dying rasp.

Despite all the hurdles put in front of us students, the language posing as an enemy, a beast not wishing to be tamed or understood; and despite all the hostility the language provided in direct contrast to the openness of the country and the deep blue air, every one of us in the class quite perceptibly and discernibly *did* improve. For me I was at last able to understand the people I had met here in Corfu: the lives they led, how they talked to me and to each other, their personalities. Up until then, most interactions I'd had were based on purely on some kind of assumption of mine. Whether they were being kind, whether I was being laughed at or helped. Everyone's personal disposition was all of my own invention. Now at last I could understand what they were saying, I could finally put an essence and an individuality to a face and to a voice. And others grew too.

One evening, as the class packed up and we collected our things, the dust falling in the shafts of Corfu's late sun coming through the school shutters, Lyudmila, the shy Ukrainian, always the first out, suddenly stopped in the doorway. She hesitated and then turned. A pause. She looked at us all, really for the first time, a long slow moment.

"*Kalispera* everyone," she said.

She looked terrified, and then the briefest sweet smile flickered on her face before she turned quickly and fluttered out through the large wooden main school doors.

We all looked at one another, and smiled. Voula clutched her heart with pride.

A sound at the back made us turn round. It was Keith, rubbing at his stubbly beard like the scratching of the side of a matchbox. He was still in his bright yellow t-shirt, still staring at his language book. Still lost. He looked up at us with sad eyes.

"Er... Do you think we could try that alphabet thing again one more time next week...?"

Part 3
Karagiozis and the Musical Island

Corfu is a strangely musical island.

Throughout Greece, music is always there, in the background, from the singing cicadas in their heat-cocooned trees to the *tragouthia tis thouleias* work songs sung by the old ladies harvesting the olives in the fields in the winter months. In Corfu, however, this Greek symphony seems even more amplified. Perhaps it all started with the philharmonic orchestras in many of its villages and towns. Corfu was the first place in Greece where anyone, regardless of social class, could learn music. Nowadays trumpets and drums are seen being carried around all over the island. Men clutching fat gold polished tubas as they travel along, hanging off the back of coughing broken-down old mopeds. But there is an extensive amateur musical tradition in Corfu too. Tavernas all around the town will have a few chairs slung in the corner where a couple of bouzouki players will be sat playing Greek folk tunes, everyone at their tables singing along to these songs. Knives and forks laid down, food forgotten, eyes closed, heads turned up to the ceilings, tears in the eyes as a tune touches the Greek soul. Greek emotions often only ever kept behind a very rickety door at the best of times and, like a deranged dog, always eager to be let out to run wild.

Every Friday night we would head to an old taverna called 'Ethrio'. Set just behind Kekyra's port, 'Ethrio' faced out with determination on the dark sea. A lit beacon on its own where, inside, a regular crowd of faces met and chatted in the accommodating chaos under the steamy windows. The patron of the taverna – the plump, aproned, Thalia – was wildly unpredictable. Sometimes, on entering, she clutched roughly at my face and planted kisses on both cheeks, sometimes she barely looked at us, jerking her head towards a spare table, the food slung down from a great height. We would join tables together with others, drink retsinas and tsipouros, and over the plates of grilled meat and tzatziki we would loudly discuss the events of the day. But the real reason for being here was the music.

Giorgos and Kostas would be in the corner, sitting underneath the black and white faded portraits of famous old Greek musicians like Tsitsanis and Bellou, swapping between themselves guitar and bouzouki. They played all night, rebetiko and the lighter *laika* songs from the 1920s and '30s.

I had heard much rebetiko from my initial introduction back in the Thessaloniki dark taverna when I had first travelled through Greece and had slowly learnt to love this world of dark-passioned Greek songs. However, Corfu doesn't really have an extensive tradition for rebetiko as the island was never conquered by the Ottomans and so always aligned themselves more towards the Italian influence of the Venetians rather than looking to the East. This sort of music, along with raki or Turkish cuisine, hasn't seeped into the fibres of the culture as in the rest of Greece. But the 'Ethrio' crowd were devotees of rebetiko and Greek folk music. As if in loud defiance to the modern *skilathiko* cheap music pumping out from the other bars around town, the congregation here would sing throatily together all night. Everyone word perfect to these arcane strains of island music, Turkish, Balkan. Songs all coated in a cloud of hashish, poverty, lost love and exile.

In Greece's mood of modern-age suffering, an instrument like the bouzouki which was smashed by the fascists during the time of the dictator due its strong rebellious symbolism, gave another edge to these songs.

Giorgos was good, but his voice always sounded a little too polite for some of the songs. Kostas was *perfect* though. Heavier-set and with a voice – between glugs of tsipouro and with a dirty roll-up cigarette, permanently dangling from his lower lip – of real rebetiko: thick and guttural, straight from the street.

The evenings stretched on long and late into the night, song after song. I would feel battered about the head with the singing and bouzoukis and eastern scales sounding out around me.

One night a violin was produced and handed over to Giristroula to play along with some of the folk tunes. A man got up to dance as she played. He danced with slow, heavy gravitas: arms held in the air, falling with a genuflecting knee, a dramatic prop handkerchief displayed in his hand as he rhythmically planted his feet here and there. Then lighter music and a lighter dance. A group of women held each other, circling with a known routine of steps: back and forth, behind and to the side. A dance learned as children, never forgotten. And then, at the very end, amongst the debris of glasses and plates, the guitar was handed over to me to play, with nods and expectant eyes. Flustered, I hammered out some old Beatles tunes, ashamed of my playing and, suddenly, of my culture. Afterwards, overly kind, the musicians clapped me on the back as they took the instrument off me and placed it back into its case.

"You must come and join our group," they said. "We're practising on Tuesday. We're going to play music for a Karagiozis show. You know Karagiozis of course... Yes?"

Karagiozis is a shadow-theatre puppet. Shadow theatre spread to Greece from the East with the plays from Asia Minor and the Turkish Empire brought over by a wandering Greek sailor. The Karagiozis puppet is the main protagonist in these plays. Comically huge headed and bald, with a bulbous nose, mischief-eyed, moustached, Karagiozis wears raggedly patched-up old Eastern clothes and trudges about his business shoeless. He is always caught up in some tall tale or other and Karagiozis shows are always entertaining, musical, even riotous.

But there is more to it than that. Lying deep within Karagiozis is also the very embodiment of the Greek character. He is the impoverished and downtrodden everyman of Greece. But eventually Karagiozis will get the better of the world, if nothing else, then just by the pure force of his cunning. He is forever hungry but permanently lazy. Caring but quickly, violently, angered. Hilariously foolish but impishly clever. Quick to fall in love, quick to break into song. He is a coward, a cheat, but, picaresque to the core, he always keeps the audience on his side. Karagiozis will end, ultimately, valiant. Or if not, he'll at least have taken the pompous and the bloated down with him as he falls.

The figures and stories are centuries old, but this shadow-theatre is still played all over Greece today. Although perhaps a slowly dying art, all children will have seen a Karagiozis performance. I myself stumbled across what initially seemed to me a very strange gathering, one summer night in the main square of Corfu. A square tent was set up underneath the old Victorian iron bandstand that the British put up when they patrolled this island. At first I was unsure what was happening, but the crowd's laughter, the preposterous characters cavorting on the lit screen with comic voices behind the canvas tent, and the up-tempo orchestra – bouzoukis, tablah drums, fiddles – striking up after every scene, drew me in. I joined the audience and sat on the ground and watched an hour of tumultuous entertainment in the hot night. The speeches and the songs utterly bewildering to me, but at the same time the comedy and the messages perfectly clear.

This was the 'Koum Kou Art' group. And my first taste of Kariagiozis.

The 'Koum Kou Art' group, named after the ever-present bright orange kumquat fruit grown here in Corfu, had been formed over 10 years earlier by a group of school teachers who wrote and performed their own Karagiozis shows. Musicians from the music department of the university established on the island centuries ago, plus the rough tavern bouzouki players had joined. Now the group had a fixed ensemble in place and were playing to increasingly large crowds on the island.

My introduction to this group took place at one of their regular meetings at the small primary school. Underneath the students' childish drawings and blackboard scrawls, countless cigarettes were smoked, tsipouro and food was brought out from hidden cupboards, laughter, long stories and sudden bursts of protracted activity on the instruments. Nothing but eating, drinking and singing happened at every meeting, week after week.

But then one evening, without warning, Ilias, the head teacher of the school who had originally formed this group and was nominally the leader, clapped his hands together and announced that they were going to play a big show at Corfu's Carnival in a few days and needed new figures for the occasion. Everyone was roped into turning up on a Sunday to make and paint new Karagiozis characters.

Karagiozis puppets are thin, two-dimensional figures, always in profile and with sticks and joints to move the body and limbs. They are painted in bright colours and with idiosyncratic costumes to show up behind the screen of the shadow theatre tent.

I was handed the task of making a new *Nionios* figure and spent my Sunday grudgingly copying and cutting and painting. But it gave me a chance to find out a bit more about the characters in these plays, and the pantomime actors behind them.

Nionios is a ludicrous dandy figure. He wears a top hat and tails, has a sculptured pointy beard and talks with an exaggerated lispy Italian-influenced accent. He is meant to come from the Venetian-influenced island of Zante and is hopelessly unlucky in love and incompetent in nearly everything he undertakes.

On the small desk low to my left the main Karagiozis puppet itself was being painstakingly drawn, and next to him was his friend *Hadjiavatis*, with his old fashioned boots and waistcoat, clutching at his beard. Unlike Karagiozis, Hadjiavatis works for a living, but always ends up embroiled in Karagiozis's ridiculous schemes anyway. Hadjiavatis has his plots and plans too, often pretending not to understand what is going on around him while at the same time conniving some trick of his own. But of course all his plans fall like a straw house, and the last sight the audience usually has of Hadjiavatis is of him receiving a beating from Karagiozis and fleeing the stage, wimperingly.

A *Stavrakas* was being made: a tough guy from the port of Piraeus. Stavrakas is a *magas* with his thick moustache bristling with tricky hostility, but he can of course never live up to his boasts of bravery, always let down by cowardice at the crucial moment.

Karagiozis's wife, the nagging *Aglaia*, and his three urchin children who are all miniature versions of himself: *Kolitiri* (pest), *Kopritis* (loafer) and *Skorpios* (wastrel) were all being painted on another table. This unruly family fight, spar, mock but ultimately all support Karagiozis. As does his honest uncle *Barba Giorgos*, with his thick accent from the mountain villages, always carrying a farmer's club and wearing the villager-style *foustanella* skirt.

Over in the corner, near the neatly stacked learning-to-read books, the grand figure of *The Sultan* was being prepared. A lot larger than the other characters, turbaned, brightly painted, the Sultan represents the despotic rulers from Ottoman Empire. The white screen, which stages a Karagiozis performance, is always decorated on either side with images of the Sultan's imposing minareted palace on one edge, and Karagiozis's shack on the other.

The Sultan's lordly, lofty authority is continually mocked by Karagiozis and is used as a prompt for the comedy.

Sultan: Karagiozis, is this really your home?
Karagiozis: Yes, sir.
Sultan: But how can you live without a roof?
Karagiozis: Oh we don't mind, we get lots of fresh air this way.
Sultan: But what happens when it rains?
Karagiozis: Oh when it rains we go outside.
etc.

Our group of workers continued the figure crafting. By the trays and plastic mugs for the primary school lunchtime the next day, the puppet of *Morfonios* was being created by Aphrodite, the teacher who would eventually manoeuvre him behind the screen, giving him life and his ridiculous voice. Morfonios is a terrible mummy's boy who, for some reason, believes himself to be stupendously good-looking. In reality he's another ludicrous Karagiozis figure with a huge melon-shaped head and long nose producing his high-pitched nasal voice and high "*whit... whit*" noises at the end of every sentence. As she painted him, Aphrodite handled him with a gentleness as though he were her own child.

The main man, Karagiozis, was controlled and voiced by Giannis. Just as they say dogs start to look like their owners, the features of Giannis, though one of the younger teachers, seemed to me to have metamorphosed to look just like his old-man stooge: both of them with a big comic proboscis nose and moustache. Giannis didn't really know about Karagiozis before Ilias introduced him to the shadow theatre group. But, like a talent spotter, Ilias saw the potential in his young teacher, coercing and goading him into attempting the voice of Karagiozis. He was a natural: the deep nasal gnarling voice with the *"hyakk hyakk hyakk"* laugh. Although Giannis insisted on hiding his face behind a book when I asked for a personal demonstration.

"I can't do it if people are looking at me..."

Another teacher, Pavlos, was responsible for the voices of Stavrakas, the Sultan and Barba Giogos. I met Pavlos and congratulated him on what a remarkable performance he gave when I first saw them play. What a ridiculous, scabrous, voice he produced for his puppets. We both looked rather embarrassed as he then spoke to me in his normal voice, which was utterly identical to these horribly spoken characters.

As Ilias and his gang of puppeteers got ready for their performance, we, the musicians, gathered in a classroom to run through the songs we were to play.

We had a repertoire of 14 songs on the night. Starting with the traditional fast, whirling Karagiozis overture which we played over and over again, the playing getting faster and faster, stirring up the feeling in the crowd as they took their seats.

It was a warm night under a black sky in Lemon Tree Square in the centre of Corfu. Surrounded by the Italianate buildings, with women watching down from high open-shuttered windows, souvlaki sellers had their stalls set up in the corners. Men clutched glasses of wine, kids cross-legged in the front rows were eating *pastelli* and drinking Loux lemonade. Karagiozis began the performance with his usual long greeting to the crowd.

"Tonight we will eat and we will drink... and as always, we will go to bed hungry..." – poverty, desperation, grim humour and resignation ever present, even in the midst of a good time.

Then Karagiozis gave the customary rambling speech as to what they will see in the performance. It was strange to be sat with the orchestra and to be staring out at the crowd, their faces lit-up by the bright shadow-theatre screen. I got a view as you would see if you turn around in a cinema: faces all un-self-consciously lost in enjoyment, concentrating solely on the performances, mouths fallen open.

Eventually the hoard of other puppet characters joined Karagiozis and the story unravelled itself in chaos up on the stage. Periodically the dialogue would end briefly and we musicians would strike up. I found it hard to keep up with some of these ancient Eastern-rhythmed tunes, all full of 7/8 time structures, and many of the words were lost on me. But when the men of our group of musicians put on women's high-pitched voices and sang to their wandering-handed lovers – "*Ochi etho!*" – no, not there! – or when we, and the crowd, all sang lustily together "We're all Corfiots, we sing all the day and in the evening... we swear!" – the Corfu crowd found it agonisingly funny and in perfect keeping with the carnival atmosphere.

The parable of this particular Karagiozis performance was based around a story where Karagiozis had got himself into the usual trouble promising the Sultan he could form a musical band. He spent his time trying to swindle and cheat many of the characters into forming a band with him but in the end we musicians sat underneath the berdeh, the tent surrounding the screen, were indicated by Karagiozis, sadly, as the final result of all he could muster. But to cheers from the audience, we played a final driving song as the puppeteers emerged from behind the screen to dance with their respective characters held up on their sticks – looking like the souvlaki sellers plying their trade in the square, twirling the skewered puppets above the heads of the crowd and us players. The music went on into the night. Long after Karagiozis was abandoned by his master, limp and lifeless on one of the wine barrels in the square, as the crowds drank and danced around. Karagiozis's ludicrously proportioned long arm had fallen down the side of the barrel as the party continued around him, but the insolent grin remained stuck on his painted face.

I found myself sat on a heap of old sacks of potatoes on a decrepit leaking boat.
We were stalled in the middle of 'The Channel', the supposedly dangerous body of water between Corfu and the small island of Paxos to the south. The old Greek skipper with a dirty captain's hat, chewing on a never extinguishing scrap of a cigarette, stood on the stern, pulling at a propeller cord and whacking indiscriminately with a spanner. I was with the 'Koum Kou Art' group again, surrounded by boxes and bags stuffed full of Karagiozis effects and paraphernalia – the humungous Karagiozis nose poking right out of the top of one open box. We were going to play another show.
There are some famous Karagiozis stories that have been written down and are performed often – Karagiozis the Baker, Karagiozis in Love – but the beauty of Karagiozis tales is that they are permutable and the performers often fashion their own stories to suit the crowd or the place where the show is being played. "You don't write a Karagiozis story. You tell it..." is the axiom, and I saw this to be true as we played further performances.
We were on our way now, on the seemingly doomed boat, to perform a Christmas show in the centre square of Paxos, where Father Christmas and the famous, festive, grotesque Greek goblins – the *kalikajaros* – were to make an appearance. Kalikajaros are horrible creatures, appearing at Christmas time, drenched in wine, infamous for urinating down people's chimneys, green and bald and hideous and always wanting to dance and cause mayhem. They were very popular when they appeared on the lit screen in this Karagiozis performance for the children of Paxos. It's an interesting twist to the

Karagiozis tales that sometimes other characters or figures, even people from history, will turn up. So, you may well come across a scene where Karagiozis will be conversing with, say, Alexander the Great or Odysseus. The folklores and histories of Greece and Greek people, played for fun, but also celebrated.

Later we played a performance of Karagiozis and the Refugees, created especially by the teachers of the school as a commentary on the situation gripping Greece and the wider world.

It was here that I saw the true uniqueness to Karagiozis and its complete dissimilarity from Britain's Punch and Judy – and I was surprised to find that actually none of the 'Koum Kou Art' group had heard of my own island's old fashioned puppet theatre. Punch and Judy may have its anarchic clowning, as of course does Karagiozis, which makes the front rows of children howl, but fundamental to Karagiozis is its satire and its political commentary, which appeals to the radicals and the thinkers also in the audience. And in these modern times of Greek difficulties, as in the periods of crisis and hardship in the centuries of Greece's past, Karagiozis as the simple representation of the everyday Greek is as significant and meaningful as ever as he plays in towns and villages across the country. Mocking authority figures, the rich, the powerful, and commenting on the injustices forced on the people, and their cursed situations. And always with the voices of those who live on their wits, the impoverished and the rebellious of Greece. And on Corfu island especially, all played out under a rare musical spell.

Part 4
Paradise Forgone!

01.06.2016

Manolis has lost his kafeneo. Never asking a single customer to pay their bill, drinking through his own stock night after night... it seems these weren't great business ideas. The warped, faded, rose-coloured doors have now been bolted. The bar is dead. Manolis has found work in Orestis's old bakery instead. He works with little Manolis – the Albanian. Giristroula and I visited two nights ago in the early hours of the morning after a night out. The two of them were in their dirty sweat-soaked t-shirts and white hats, throwing the bread into the scorching primitive stone ovens. Manolis kneading and pulling at the clingy sheets of flour with a cigarette burning in his mouth, the ash bending long over the dough. A blackened silver Madonna ikon sat above the ovens on the burnt, heat-stained, wall.

Manolis the Albanian wants to move to England. He wants me to write him a testimonial for his visa. Every day we find he has left something from his garden on our doorstep: a bag full of tomatoes, a pyramid of balanced oranges, a headless chicken. The other Manolis took me into his confidence yesterday, pulling me to one side as I walked through the village.

"Eh, are you thinking of writing him the letter? I wouldn't do it..." he said of his best friend. "He's a bad man, a very bad man. He'll only get you in trouble..."

This morning a fresh gift of three giant watermelons have been left on our doorstep. I saw Manolis the Albanian down by the church. He smiled and waved, and acted out a hopeful mime of a letter being written.

21.06.2016

Summer in Corfu is too rich, too full. Like a song that's all chorus and no verse. Spring had been good – the flowers appearing rapidly in ones and twos on the hillside like firecrackers going off. Hundreds of new insects I'd never seen before and couldn't recognise. The re-emergence of the lizards: darting across a hot wall, pausing at the sight of me, frozen with one leg in the air. The sun returning like a briefly deposed king.

Easter had come with the raining down of pots thrown from the windows of the high Venetian houses in Corfu Town. This unique tradition on Easter Saturday is either to wake up Persephone, the goddess of Spring, or a good way of getting rid of the old so that the new year will bring new, better, things. We had watched the sombre Good Friday procession: coffins and slow drum beats and mournful brass bands. Crowds lining the paths. I saw one old woman staggering back and forth with her husband on her back so he could get a good view over the heads.

Easter is a far bigger deal in Greece than Christmas. The dark drama of death far more appealing to Greek senses than the light serenity of Christ's birth.

While we packed the square watching the sky fill with falling pots, I had recognised a woman who has a shop in the narrow tight lanes by the island's main St Spiridon church – one of the hawkers who set up their stalls next to the church. The large yellow 500-year-old church always looks as if it's been surrounded, attacked, like an old elephant by a tenacious pack of hyenas selling their carved wooden trinkets, football shirts or bottles of Corfu's kumquat liqueurs. The woman clunked Giristroula on the head with her umbrella.

"*Anepithimiti...*" she said – You're not welcome. "You outsiders coming here for our traditions, getting in my way, stopping my enjoyment... Why don't you just go home?"

A week or so later, as we had passed her shop I saw her again. She grinned and stretched out her arms for us to come in and buy some of her tourist tat. "*Kiria mou...*" she sang in a sweet imploring voice.

One late evening in early May, Olympiakos lost the Greek football cup final. There was a huge ringing commotion in our village's church square. Everyone came out of their houses to see what was happening and found Markos, the old villager with his black and white beard down to his navel and bald head, swinging high in the night sky from the church bells. Markos is an avid fan of Panathinaikos, Olympiakos's rival. He has painted his centuries-old stone villagers' house with huge green shamrocks and big daubs of Panathinaikos slogans. Markos was drunk as a skunk, hanging from the bells, the priest below shouting up cursed words at him. Markos, uncaring, swung to and fro, his blissful sozzled face emerging and disappearing in the moonlight. The bells clanging out late into the night, celebrating his enemy's defeat.

27.06.2016

Stavros seems to have given up on his acting. He was furious when his one small scene in the Durrell's television adaptation was left on the cutting room floor. He had gathered the whole of the village round his house and brought a TV set outside for us all to see his performance.

"*Erhete...*" It's coming... "*Kodevee...*" It's close... "*Tora..!*" Now..!

His face then went through his whole range: twisting confusion, bafflement, realisation, anger, as his walk-on part in a crowd scene didn't appear.

"Ok. You all go home now," he said as he snapped the tv off, stomping back inside his house, slamming the door.

He has now opened a taverna higher up the road in the village under the stone bridge with a deep well outside. No one ever seems to visit. I walk past in the evenings, the restaurant is always empty. Framed pictures of Stavros on stage, acting in Greek tragedies, holding up a skull to the spotlight, clutching a sword to his breast, line every spare space on the walls. I wave as I pass but Stavros, surrounded by empty wine bottles, has his eyes closed. He's wearing long blue robes and his face is plastered with make-up and theatrical greasepaint. He strums a small mandolin and sings deep and low to himself.

06.07.2016

Giristroula and I climbed to the tiny 10th century church above the village on the evening before the village Saint's great feast. A white chapel all alone up a steep mule path, Byzantine frescoes on the walls. We stood and stared as the whole island spread underneath us in a vivid sweep, glowing and altering in the final leaking light of the sun. There was a rustling noise behind us. The village priest was up here fixing the church for the celebrations tomorrow. He raised a hand but didn't say a word to us. Out of his priest's robes, the flies on his trousers bust and gaping wide open, his filthy shirt hung down low. Seventy years old or more, prodigious stomach, hair fallen straggly out of his Orthodox ponytail, his beard soaked in sweat. We tried to follow him back down the steep hill to the village over the rocks and stones but he was uncatchable. Like an ibex gambolling nimbly over the loose crags.

The heat of the day has become extreme lately, not comfortable to be out in the sun for more than 10 minutes. The land is baked and cracked. There is no wind and the blue sky sits like the sealed lid of a box oven, leaving us sweating and poached below. The sea is just a warm flat pool.

29.07.2016

We caught a boat to sail out to the three small islands north of Corfu, the Diapontia Islands: Erikoussa, Othoni and Mathraki. A population of less than 300 on each one. The ferry had slowly plodded along from Corfu like a fat man after a heavy meal, occasionally burping on the hooter. We landed at tiny Erikoussa island and disembarked alongside all the goods from the real world stacked up and wheeled down the ramp to sustain this small community. A man with his whole life piled up in one tiny broken-down car: bags, beds, family, fridge, bath tied on to the roof.

We were stared at by old men from chairs outside a white stone old café a few yards in front of the dock. The rest of the island appeared completely asleep, just a filthy dog having a long and satisfying scratch in the sun. So we joined the few there in the café. Eventually the island woke up to its new visitors, shutters opened, vans spluttered into life to take people to one of the very few places to stay on the island. I was struck at how many American accents there were as we made our way from the port area, some people easily swapping back and forth between Greek and American English. Apparently this collection of small islands north of Corfu figured heavily in the great 20th century emigration trail of Greeks fleeing poverty to America. Almost the whole of Erikoussa was emptied by people moving over the Atlantic. Now relatives come back to visit the land of their ancestral home. Coca-cola and ouzo bottles sat side-by-side on the café tables.

We spent the night camping on the long sweep of beach and the next day caught the early boat to the next island, Othoni. The Othonians stood at port side, awaiting their essential deliveries, staring at our arrival. A strong scent of Cypress hung in the air. This island is where Odysseus was washed up on his long trek home, imprisoned for 10 years by the nymph Calypso in her cave, unable to leave and make his way back to Ithaca. I was imprisoned too. For two days I was struck down with food poisoning and stuck in my white cell of a hotel room, a generator rumbling loudly outside all night and day. A storm blew up while I was on my sick bed, rain and wind lashing the island. When I finally emerged I found there was no one who would be prepared take us to Calypso's beach to see her cave. We walked from person to person, shop to tavern, all the old men with their beards and their sea-dog tales had been scared by the storm.

"The sea takes three days to calm down. Don't you know this? No, no, no. There's no way I'll risk my boat..."

So we told them we'd try and swim it. The cave was only a few miles from the town, round the rocks, down the coast.

"Swim!" they said, throwing their hands up. "It's too deep... No, no, no... The seals will get you..."

Eventually we found one man who would take us in his clapped-out boat. We had to slop out the sea water continuously from round our ankles as we chugged our way to Calypso's beach. But then, there it was. The cave where the nymph goddess kept Odysseus, forcing him to stay and make love to her – apparently reluctantly and to his great mortification – again and again and again. The shore where he sat and watched all those rosy-fingered dawns. The clear turquoise waters, the ribboning cliffs and white sands. Even an immortal visitor would gaze in wonder.

When Odysseus was finally released, it took him 18 days to get to Corfu, with the island looking like a shield on the misty sea. We are back, passing Corfu's Mouse Island – Odysseus's boat turned into rock by an envious Poseidon, so they say – five hours after leaving Othoni, having crossed the wine-dark sea from Greece's very most westerly point. I can't think what kept him so long.

09.08.2016

Manolis has seen me reading under a tree in the olive groves outside of the village. He approached Giristroula to tell her what he had seen. She said he was embarrassed, as if he had caught me with another woman. "Reading…" he said to her quietly, disgusted.

Manolis has lost his job at the bakery. Falling foul to Orestis's capricious ways, he is now watering olive trees all night for 20 euros. He also goes out fishing after his watering, but he can never seem to catch a thing. Giristroula and I often watch from the hills of the village down over the roofs on the nights when the moon isn't crawling across the warm tiles and lighting up the sea. The dark water is best for the men to go out fishing. We look down towards the sea and their rows of fishing boats with the suspended light bulbs pointing down into the water illuminating the fish, and we think of Manolis out there, catching nothing.

15.08.2016

Giristroula and I had been getting tired of life in the small red house here in the village. Getting fed up of our neighbour – Orestis's son – treating our house like his own. We would find him most days in our garden digging up our vegetables and plants. Never smiling, never saying a word apart from telling us of things he had seen us doing around the village from his window that he didn't agree with. The rent was too high for such a small house so far from the town. We told Dionysis we wanted to leave. We gave him plenty of notice.

"*Mia hara*," he said – fine. "There are plenty of other people who want to live there." He put on the great Greek act of not being bothered, even a little scornful about why we would even bother him with such trivia.

It was leaving day today, and we packed up our things to be taken away by some men with a van. We drove off in our own car. When we were later reunited with our belongings, the workmen told us that Dionysis had been hiding behind a wall as we left. He had come out and said to them "Where are you taking these things? Where are they going? They can't just leave. Who will rent this..." he waved his hand at the house, "This..." His anger getting the better of him, "Who will rent this *paraga* off me? Where will I get my money?"

He had grabbed one of the workmen by the collar of his shirt. He had rooted through the boxes, tried to take some of our things but the men wouldn't let him. The van drove out of the village down the narrow road with old man Dionysis clinging desperately to the back, his wooden leg trailing behind him.

"You can't go!!"

13.09.2016

North of the island. This time we wanted to find somewhere to live north of Corfu Town. We were driven around by a grossly fat estate agent. On the dashboard of his seedy blue Mercedes was the Holy Trinity of pictures I often see in many Greek family men's cars: The Virgin Mary, beside a photo of his daughter, next to a topless model.

Kodokali. A yellow sprawling villa. Its own little church built in the grounds.

"This is a *very* nice house. Peaceful," the estate agent said, breathing meatily.

We said we'd take it.

"Vasili!! Eat something. You haven't finished your food. Eat!"

A small boy slammed out of one of the doors, his mother chasing him out of another holding a spoon.

"Eat!!"

A man in his underpants and a vest then appeared, shouting, singing, neighing at all his other children pouring out from behind him.

"Oh ho!" he said, spotting us. "You must be our new neighbours!"

Wiping his hands down his thighs, he gave us two great garlicky hugs.

"*Kalos irthate!*" he boomed. "Welcome!"

This is the Lappas family.

The chickens of the Lappas family walk freely through our house at all times of the day. Followed by the strutting cocky rooster. We have a bare couple of rooms. The Lappas house is decorated with perhaps a thousand religious ikons.

It is hard to exactly gauge how big their family is, there always seems to be another child added every time I try a headcount. Each time I pass through their open door, a baby is planted in my arms. Lappas, a large upended sofa of a man, will appear and set me down at the kitchen table, pouring out big tumblers of tsipouro. Always wanting to argue. Pounding the table with rage one moment, gurgling with laughter the next.

Back in June, Britain voted to leave Europe. I have grave misgivings about this. For immigrants like me, life living abroad is going to get very precarious. The pound plunged straight away, making Giristroula and I poorer still. The Greeks seem to think Britain has done something heroic though. People come up and congratulate me.

"We couldn't do it, but you can. You'll bring the European Union down for us…"

I tell them it's not perhaps the noble fight they think it is. Greece may have suffered terribly at the hands of the EU, with the forced austerity crippling the country, but back in Britain people have voted to leave for many different, many dishonourable reasons.

"We were ready," Lappas said to me, brandishing a fistful of his collection of old drachma notes. "When we had our own referendum, we were ready," he bashed his fist into his chest. "We were ready to starve if we had to!"

Lappas is always wiping wine from his beard, always wiping a piece of olive oil soaked bread round a bowl.

I'm woken every day by Lappas, down below my window, rolling out of bed, roaring at his children. The children that he loves more than life itself.

31.10.2016

I've been asked by a friend who edits a magazine back in London to write a few observations on Corfu, so I send a few vague thoughts on the look and sound of the Corfiots.

Tourism has altered ways of doing things here. Altered the pace of life. The openness of many in Corfu is now often only an exterior, not durable to anything more than just loose association – as opposed to Corfu of the past, or the ways of Greeks in other, wilder, less mercantile areas of the country. But the Corfiots can't avoid the long line of history running through them, back down the years. It's there in their individual look: the distinct chubby round faces. It's there in the blue eyes and blonde hair that many Corfiots have – uncommon in Greece – coming from the years of Venetians in Corfu, and the British (both now and then) and the Albanians just across the Straits of Corfu.

The Straits of Corfu, in the north of the island, seems almost a swimmable distance from Albania. And many refugees put this to the test during the era of Albanian dictator, Enver Hoxha. The island has a hundred stories of desperate young men clinging to tyres, old ladies in bath tubs coming across, aiming for Corfu's rich shoreline.

The Corfu language is full of idiosyncrasies. The common "re" that all Greek's use to prefix every conversation, to express surprise or get attention, is replaced by an "o re" here in Corfu. Corfiots will also call anyone they meet "agapi" – my love – they say this to strangers, children, old people, anyone. Even during arguments with their most hated foe. And fools or stupid people get their completely-specific-to-Corfu word "niorandes." The muja – the open-palm, splayed-fingered contemptuous hand gesture that all Greeks sling in the direction of someone who has just cut-up their car, made an idiotic remark or generally got on their nerves – is replaced on this island by a bunched fist with the thumb poking through the first and second fingers. And Corfiots like to swear. More so than in other parts of Greece – and Greeks as a whole are never really that shy with a bellowed malediction – the Corfiots will turn to the sky with an inventive series of profanities. But unlike in other parts of the country, it's the island's patron saint, Spiridon, who receives the most profanities.

The Italian influence is always slipping in again and again, unheeded, on this island. For example, Corfiots will say "Libretto" of their shutters if they are partially closed – Italian for a half opened book. "Liberta!" if they're flung open wide. "Tsito!" the café owner shouts at the stray cats around his doorway "Tsito!" What is this word? Only heard in Corfu. Again, some strain of Italian I guess. I'm told there are over 3,000 words that are particular only to Corfu, not heard anywhere else in Greece. "I'm going to write a dictionary of them all…" says the unshaven Corfiot I see most days sat in a bar in town. Of course he never will.

There's the accent too that is also so unusual and peculiar to this island. 'Tragoudista' Greeks from other parts of the country call it – a singing voice. Rising and falling on syllables, like a musical tide. Maybe this is connected to the Italian influence as well? Or the unique musical aspect that exists here…"

11.11.2016

Kodokali has a large community of British people. Many of them spend their time drinking their days away in 'The Old Barrels' pub. Lappas can't understand the British at all. He stands outside the windows of the Old Barrels, his face flushed with excitement.

"What are they doing in there?" he points through the glass. "What are they doing?!"

It seems to me that a few old men are just sat in the darkness, drinking in silence. An air of Tuesday afternoon alcoholic gloom hanging about the place. But Lappas is astounded, bewildered.

"What's happening? Is this normal in Britain?" he asks, pointing again through the window.

"Well why don't we go in?" I say to Lappas.

"Nooo..." he recoils, waving his hands in the air, smiling nervously at the idea, as if I've suggested the most inappropriate, unbelievable proposal. He goes back to looking through the window.

"What are they *doing* there?" he shakes his head, stupefied.

The magazine has rejected my article.

15.11.2016

Before Corfu's damp green winter sets in, the olives have to be harvested. It is said that Corfu has two million olive trees on the island. But they are unruly, not cultivated well. The olives aren't the best. Back in Venetian times they used the oil for fuel and rewarded the Corfiots for planting as many trees as possible and growing them as high as they could. Now the trees push up with clawing fingers into the sky. Many Corfiots lazily leave nets down on the ground to collect the olives, but this isn't good. Once they've fallen they're already going bad.

I walk past some olive groves on the hills above the sea. Old women in headscarfs, dungarees and thick socks stand on stepladders, whacking at the branches with sticks trying to knock the black bullets down. We wave greetings as I pass.

They were probably great beauties once upon a time, back when they met their husbands, the farmers and owners of these little plots of olive trees. Now the women look tired. They are bent with pain and spend their days smelling of animal droppings.

I offered the other day to take the Lappas children into town to visit the old cinema. Watching a film in Greece is a ridiculous experience: no one stops talking throughout the screening. The audience compete with each other to shout out spoilers as loudly as they can, everyone cackling along at this routine. I sat in the cinema on ancient maroon velvet seats watching the latest Hollywood film as kids ran and shrieked all around me. One father chased his son up onto the high-rise part at the front of the cinema, put his boy over his knee and thwacked at him for an age, all magnified and silhouetted up on the screen. Almost like a Karagiozis performance. Then, halfway through, the projectionist just stopped the film, mid-dialogue, for 20 minutes. He put the lights on so everyone could walk around and chat with old friends, gossip, greedily smoke cigarettes, happily forget why they were here in the first place. And then the film just started up again, everyone back to their seats, to shout out as loud as they could for the rest of the performance.

I left the Lappas home with five kids. I had a feeling I returned with about eight or nine.

02.09.2017

We have been away, living in different parts of the country while Giristroula has been researching children's playground games throughout Greece. We returned to the chaos of the yellow villa just as the Lappas' were having a baptism for a new addition to their family.

In the church the priest blessed the water, dunked the baby three times, and then slathered the child in olive oil.

"Where did you get the oil?" someone asked the *nonos* – the godfather. "Is it good oil? If the boy has problems later, if he goes crazy, it will be your fault, you know, if that oil wasn't good…"

"*Apetaxo to Satana?*" – have you renounced Satan? – the Priest asked three times.

"*Emfississon keh emptyson afto!*" – Breathe and spit upon him!

The crowd stood pressed together, clutching candles. The baby's hair was cut.

"God grant you many years!" we repeated again and again.

Out in the garden, which had been laid out with tables, forty of Lappas's hens had been slaughtered for the guests. Great big barrels of wine. A band played under the trees and guests danced in circles under the bright sun: adult, adult, child, adult, all gripping each other's shoulders, kicked steps forward and back. A man slapped at his full belly next to me making the sound of a bass drum.

I met Lappas's brother who played with the musicians with his clarinet. He had come from Thessaloniki and told me of a gledi he played at on a farm outside the city to celebrate the making of the year's tsipouro. There had been a terrible tragedy as, while they played and drank and danced, the farmer got trapped in his huge vat of tsipouro and drowned.

"What a way to go..." Lappas's brother said, shaking his head, draining his glass of tsipouro.

The party went on late into the night, bodies were laid out on the ground as I wound my unsteady way to bed. I saw Lappas under the trees, striped by the moonlight, holding his latest son in his arms. He was flushed with the most enormous pride and joy.

11.09.2017

A new school term at the free Greek classes that are run in the evenings at the primary school in the centre of town. The priests arrived and blessed the school for the year, shaking bunches of basil dipped in holy water into every corner. Greeks will ask a priest to bless anything that's new. I've even seen priests gathered round the open bonnet of a new car, crossing themselves and granting the engine a hymn of blessing. I turned up at Voula's class but it's a different crowd to the last time I was here. Now at the front of the class there are groups of Syrian and Afghanistani men. Refugees who had taken boats over the Aegean Sea in the summer and had been relocated to Corfu while they waited to be granted permission to continue their travel further into Europe.

They are keen students. Despite the fact they don't necessarily want to stay in Greece, and don't know how long they will be here, they want to learn the language. Compared to the refugees, our slow attempts at learning Greek look lazy. They have questions for Voula, they write assiduous notes, they want to learn this language quickly. They don't want to be dragged down by our half-arsed efforts. What's wrong with us, why don't we take it more seriously?

16.10.2017

I walked past the marina in Gouvia, along the promenade, past all the masts and yachts and moneyed foreigners sipping in the cafés. Suddenly I heard the clack of leather on willow. The main cricket pitch in Corfu has moved from Spianada Square – they've built a car park in the covers and down at fine leg now – to here, by the marina. The Greek national team were practising. I stood and watched for a while. Eventually they asked me to join in. I sent a few balls down. The first in 10 years or so, my body creaking like an old gate. Then they asked me if I wanted to play for them in their next game. This seemed ridiculous, but they told me many of their players were away on holiday, they needed extras.

"I'm not Greek," I pointed out. They brushed this off.

"Your wife is Greek, yes? It's enough, it's enough..." the captain said, wafting a hand in their air.

The next game was against a Rest Of The World team. There were riotous scenes as one of the Greeks was given out for the little known, but perfectly legitimate, law of hitting the ball twice. The Greeks suspected crookedness and players rushed from the pavilion onto the field, pushing and shoving, accusations of cheating, fingers pointed in the umpire's faces. "*Malaka! Malaka!*" It took half an hour to calm things down and for the game to continue.

"Eh Spiro," one of the players called to the man putting the scores up on the board. "It's 183 for four, nor three."

The man was offended, slung the numbers down on the floor, pushed over the board.

"Are you trying to tell *me* my job?"

After the match, which the Rest Of The World won comfortably, I listened in as an Australian told one of the Greek batsmen who had clearly known earlier that he was out but didn't admit to it, that he should have walked. How it was in the spirit of the game, the spirit of fair play. The Greek stared at him dumbly. The Australian might as well have been explaining neuroscience to a penguin. The Greek batsman obviously long schooled in the old saying: 'Better to be a cheat than a fool...'

I took no wickets, scored no runs. No one asked me to come back for the next game.

12.12.2017

Saint Spiros's day. The saint of the island. Spiros was a simple shepherd who dedicated himself to God and was given the power of healing. After his death in 384BC his body – remarkably preserved, still at normal human temperature – was moved around and around: Cyprus, Constantinople, northern Greece. Since 1453 though, he has been holed up in his great silver sarcophagus in the main church in Corfu Town. Today he was brought out, small and black, mummified and frightening-looking, crouched in his glass box. He was carried on an ornate stretcher through the town. Corfiots gathered and jostled and fought to get to see the saint, to kiss his feet. He is the hero of the island, saving it from fires and plagues and, in 1716, driving away the Ottoman invasion – his apparition flying at the Turkish fleet with a flaming sword. Most boys born on the island will be given the name Spiros.

Saint Spiros Church, dark and decorated inside, is a place I like to come and sit in the peace, out of the sun and the heat. Saint Spiros always lies there, closed and locked up in his case in his sanctuary. People leave little silver ikons – *tamata* – with the image appropriate for whatever prayer they want to be answered: a little silver boat hanging above Saint Spiros if someone's husband has gone on a long dangerous fishing journey; a silver representation of a leg if someone's child has been born handicapped; a pair of eyes engraved into a square piece of silver hanging from a silk string if their eyesight is failing. The Corfiots are sure Saint Spiros will do what he can. Chanting goes on at the front of the church, a small humming drone like a bluebottle caught on a window pain. Christ looks down from the ceiling on the few of us sat on the pews here: the farmer, the fisherman, the rich Corfiot businessman.

Once I saw a man sat at the front with a pile of scratchcards, slinging them to the ground as each one revealed nothing, swearing under his breath as he slung. Then he got a winner. He rose to his feet and cried out in joy and rushed to the altar, falling to his knees, kissing over and over again at Saint Spiros's silver coffin.

23.12.2017

We climbed up Pantokrator today – the tallest mountain of Corfu – to take a look down at the island below us. As if to make sure everything was ok. Just like Kaiser's Throne in Pelekas, or the unmarked path that leads up between the small towns of Doukades and Agia Anna, up to the ancient miniature white-washed church of Agios Simeon clinging completely on its own over a sheer drop towards Paleokastritsa and the surrounding ribs of mountain rock alive with birds – Corfu has some incredible peaks to stand and to contemplate.

I have been involved in a Christmas panto the British community are putting on down in the town in the Anglican church. Greeks don't know what a panto is, the Dames and Widow Twankys all quite baffling to them. A few Greeks have been roped in to help, but predictable arguments spill out in the old church hall. Two Greeks in a pantomime cow costume was never going to be a good idea. But even though they don't really understand it, the Greeks love acting. A large swarthy Greek, Kostas, is playing the evil Count. There is no need for a fake moustache to twirl, he has his own. We will give a performance in the main Corfu theatre. It could either be brilliant or unimaginably awful.

01.01.2018

New Year's Day arrives and Lappas greets it with the tradition of hurling a fat pomegranate to smash on our doorstep. The seeds spilling out for good luck. We are going to be moving in the next few days. Moving back south of the main town again, to rooms in a white villa in the middle of an olive grove looking down over the sea. The owner has cats and dogs she wants looking after while she's not around. We will miss the Lappas family terribly.

Moving back to our old area has alerted Dionysis our old landlord, who had felt personally wronged when we left his house. As we were being shown round the white villa I could see that Dionysis had sent one of his spies to see what we were doing.

Unfortunately for him, he had sent Adonis the fat fisherman. Adonis tried to hide behind a tree to see what was going on. His stomach stuck out a mile.

15.01.2018

There have been storms this new year. Storms always seem to bring electricity cuts to the island. I once had an appointment at the dentist when all the power went. Unperturbed, the dentist just carried on doing his rooting around in my mouth by the light of his phone's torch. He appeared very used to power cuts. Then, as I was sitting back in the chair, with his phone hovering above my wide open mouth, his torch died too. He continued the rest of the routine clutching a candle.

Visiting the hospital can be a challenge too. I was once walking on Kodokali's empty beach when a stray dog appeared from nowhere and bit me hard on the backside. I went to the Corfu hospital casualty department and they told me I should have a tetanus jab. I was reluctant, but eventually they talked me into it.

"You should have the tetanus jab," they said.
"I don't really want to."
"You must."
"Really?
"Yes."
"Ok then."
"Ok?"
"Ok."
"You'll do it?" they asked.
"Yes," I said.
"Good... Now can you go and buy us the tetanus jabs. We've run out..."

So I had to go to the chemist and buy a stack of tetanus jabs. When other doctors in the hospital realised I was going to the chemists, they came with long lists of other things I could buy for them too.

The rain has ruined the road in the hills above our house. Half of it has fallen down the hillside. I gingerly walked along the edge and met a car coming the other way.

"Can I get through?" the man said.

"No," I said. "Look…" I pointed at the 'Danger – No Entry' signs.

The man gave me the Greek sagging shoulders, the mouth pulled down in a scoffing pose…

"Yes, but *can* I drive through?" he said.

"The road really is very bad," I told him.

I could see him looking over his steering wheel. I could tell he still thought he could make it.

I walked back half an hour later. His car was stuck, two wheels hanging over the edge, workmen pushing at it to get the whole car back on the road. The man shouting and plunging his arms down low, angrily, as if it was all someone else's fault. One of the workmen giving him the Greek sign he was crazy, clutching his hand into a claw and twisting it by the side of his head.

16.02.2018

It is Carnival time here in Corfu, in the run-up to Lent. My favourite thing, only seen on this island, is the *petegoletsa*: The Gossips. Woman lean out of their windows in the old town, on their balconies over the alleyways and squares, hanging out their washing and discuss loudly and indiscreetly all the secrets and perceived failings of various famous figures around Corfu. Or their husband's bad behaviour and poor efforts in bed. Or the state of other people's laundry. All in the thick Corfu City dialect, which is different from all the other unique dialects of the rest of the island. Sometimes the women will lean back and sing an Ionian serenade. It's all recreated by actors nowadays, brightly made-up, wearing old women's cleaning clothes and headscarfs, but this is a real tradition stretching back hundreds of years. The crowd gather below to listen to the lewd conversations, cackling with their red round Corfiot faces turned to the high Venetian balconies. On an island that has lost so much of its identity through tourism, I find this all a great spirited connection to Corfu's past.

12.11.2018

Above Argirades – Silver Town – an old village down in the south of the island, an ancient old woman stood in the doorway of the church, her head tied tight in a blue headscarf.

"*Apo pou ise?*" she said to me – where are you from.

"Londino," I replied – London.

"Londino?" she said, absolute confusion on her face. "*Londino..?*" she repeated to herself quietly, looking at the ground.

"Paliohora," I try again, the village just a few kilometres down the road.

"Ah Paliohora!" she brightened, "*Kala! Po, po, po..!*" she was impressed. "He's from Paliohora!" I heard her telling the other old men and women who appeared in the tiny village lanes.

"Paliohora. He's come here to see us from Paliohora!" I heard floating down the hill as she called up to her friend in a top window, a voice of utter amazement, as if I'd arrived from somewhere in central Africa.

We passed an old woman walking up the slope as we went down. She had two very large logs that she was taking back to her fireplace balanced one on top of the other on her head. In these real rural parts of Corfu the Corfiots still, even today, use the duration of a cigarette as a record of distance. I've asked someone before something like "*Poso makria ine Corfu Town?*" And got the reply "*Eh... Ochi makria. Thio tsigara thromos...*" – Not far. You'll smoke two.

01.05.2019

We stand out on the veranda. Stripes of moonlight on the sea, the warm wind blowing up onto the balcony through the olive trees. The occasional thud of an orange falling to the ground somewhere out in the dark. It could be paradise here, I'm sure of it now.

During the bright days I also stand on the balcony and look out over the cypresses trees hanging on the sky like long thin puffs of dark green smoke. I look past them to the honey-smooth sea with the Greek mainland and the mountains of Albania, both just a gleaming distance away.

I feel incredibly lucky. I watch a pair of eagles languidly fly in circles overhead and remember how excited I used to get just seeing a magpie in the London plane tree outside my Streatham window.

28.06.2019

Thalia won't have music in her taverna any longer. Ever since Giorgos the bouzouki player ran away to Paris with her daughter, she won't allow any of the musicians to set up and play. So nowadays we all pile into the small dark bar 'Berdes' in the centre of town. The bar is named after the tent of a Karagiozis show, and this great bar is festooned in old Karagiozis and rebetiko paraphernalia. Musicians play, there is always smoke and laughter and thrown-back bottles of raki.

Giristroula and I went into town this evening. We walked along the old Venetian lanes and got souvlakis and gyros pitas to eat. Weirdly, only in Corfu, this classic Greek takeout always gets served with a tangy red sauce, like a spaghetti sauce. I don't know why they do this, perhaps it's the Italian influence once again? After eating, we joined the crowd in 'Berdes'. Everyone was there. Lappas was free from his children for the night, a collection of bottles in front of him already. He was shouting something to me about God. The Karagiozis theatre players were all there – Ilias, Giannis, Pavlos, Aphrodite. Giristroula joined one table to talk to some of her students from the music university. Other musicians plucked down instruments – a bouzouki or a violin – hanging from the ceiling and started to play. Spiros, the son of Voula my Greek teacher, poured me out another drink.

We will leave this island tomorrow. There are other places in Greece we have said we must visit, other places we must see. I will return, I'm sure of it. But I know I will always be thinking of those Corfu days that were not to be.

Chapter 4
Travels in Northern Greece

One summer, while we had still been living on Corfu, Giristroula and I crossed over the thin strip of sea that divides the island from Greece's mainland to take a tour around the northern part of the country. We travelled the northern lands that run from the Ionian in the west to the Bay of the Sacred Mountain in the east; from the southern Balkan borders down to the top of the Thessaly Plain. Journeying down the roads that once linked great Byzantine cities, over vast mountain ranges, and through dusty *vorioelladitika* villages.

We had no real purpose, we were travelling just to see what we would find. The way of all great journeys.

Part 1
Epirus

We were looking for a place to speak to the dead.

Having left the port town of Igoumenitsa, where our boat had docked, we faced straight away the foothills of the Pindus range. Mountains lying like gigantic sleeping dogs, curled up with heads resting on enormous paws. We cut into this range and headed for Necromanteion, an ancient Greek temple looking down onto the banks of the Acheron River. A temple dedicated to the oracles of death. Travellers in ancient times would make pilgrimage here to contact those who had passed away. Wily priests would lead these believers into the dark crypts and then, having taken their money, starved them for days and given them hallucinogenic plants to chew, would bring them back up into the daylight. Staggered and dazed, the followers would see the dead before them, larger than in life.

The sanctuaries and the black oppressive underground crypt, 3,000 years old, were open for Giristroula and me to climb down into. The pots where visitors left their dedications still stood preserved. We clambered down and waited in the open tomb, but emerged out from the dark crypts, blinking into the light, with a disappointing lack of any obvious signs from the other side. So, instead, we made our way down onto the plains we had seen from up high, and to the Acheron River. The river which took souls from this world to Hades.

You no longer need the sordid ferryman Charon – foul with grease and eyes like furnaces of fire – to transport you across the river to the underworld. There are now zipwires and hoardings and boards advertising pony trekking and red and yellow helmeted kayakers and loud families splashing about in the water. Hell is not down this river, Hell is right here.

Giristroula and I headed along the bank, upriver to get away from the organised holiday fun, passing the weekend hippies camping and playing guitars. After a 20-minute walk, we set up a tent ourselves, just above the gushing springs and the cave that opens up into Hades.

The river was clear and frighteningly cold to stand in. The noise downriver slowly ended as the sun died, and the river was left alone just for us. And perhaps some passing empty souls.

Early next day we headed away from Acheron higher into the mountains. The road wound round the toppling views up towards Souli. Giristroula told me of a dance she did, and every Greek girl does when they are at school. 'The Dance of the Souliotisses.' School girls learn this dance in tribute to the women of Souli, who were caught in the Greek-Turkish nineteenth century war. The dance ends with all the girls flinging themselves and their doll babies off the edge of the school stage, copying the heroic mass suicide of the women who plunged to their deaths from mountain tops to avoid the terrors of capture and slavery at the hands of the barbarous Ali Pasha. They fall with the song: "The women of Souli have learnt how to survive, and they also know how to die..."

As we approached the top of the climb, and a vast expanse of field hemmed in by a ring of huge mountainous rock walls where battle took place between Greeks and Turks, there was an eerie silence. Despite the now gentle peace sitting over these fields, I could hear these hills reverberating with ancient gunshot.

Dodoni, on the other side of the Souli mountains. Three centuries before Christ, a theatre was built here where festivals were held and sports played. Dodoni even rivalled Ancient Olympia in its contests and entertainments. Before this, though, Dodoni was known for its mysterious rites with its sacred tree. Pilgrims would come to the oak tree and priests would deduce the prophetic messages for them from the rustling leaves and the cawing of the birds in the branches.

Giristroula and I passed the ugly warehouses and bottled water factories on the modern Dodoni roundabouts. Suddenly the theatre was there. Old as time but still able to house audiences for performances in its sturdy but misshaped stone arc. Performers in robes and togas were milling about getting ready for a rehearsal that very afternoon. Walking the parched grounds between the broken columns, stones creaking under foot, Giristroula and I saw the oak trees were still standing here. The birds still making their noises, holding portentous branches in their claws. Even on this still dry day, a strong wind inexplicably rose and the oaks sighed. Though what exactly they were trying to tell us about our future, it was a little difficult to say.

We continued eastwards, rolling down towards the city of Ioannina, the capital of Epirus. Ioannina is Epirus's jewel. Roads full of old silver shops, spilling out with produce from old wooden fronts. We were looking out for the family home of our *koubara,* one of the two bridesmaids from our wedding, an Ioanninite from these parts.

The city seemed a peculiar mix. Byzantine churches and eastern minarets in the castle; then alpine-looking buildings in the central streets: stone-built with dark wood beams and hanging roofs for the snow. Unlike the rest of Greece, there were few balconies: usually vital places for Greeks to pad around after their afternoon sleeps, men soaking up the sun in their white underwear and smoking so deeply it looks like they are trying to suck the nicotine down into their feet; woman slinging dripping wet rugs over the railings to pour down onto the street below. There were even wide pavements in Ioannina for pedestrians, very rare in Greece. It struck me as more of a central European city.

We met our koubara and took a short bus-boat ride over the mountain-reflecting lake in the centre of Ioannina to the island with its small community of little homes and monasteries. There's a small lopsided house where a bullet hole in the floorboards indicates where the Turkish tyrant Ali Pasha finally met his justice. We ate at a taverna where they served us Ioannina's signature dish of frogs' legs straight out of the luridly luminous green waters that surrounded us.

"Vrekekex quacks quacks..."

The noise that Greeks think frogs make is different to how people think it sounds elsewhere. They're not any tastier to eat here than I imagined they'd be elsewhere either. We sailed back to the centre of town. I was struggling with the Greek I was hearing around me in Ioannina – the *people* seem to make different sounds here too... Epirots seem to cut the syllables from the end of every word. The word, say, for table – *trapehzee* – becomes *trapehz'*. And then other speakers cut the sounds in the middle of the word too, so it becomes *tra'ehz'*. I was frequently lost by this. I asked why they do it and was told that it can get so cold in the winter that people just don't have time to hang around talking. So they cut words down to the minimum length possible.

The three of us sat drinking on Kalari Street, with its stained old stone buildings. Eleni, our koubara, complained about life in Ioannina and pulled a face as she discussed the city, unimpressed by anything it had to offer. However, like all the Greeks who enjoy their pastime of condemning their hometown, as soon as I nodded agreement she snapped at me and couldn't believe I wouldn't want to live here myself. I *did* like Ioannina though, and as I watched the cheerful crowds throng the streets I thought how the common Greek saying 'San tin Arta keh ta Ioannina' – Dressing like Arta and Ioannina – a saying perhaps best summed up in English as 'mutton dressed up as lamb' didn't seem at all fair in this easy, unpretentious, genial little city.

Our koubara's grandmother, Labrini, was a strong-faced, strong-willed, widow well over 90 years old. She arrived at the family house the next morning, bent double, black headscarfed, worrying the cat with her stick, grumbling at everything and everybody. She was utterly discontented at having to be here in Ioannina. She hated the city, living her whole life outside in a small mountainous village. She had been brought to the city today for a hospital appointment. She was not interested in introductions, but placed a horny hand on my shoulder and lent towards me to tell me something.

"Then echo dei tin thalassa   pote..."

I wondered if my often faulty Greek was amiss here... She had never seen the sea? I double checked, but it was true. Living in central Greece, up here in these highlands, she had never set eyes on the sea in the whole of her extraordinarily long life. She told me she never wanted to. I imagined now, she never would. I tried to chat a little more but without warning she was off, up the street, shaking her stick at the cats in the road making them flee under the cars as she passed. So, with thanks and kisses and baskets of food forced upon us, we said goodbye to the family and left the overflowing home and headed out of the city.

Giristroula and I drove up sinewy slopes beyond Ioannina's edges and then, as the trees around us turned a russet brown, we started to plunge down again. Down to meet the Vikos Gorge.

Initially we missed the path into the gorge and instead walked straight into a small uneven stone church, the 15th century Saint Paraskevi monastery, clinging desperately to the rocks, with the gorge flowing an alarming thousand feet below. Seemingly abandoned for any religious use, with empty rooms and faded frescoes, a priest was sitting outside the church painting ikons on pieces of wood. He appeared to be hoping to sell these tatty items. We asked him for directions for the path down to the gorge. He placed down his brush and slowly stood up.

"Are you sure you want to go?"

This was unexpected. I told him we were very keen.

"Are you determined?"

I told him we were.

"How determined?"

He fixed me with a long stare. I told him we really wanted to walk the gorge.

"The path is there," he broke off, and pointed down the track between the trees, picking up his paint brush again and going back to his ikons.

As we turned to go, he called out to ask Giristroula where she was from. It surprised both of them when they found out they were from the same small town of Amaliada, way down south in the Peloponnese.

Giristroula and I set out on the path, shepherded along by a hard sun straight above us. A fast moving tortoise came out from the undergrowth and kept pace with us for a while. The scalding heat at the top of the gorge was then slowly replaced as we lowered ourselves, cautiously, into the bath tub of thick green trees, bush and shrub in the valley below.

The Vikos Gorge is, by some measurements, the deepest in the world. I found this surprising as I thought I would have heard this said somewhere before, but sometimes Greece doesn't like to boast. So, there I was, scudding down hundreds of feet on a steep loose path to the dry rocky riverbed at the bottom. Then, as we started on the long walk from Monodendri to the village of Vikos, along the base of the gorge, we were annoyingly thrown upwards again. And then down again, to the chaos of boulders at the bottom. And then up again, and then down again. The gorge's path was sometimes clearly laid out, sometimes it just required sheer guess work. Fallen trees needed to be vaulted; a rope was left out to haul ourselves up a bare rockface. The bleached stones of the empty riverbed acted as a weaving guide. The river must rage with water when the snows here fall and then melt. The shade of green changed every few hundred metres as fir trees gave way to pear trees, then thin reedy saplings which were then brushed aside by tall spreaders. And all the time we were continually looked down upon by the great jagged skyscrapers of towering rock above.

We finally lifted ourselves out of the gorge and up to the few scattered buildings of Vikos village about five hours after we started. The sun was setting as we stood outside an old kafeneo for an age and tried to flag down a lift. The fat lady owner of the café stood in the doorway of her bar, smiling at our efforts. Her cloth-capped clients raising an eyebrow at each other over their tsipouro and game of backgammon. Finally, having managed to cadge a lift in an old truck and having taken the endless hairpin turns climbing up Mount Tymfi, ears popping, tired slacked-necked heads banging on the truck window, we reached the village of Mikro Papigo.

The old stone hotel we fell into was still open and serving. We sat down at a long wooden table in the open terrace. Giristroula looked over and thought she recognised one of the other hikers sat eating in the courtyard.

"Nikos?" she said.

I told her she was making a mistake as I'd heard them speaking German to each other. But it *was* Nikos. A boy from her old town of Amaliada that she had gone to school with, who had left years ago to work in Switzerland. He had now brought his Swiss friends to walk the Zagoria.

"*Ha! Mono vouno meh vouno then smigi!*" laughed Giristroula – only mountains can't meet each other! An old Greek saying on the very common chance in this country that you will run into someone again, somewhere, sometime down the line...

We had met two people on the same day from Giristroula's small insignificant seaside Peloponnese town, 400 kilometres away to the south, here in this remote, impermeable, mountain-locked region. It seemed incredible.

Reunions were made and as we sat and ate late, and listened to the friends' stories of walks and climbs in Germanic countries, with the orange lantern lights making the courtyard dance in the darkness, I could have sworn I was in the Alps. The thick stone buildings surrounding us in the village all adding to the illusion. We asked if they knew of the priest from Amaliada in the monastery on the other side of the gorge. Nikos, who regularly comes back to Zagoria – this area of hundreds of square miles of untouched nature – said he knew him well. Everyone here talked about him. He was known for his drinking and his carousing and his womanising, bringing shame to the name of their old hometown.

We drained our glasses and toasted Zagoria. We toasted Epirus... this great little hotel... the hotel owner, who kept bringing us more and more bottles to drink... the mountains we would tackle the next day that hung over us now in the dark... Switzerland... the rascally priest... until there was nothing left to toast and we all fell heavily into our beds. The huge Papigo rock towers glowering at us, reproachfully, through our cracked wood and solid iron-crossed bedroom windows.

The morning came early. We set off, after a climber's breakfast, to tackle the mountain of Gamila, a short pathway walk from the village. A man passed with his family in tow, coming back down from the mountain. When had they started? How long had they been on the route?

"The end of the path," he puffed at me as he staggered closer, with a frail smile. "It's... it's like Ithaki..." he said, channelling Odysseus and his epic interminable journey that never seemed to get any closer.

"I don't know where I end and where the sweat begins," his wife said as she passed. Her face looking like an old red cabbage.

The climb up Gamila was hard: 2,500 metres, the fourth highest peak in Greece, with camping gear and tent on our backs, and in truth it was a fairly unenjoyable hike. The scenery was plain, the sweat ran into our eyes and we were buzzed endlessly by huge black rapacious flies. But then after slogging for hours, with only stops for water from the natural wells along the scrub-coated slope, we reached Drakolimni – the dragon lake. This stunned us to a halt. Rocking us back on our heels. An ecliptic lake, floating over 2000 metres up in the sky, set down in an amphitheatre of rock. All the effort was worth it for this alone. Legend has it this was where dragons fought, viciously sculpting the landscape. The lake now contained hundreds of miniature dragon-like newts, black with bright orange stomachs and angry nefarious faces that twisted angrily and looked as if they wished they could burp flame and smoke at us as we picked them up by the tail and inspected them.

Beyond the lake was a yellow grassy elevation that we climbed and which suddenly fell away and an enormous prospect of the Pindos mountains opened up and stretched away from us. Our stomachs fell and recovered as we stared across the land, as if we were looping in the sky. The evening was stacking up in streaks of purple above us. We set up the tent and spent the night alone on Gamila. Except even here, miles from civilisation, wild deer pecking at our tent as our only neighbours, we were still under the flight path from Athens to Europe. So we lay and watched the constellations move, heard the plop of the Lilliputian dragons falling from their stones into the lake, and counted the distant 747s taking people somewhere else, worlds away.

On the way back down to a distant Papigo village next morning, we were accompanied and ushered along by a series of shouts and yelps. I used these shepherd's urging barks and bawls to keep me going along the hard path. I enjoyed his constant presence, even though I couldn't see him. I realised that he must be one of the fabled nomadic Vlach shepherds, the community of herdsmen, stretching back to antiquity with their unique customs, language and ways, who climb these mountains to graze their flocks during the good summer months, living alone on the peaks and returning back to the plains only when the weather turns in the winters.

We carried on with our own toil and lumbered back down the slope, the landscape toppling down alongside us. Then I suddenly caught sight of him. The shepherd was far away, stood on a high crag of limestone rock, black and thin, crow-like, surveying the scene. I caught my breath a little at the sight of one of these mythical men, living with seeming ease in this highland that we had laboured to reach. And then, just as quickly, he was gone. Only his cries, following us back into the Zagoria villages.

There are 46 villages, lurking in the 1000 square kilometres of the Zagori. Quiet, thinly-peopled villages. Heavy solid stone buildings with loose slate roofs, cobbled streets, ancient schools and churches. Famous for *tyropitas*, *spanakopitas*, cheese, spinach pies. The best in Greece, so it's said. We sat in one peaceful Zagori village square and tucked into one. It was expensive and tasteless. The misery of cheap tourism had crept even into this idyll.

Zagoria is also known for its old stone arched bridges. Konitsa has the most picturesque and, since an earthquake in Tzoumerka recently felled the stone bridge there, the tallest in Greece.

Giristroula and I stood, necks craned, admiring the bridge for a while before noticing two rather dirty tatty figures chatting, eating together on a bench. We approached to ask these two apparent Konitsa veterans if they perhaps knew anything about the area. One of them turned out to be the priest of the town, the other the mayor. They told us not to eat a pita now in Zagoria, the tourist industry has ruined them for good. We know, we said. Instead, they advised us to go to Bourazani to eat.

I recalled sitting in the old, impressively-decayed Epirus Club in the old town of Corfu, with good cheap Epiros food and walls covered in posters of old bridges and wooded mountains, populated by the few Epirotes who had been forced over the 20 miles of sea to Corfu from their homeland. We had been advised there to go to Bourazani to eat too. The priest, sat here by the Konitsa bridge, also insisted we go and see the village of Molyvdoskepastos on the way.

Konitsa looked a sweet town. Sat small and round on the lower part of a tall wide mountain, it looked as if it had slipped down the mountain side with the winter snow. Inside the old market streets, life moved at an easy-going plod. Everyone seemed to have washed their carpets on this very afternoon. Bright coloured and zigzagged patterned rugs hung dripping over balconies, reds and blacks and golds and greens, watched over by weathered-faced old women and their learning young grandchildren.

Giristroula and I kept going, onwards to Molyvdoskepastos, and found an empty village, a shut tsipouro distillery, old signs advertising long-passed fairs, closed 'sweets of the spoon' shops and a large guidepost declaring its important significance once upon a time as a stopping point on the old Imperial Road – the road linking Constantinople to Ancient Rome, through Macedonia and Epirus. Quite unbelievable now. There was no one on the streets but every hundred metres or so there was a monastery. Again and again, as we trundled along, a different large canonical monastery reared up. One of them, the Apostles church, was a busy working monastery with restored 10th century frescoes, and had been built exactly on the Albanian border.

Back up in Molyvdoskepastos, we could see high over the Albanian checkpoint and down onto the border line along the river, just after where the Greek mountain ranges end, and just before the Albanian ones start. Walking around, we stumbled on an army barracks. A solitary guard on duty, protecting his whole country from the menace of Albania beyond. He was dozing, feet up on a chair, his cap on his lap. Slowly he caught sight of us walking past and snapped to attention, grabbing at his gun. Then turning it the right way round. He stood up, looking out towards Albania and any great threat. Every so often he would look sheepishly at us from the corner of his eye to check if we were still watching him.

When we found Bourazani, it was with a disappointment. An area of woods and lands for hunting. The owner of the large restaurant proudly showed off the heads on the wall of huge wild boar – the main ingredient of the signature dish they all sit and dream about back in the Epirus Club. A smell of death covered the place. We left as quickly as we could and headed away into the country, further on, northeastwards.

Floating birds of prey hovered in the sky above us. The solid shadow of a powerfully-winged bird enveloped the car and followed us for miles, darkening the brightly lit deserted road all around us. We passed graffiti: 'North Epirus is Greece!' scrawled on tunnels and rocks. A reference to the loss of a part of Greece on the creation of the state of Albania. Greeks have long, strong memories. Memories that stretch back further than they do. Further back than their parents. Their parents' parents. Memories that can stretch back, if needs be, thousands of years.

North Epirus is one of many contested issues of lands and borders and peoples and history. A neighbour we had back in Corfu was a Greek-Albanian, from this area just beyond the Greek border. As I met her one stingingly bright day, outside her house sweeping her step, I asked her where she came from. She seemed ashamed to say she was Albanian, telling me she was a Northern Epirot. I smiled and nodded, not knowing quite what that was back then. Now, as we drove along the border, I looked out and felt sad knowing that some Greek-descendant Northern Epirotes felt the need to disguise themselves in Greece, and how many of them were not welcomed in Albania either.

Giristroula and I tracked along Greece's long northern perimeter, the sun beginning its evening climb down into a deep orange cast. The journey had only just started, but already a strikingly unfamiliar land was revealing itself.

Part 2
Western Macedonia

We were aiming for Grammos mountain, driving through the northwestern part of Greece. Like a low rumble, turning into a rolling boil, the ground started rising up dramatically all around us. We stopped and asked a man at a precariously tilted petrol station the way to Aetomilitsa. Aetomilitsa, somewhere ahead up the mountains before us, was once the headquarters of the leftist rebels during the Greek civil war, the operation area for the displaced guerrilla fighters. Holding the nozzle in his hand, petrol dripping on the floor and over his feet, the man turned to us, his face struck in trepidation.

"*Min pate!*" – Don't go! He implored us. "Aetomilitsa? No, you mustn't go!"

"Why not?" I asked, now a little unnerved.

"The roads," he said, shaking a sad head. "I went there once. Only once" he reminisced, about this journey of less than an hour. His voice fell to a rasping whisper as he leaned a contorted face into the car window. "I would *never* go again."

The man had a point. The roads were treacherous. Up here in the most northern remote reaches of Greece, no one seems bothered to maintain any of the infrastructure. Even the small roadside shrines that you see all over Greece have fallen into disrepair. These small raised-up little basilicas are usually painstakingly maintained. The miniature domes with glass frontages that hold candles and tiny wooden religious ikons are placed at the sites of supposed miracles or, more tragically, by families where a road accident has happened and a family member has been lost. Usually a fresh candle will have been lit every day, but up on this forsaken road, even the fixedly-devoted have given up looking after these dotted monuments.

Giristroula and I drove over falling down bridges, picked with wide collapsing holes, climbing further up one side of Grammos mountain. The views behind us rippled away for as far as we could see.

We thought there was an end we were aiming for: a refuge we'd booked into. But we couldn't find it. We abandoned the car and went searching on foot and started walking over fields, blissfully ignorant of the mines left during the Greek civil war 70 years ago. The mines were designed for ratted-out skulking insurrectionary rebels but nowadays blow unsuspecting goats sky-high in the air. We continued ploughing on through these danger fields, searching for our hostel and headed towards a farm house we'd spotted glowing in the dying sun.

As we crashed onto the veranda, demanding to see the owner to complain about the awful directions, something seemed wrong. The light in the open room was dim. Furniture was pushed up against the dirty windows and a ring of bodies were sat on an unswept floor, eating from an old saucepan. Mohicaned heads turned to us. They wore tattered military-style uniforms. The apparent leader of the gang rose up to meet us, to see what we wanted.

"Er... I don't suppose this is the Grammos Hostel is it?" I said.

Of course it wasn't. We had instead landed on an anarchist co-operative group squatting in this old, holed-out building. The group showed great concern for our plight, pouring over their old, torn, battered map of the area. Some arguing and pointing, others at the back kicking stones with big boots, offering us smokes.

"You can stay here if you like," said one of the anarchists, pointing to the shared quarters and grim camp beds. They offered us the food they had and it was all very kind of them, but we said no. We were determined to reach our booked accommodation. Having come up the wrong side of this towering 8,000 foot mountain, there was nothing to do but go down and try again.

Night had fallen as we climbed closer to the real location of the hostel. We managed to get the owner on the phone and were told to take a tiny dirt track.

"Just to tell you," the owner said, "You will probably see a bear. It is possible. Likely, in fact. The thing to do is not to panic."

Panicking the whole way, we saw no bears in the end only fleeing long-legged hares followed by purposeful head-down badgers scurrying from our headlights. Distant thunder rumbled and the mountain top was illuminated by odd flares of lightening as we finally arrived in the village of Grammos.

The next morning, the sun-lit uplands we had seen in the late afternoon the day before were wreathed in clouds. Bursting to let go with their downpours within. We sat at the breakfast table with a miserable-looking couple in their waterproofs. They had tried an early hike to the cave on Grammos, which had served as the civil war rebels' hospital, but told us that a family of bears had set up their own camp in front of the entrance to the cave. As they'd tried to get closer the mother bear had risen up on her hind legs and the growling of the father told them he must have been close-by too. It was safe to say the cave was out of bounds. So instead, Giristroula and I took a walk up to the see the remaining walls of the anti-aircraft bases built by the communist rebels at the top of the peaks.

The climb looked tough, but on the early paths we were accompanied along the way by an 80-year-old named Eudokia. She told us she was a descendant of the Vlach shepherds. Old Eudokia was dressed in one long dress of black and tough material, dated by perhaps a hundred of years, with just a belt tied round her waist and a slapping pair of wellington boots on her feet. Her Vlach family had died out and she alone now looked after a herd of 200 cows. She was happy to chat for a while as we walked briskly along, but clearly bored by the pace we could offer, soon vaulted a fence and was off, haring up the steep camber. Uncatchable.

The rain set in and Grammos looked as bleak as its history. We made our way back down the side of the wet mountain to the hotel, and sat eating bread and homemade honey with the owner's parents and listened to stories about the village.

There were only 25 people living in the village now, at one stage there was 3,000. Grammos had suffered two monstrous tragedies in its history. The first was when Ali Pasha – that man again: the butcher of the Ottoman empire who had previously haunted us through the state of Epirus – had fallen in love with a Grammos village girl on one of his raids through the north of Greece. When she spurned his advances, Ali Pasha burned the village to the ground in revenge. Then, a century and a half later in 1949, with the communist fighters battling the Greek government forces in the hills, the government turned to its backer, the United States, who had just developed a new weapon. The US were looking for a place to test this weapon and believed it could quickly finish the ruinous Greek civil war. And so it was that one August day the Greek government dropped napalm on this village, and on its own people. This barbarous act enough to end the war, and the communists' last stand was wiped out. As was the village. Only the church left standing. I stared out the window at an angry sky, the clouds sat solid on the unhappy scene. The landscape has been a sad backdrop to the conflicts caught deep within it.

Vasilios, the old man of the hotel, brought out an old, thick tin drinking flask. With a shaky hand he showed it to me. "*Kita…*" he said – look – and he pointed at a bullet hole that had pierced both sides of this flask. Vasilios pushed the flask to his breast where it would have hung when the soldier wore it. He turned the old vessel over and showed me where its owner had scratched his name. 'Georgio Fabritsi'.

Vasilios was a boy when the Second World War was played out in these highlands and gullies. When the Italians came into this village, his father and the other men had tried to fight them back. Vasilios found the flask while digging the land 60 years later. He told us he now spends his time trying to find the Fabritsi family back in Italy to let them have back this piece, a memorial of their relative.

The old man scurried off again, and when he came back he produced a photo.

"*Kita…*" he commanded again.

It was a colour photo and it appeared to be of a snake. A snake poking its head out of a hole.

"Ah. My father wants to know if this is true..." his son said to me, walking over and taking hold of the photo.

"You are going to the Prespes lakes I think, yes? You will see a church there. In the small town of St Germanos. There is a famous legend about this church," he said, tapping his finger on the photo. "On the 15th of August, *Panagia's* day, the Madonna's day, snakes come out of a hole in the floor. They come to protect the church, to protect the Holy mother. When my father went to this church on that day he *saw* the snake."

"It was there!" said the old man "I took this photo of it… but can it really be true? Can you find out? Can you tell us?"

The weather cleared slightly and so Giristroula and I decided we should try and make a move away from these rain-cocooned mountains. Vasilios stood in the doorway to say goodbye to us with his arm around his wife.

When a baby is born in these rural Greek areas it is the job of one of the boys to race around each village to tell everyone in the squares and bakeries and cafés the news. When his wife was born, it was the eight-year-old Vasilios's job to spread the word of her birth. He did it by telling everyone in each nearby village *"Ine koritsi! Ine koritsi!"* – a baby girl has been born. "And one day I will marry her!" The baby girl's family moved away, but 18 years later she returned to this village and, of course, Vasilios fell deeply in love. One father asked the other father, as was the tradition for arranging a marriage, and sure enough, the eight-year-old Vasilios's prophesy came about. Sixty years on, the hugging couple waved us away as our car picked up speed, freewheeling down the mountain dirt track.

We had an appointment to keep with a musical professor friend of Giristroula's in the village of Kryovrisi. The large dark house, full of books, lamps, rugs and musical instruments was one of just a small scattering in the village. Kryovrisi looking down on a great sweep of checked fields, with pylons and chimneys clumsily trying to hide behind the hills. This area is the centre of Greece's real power – four gigantic electricity stations providing three quarters of all of Greece's electricity, pumping and burning all day and night.

While Giristroula worked on a book inside the house, I sat drinking with the professor's husband on the porch. He had lived many years in the area, working his way up from apprentice to one of the directors of one of the power plants. He told me about the village.

"You see this school..?"

Christos pointed with his glass towards a sweet-looking old school building sat in a small copse of trees.

"There was no school there once upon a time. One man built that school. Built it with his own hands. Taught the few kids here on his own. Then one day he left. He left to join the fighting in the civil war. Later his sons joined him too."

My storyteller shifted his seat round and pointed his glass close behind my head.

"That was his house, over there."

I turned to look at a broken-down old building.

"His wife looked after it when they were gone. Just her and her young daughters. She would tell people in the village 'I wish my boys would come back. Just for one day. I wish they would leave the fighting just for one day and come back to see their mother.'"

Christos went quiet, looked at his drink.

"One day there was a knock on her door. Two men from the rebel army. 'Your sons...' they tell her 'They're here...' 'My sons? Here?' the wife said. She's overjoyed. Looking over their shoulders, desperate to see her boys. 'They're over there,' the rebel soldiers say, 'waiting in the woods for you...' There were thick woods here once upon a time."

Christos did a sweep with his glass in a long arc in front of his house.

"So she tells her daughters to set the table 'Your brothers will be back home soon!' She rushes to join the soldiers already walking into the trees."

Christos took a sip of his drink.

"The daughters were waiting by that table the whole day. Later the priest was walking back to our village through the woods. He sees the wife. Calls out to her. Wonders why she doesn't reply. Walks over to see what's wrong... Hanged. Hanged out there in the trees. Just for wanting to see her sons."

Christos' glass went down cheerlessly on the table.

"This country has much shame in its history. Much beauty, much glory, but so much shame..."

Giristroula and I spent the evenings in the nearby city of Ptolemaida. A beautifully ugly place. The large main square, with white pavestones and marble sculptures, was heaving every night. Adolescents parading in their best cheap clothes. Girls made-up with bright red lipsticks, walking up and down, catching looks from the boys. Dark skinned, dark hair and eyes. Exotic-looking attractive kids. The sons and daughters of the electricity workers. A vivid working-class community. Everyone seemed happy to see us here: us, two unpolished strangers. People wanted to talk, wanted to share. I instantly warmed to the place. Even the middle-aged ladies working in the mini markets were remarkably dressed-up and flirty.

We stopped for pitas, the usual Greek take-out. However, up here in this part of Western Macedonia, rather than the pita bread they use the unleavened *lagana* bread that everyone else in Greece only eats on the first day of Lent. We sat and ate and I was sad that we would soon have to say goodbye to Ptolemaida, an area looked down on by everyone I'd told we would be having a stopover here. The wisecracks they made about how, living under the shadow of the power plants, everyone dies young around these parts and that we should take care not to stay too long, just in case, didn't seem funny at all to me.

We left this kind, congenial city with a sense of regret, but we had to keep moving. Northern Greece is not small.

Navigating round mountains meant we had overshot slightly on our route. We were looking for the Prespa Lakes.

We back-tracked a little west and then headed north towards the lakes sitting on the Greek border. On the road on the way there, we hit the smaller, but still vast, lake at Kastoria.

Approaching the town of Kastoria, coming round its tray-flat water, a rising and falling yelp of houses, all coloured only white and orange, sat before the mountains beyond. As we entered, every other shop was a large windowed store selling fur. Incongruous pictures of female models clutching fur hoods pulled tightly around pouting faces, under the stingingly hot sun.

Kastoria became rich years ago on the fur trade and now looked unlike any other Greek town I'd travelled through. Prosperous, clean, tidy, a little pleased with itself, a little unwelcoming. The old town, higher up, was full of handsome Italian-esque villas built by the first men to have made their money on the fur trade in the 18th century. Attractive as they were, I didn't enjoy looking at this beauty in these small squares. There seemed something soulless here. But it was only from high up that I realised that the enormous expanse of water I looked over in Kastoria was only half of Lake Orestiada. Kastoria is just a spur sticking out into the lake. There's thousands more litres of ridged freshwater and hundreds more gabbling flamingos, all on the other side. As big as Lake Orestiada is though, we were soon on the move northwards to a lake ten times larger.

We pulled into the small village of Microlimni and stopped at a quiet taverna on the Prespa lake front. It was satisfyingly tranquil: a few diners having a quiet late lunch, a dog asleep, breathing deeply, under a heavy sun.

Half an hour later, however, we noticed things started getting busier. People were arriving. More people than could fit in the taverna. Peculiar looking people. People who look like they hadn't been out of their houses in ten years. Village men uncomfortable in old suits, farming women awkward in smart clothes. A large headed man sat next to me, sweating heavily in his old, thick, Sunday-best clothes, his bushy eyebrows wringing out like two wet rugs. Then at the next table, a young military brass band sat down, dressed in full fatigues, fussing and banging about with big gold instruments. They were in turn shooed away by four medalled generals in large hats, carrying sticks, who sat down importantly in the seats instead. What could be happening?

A crowd had gathered around a covered statue in the small village square outside. A row of rigidly-stood soldiers had appeared and started singing, remarkably out of tune, the Greek national anthem. A black collection of priests gathered and anointed the crowd with swung smoking thymiatos. I walked over to see what was going on just at a moment of stirring in the crowd. Darkly dressed ladies who had been soundlessly crying into handkerchiefs lowered them for a moment and stood aside with reverence to let somebody through. It was a small shock for both of us that I suddenly found myself face-to-face with the President of Greece. No one quite knew what to do. Prokopis Pavlopoulos, his bodyguards, or me. Eventually the large nosed, slightly grotesque-looking President stuck out a hand and I shook it.

"*Bravo*," I said. Though I wasn't sure why. I couldn't think of anything else to say.

He paused, a little puzzled, and then made his way to the statue and said some words to the crowd and the few television cameras that had arrived. Pavlopoulos unveiled a man's face carved in solid rock, as the sombre ladies grasped at their handkerchiefs again.

And that seemed to be that. The president made his way back to his car, turning to look at me one last time with a brief wave of confusion crossing over his face before he ducked inside and was gone. The police guard followed him with a roar down the quiet road, and a second tuneless rendition of the national anthem. The tiny village was left silent again. Resting unattached and trivial on its huge lake. The residents filed past me, some giving me dark looks. Eventually I found out that a local policeman had been shot and killed on the lake when he had uncovered, by unlucky chance, a smuggling gang out on the waters. Pavlopoulos had been here to honour the local man with a statue. I watched the villagers take off their old suit jackets and slowly start to breathe again. Plates and bottles of ouzo appearing from where they had been hidden under the tables. A backgammon board was opened and cards were dealt. Prespes village life re-ordered itself back into its usual sluggish shape.

Having raced against the darkness stacking up over the water to get our tent pitched under trees on the lake front, Giristroula and I set off to explore the island of Agios Ahillios. We drove along the strip dividing the smaller Mikri Prespa lake from Megali Prespa and walked across a floating pontoon bridge onto the island, enveloped now in a black night. We cautiously circumnavigated the marshy area of reeds, the looming churches and the few old, large residential houses. Groping our way in front of us in the dark, then pushing through a thicket of trees, we were suddenly confronted by the sight of a few hundred people, lit-up by blazing spotlights, facing us on a large grass sloped hill clearing. A stage illuminated in front of the bashed-about 10th century basilica of Agios Achillios. Not knowing what was going on, we took a seat with the crowd on the grass and waited. Out from the wings came Savopoulos, the white bearded singer – the Bob Dylan of Greece, so people say – and for the next two hours he played a set of Greek classics. President Pavlopoulos sat in the prime seat in the front row. By chance we had stumbled across a performance here on a lonely island in Prespes, an area that only 30 years ago or so was completely deserted. The closeness to Albania and the history of the civil war meant that anyone wanting to visit this area had to be accompanied by a soldier at all times.

Pavlopoulos left before the halftime interval.

Giristroula and I woke next morning on the strip of beach separating the two parts of the lake, a sweeping grove of tall golden reeds fortressing the water under a bright sun. I opened the tent to this scene, and found myself face-to-face with a pelican looking in at us, framed between the tent flaps. Behind him a long row of cow arses were lined up, left to right, the owners drinking deeply from the lake. Dwarf cows peculiar to only this one area of Greece.

The pelican took wing, flying away from us, over the lake towards the country of Macedonia straight ahead over the horizon. Mosquitos sailed past us with a high-pitched whine as we sat on the shoreline and stared at the scene and drank camp-stove Greek coffee.

After gathering ourselves together, we headed towards the village of Agios Germanos. Old buff-coloured stone houses dotted in scanty collections in the small villages, a water mill, the odd sun-dappled tavern, and finally the 11th century church that our old host back in Grammos had asked us to check for snakes. It was a tight fit inside. The walls were completely covered in frescos. Colourful Byzantine graffiti. I swivelled my head round and round to take it all in. And then on the floor was a familiar looking hole... But any sign of a snake was sadly very absent. I asked one of the villagers outside, tending the grounds about the snake rumour. He seemed amused.

"The children round here," he pointed, circling his finger round the scorched mountains surrounding us. "They go collecting snakes before August 15th. The priest gives them a few coins each time. And so out they go again into the fields collecting more and more. The priest puts all these snakes into the hole when he sees any people approaching his church."

Another villager denied this. "No, no. *Ine i Panagia!* – It's the Madonna..." He wafted his friends away and clasped my arm and patted it reassuringly *"Ine i Panagia..."* he repeated, nodding and smiling at me kindly.

"They have sacks full! They come to the church with sacks full of snakes!" shouted his friend from his grass cutting, laughing. "It's not the Madonna... it's just kids!"

I decided not to tell the old man back in Grammos anything. Let him believe in his miracle from this small town of stone and strange witchery.

Heading back eastwards along the lake, we passed Agios Achillios island again. We could see it now in the daylight, with its churches and the residents who say they regularly see the ghost of Greek hero Achilles, strolling slow and thoughtful, on the enclave. The village of Psarades, further on, was busy. Busy, that is, for an area that only has one bus each week: a scant service that often leaves the locals here completely stranded. We sat in a humming little taverna and ate *gigantes* beans and carp and got into an argument with a local fisherman sitting on the taverna's   terrace.

The fisherman was swaying drunk, in a skewwhiff dirty white captain's hat. We debated a price with him for a trip onto the lake in his boat before he eventually gave in, slapped the table hard, and for 20 euros jerked his head towards the path and lead us unsteadily down to the small wooden wharf and onto his small boat.

The lake was green jewel-glass, reflecting a sky holding just a few silver-rimmed clouds. Deep and calm. The boat chugged us out past the frowning cliffs. The old fisherman stopped and pointed up to the high cascading rock. There, next to a hole which had housed a lone 14th century monk, was a large perfect portrait of the Virgin painted on the rock. Still clear with deep reds, like a 700-year-old advertising poster. We rounded a bend in the cliffs and the captain brought his boat in towards land and a hidden bay. He nodded us up a high flight of steps cut in the cliff. While he stayed in the boat, lying back with his cap over his eyes, Giristroula and I pushed up the way the fisherman had indicated, climbing the steps, not knowing what to expect. In a deep crevice in the rock was a cockeyed ancient church, jammed tight right into the cave. Built again by hermit monks up here 600 years ago, it was a sweet sloped church – the Church of Panagia Eleousa – crammed in whole, below the rough cave slabs. More frescoes inside, and hidden in these ancient paintings, sneakily tucked in among the Christs and the Virgins, a self-portrait of the two beaming monk artists responsible for the work.

Our old captain of the fishing boat was a proud Greek from Psarades. However, along with Greek he also spoke an inherited Slavic language. He spoke nothing but this Slavic language at home to his equally Greek wife. He told me this mix of languages and cultures came from down the years and the confusion and turmoil in this area just before the First World War, at the end of the Ottoman Empire's days. Lands had been taken, new borders drawn. Ethnic Slavs – people who identified themselves not as Serbs, or Greek, or Bulgarian, but called themselves Macedonian – were pushed out or became minorities here. After the Second World War, despite the Slavic Macedonians having fought the Nazi occupation in Greece, even more were exiled. The ethnic Slavic Macedonians that remained became Greek, but never forgot their roots. For a long time, speaking this Macedonian language was dangerous. State-sponsored harassment could follow. The Macedonian minority had pretty much been written out of history and existence. But the older residents of this area still held this language, and held it passionately. The old man told us, in defiance, he made a point of speaking Slavic when out and about, singing old Macedonian songs. He said he spoke it particularly loudly when surrounded by young people.

We sailed further on along the lake in the old man's boat, and then without warning he suddenly cut the engine all together and we drifted forward silently. He pointed down on to the lake. We looked down into the water, and then back at him again. Here, he said, was the point where the three countries sharing this lake – Greece, Macedonia and Albania – all meet. We bobbed for a while, in silence, the lake lapping at the hull of the boat. All three of us thinking our own private thoughts, floating listlessly from one country to the other out on the tranquil waters. Then, with a sigh, the old skipper started the engine up again. It coughed into life slowly, reluctant to start, and chugged us back over the rippled water. Back towards Greece, and the huge sweep of land and mountains waiting patiently for us to continue our journey.

Part 3
Central Macedonia

We had carried on through the state of Macedonia, eastwards. Florina had been a sweet spot to stop at: a town set down in a gap in the forested hills, a nicely run-down centre. The buildings looked more Greek-like than many we had seen on our days travelling through northern Greece with open balconies and a southern look, as if ready for the sun rather than the snow. A river flowed through the town, which was rare for Greece. Usually rivers have dried up in the towns or flow somewhere away from sight, covered and concreted over. But in Florina they'd used it well, building a little walkway, café tables sitting by small bridges on the river edge. If you squinted hard enough, held a hand over one eye, Florina had almost a Parisian feel.

Edessa old town looked as if it had been left to rot and decompose in the sun. But there was also a new district of prosperous-looking tree-shaded streets and modern squares centred round a huge waterfall plummeting to the ground with a sound of thunder. The waters running and crossing over dams and down into streams. The old men stared at us from the cafés as we passed. The same stares you get as a stranger whenever you enter a town or village anywhere in the country. Half curiosity, half challenge. I never really knew how to respond. The twitching whiskers of the squinting local ladies; the children gawping with bulging eyes; the men who stop dead in the middle of the road and whose heads turn a full 180 degrees to follow you as you stroll by. The blue circles of the hanging Eye emblems that dangle on strings in the windows of cafés and shops to ward off bad spirits seem to stare with defiance and interrogation too.

Edessa's station, built back when Greece was under Ottoman rule, was a pretty but sturdy old depot. It resembled a painting with the building set back on its own, away from the town, under large trees which allowed only the most tenacious rays through. An unelectrified train rolled in, burping diesel steam, but it had come in on an unexpected line, so we watched as old women lugged overflowing trolleys over the rails to get a foot up on the ladder and haul themselves into the old carriages. No announcements, just a flapping piece of paper tacked onto the porter's wooden door detailing the trains: one every few hours. The train felt no compulsion to keep to any sort of timetable anyway. The driver waited for everyone to finish their conversations, finish their cigarettes, before leaving half an hour late. The station master in his old peaked hat roused from his slumber on his chair to wave his green flag, long after the train had started its painfully slow departure out from the town and into the countryside beyond.

The road Giristroula and I took shimmered in the heat like a mirage. Sunlight detonated like explosions off the windows of the rare few cars that passed us. Giristroula had taken her childhood holidays up here in northern Greece. Driving holidays in her father's cheap old Zastava Yugoslavian-built car, frequently breaking down so close to its original birth place and roared past by the Mercedes and Audis that Greeks were buying with the totally new notion of loans. As the two of us now drove over mountain ranges, the thickly wooded trees died away as we passed the mountain brow and started to descend towards an abrupt harsh flat land on the other side. A land of utter nothingness. We came down slowly, a little unsure of ourselves, into this dry plain, towards the border with the country of Macedonia. And towards the camp of Idomeni.

The town of Idomeni was insignificant. A handful of houses. Disturbingly though, as we entered this small village, I saw at least two of these houses were flying a 21st of April Greek junta flag: the phoenix. The celebration of this date is the marking of when the fascist dictatorship took grip of Greece for seven extreme, harmful, years in 1967. It was troubling to see these flags flying in this town that was recently the focus of the world's attention when, just before this summer, up to 15,000 refugees from Africa, the Middle East, Afghanistan were massed, desperate to cross the border. The very border Giristroula and I could now see fenced off and guarded.

This flat open land was a cauldron of heat. We walked in the mid-afternoon glare, along the fences between Greece and the country of Macedonia, all the time very aware that we were being observed from station huts on the border. The refugees had now been re-located from this iniquitous space, but there were still reminders of what had been here. Wooden tent frames, canvases, clothes, cooking things, long forgotten possessions. They had   all been swept up and piled into huge hills of debris. I looked down on the dusty ground as we walked around and saw one small pink shoe lying abandoned on the floor. It felt a dismal, melancholy place.

Idomeni is the last station out of Greece. The whole of Europe sits on top of this train line, which was also fenced and protected. We walked along to the large, old station.

"Were you here when the refugees were here?" I asked the two train guards on the station platform – one short, bald and, bellicose; the other tall, grey, bespectacled and hostile.

"*Nai...*" Yes... they replied slowly.

"What was it like?"

"Bad. They were bad men. Scum. Fighting with each other. Wanting to fight with us. They shouldn't come here. They should have stayed where they came from."

Their answers shocked me. I hadn't expected such a lack of compassion. Naively, I somehow imagined there would be some sense of empathy as they had seen the refugees first hand.

The two rail workers start to eye me up and down.

"Where is he from?" they asked Giristroula. "*Ine apo kee pano?*" – Is he from 'up'? Up as in, from up there, Europe.

Giristroula told them I'm from England.

"England? And he's your husband? Why did you marry him then?" they started to snap. "Why not a Greek, eh? *Se tylixe*?" – did he trick you..?

I pointed to the land along the straight railway line running into the distance with a glimmering dance of heat "So that's Macedonia then is it?"

"What?" They both stopped dead.

"The land over there. I guess that's Macedonia is it?"

"What did you say?" they repeated, staring at me.

"Oh..." I said, realising my mistake "Sorry I mean, as you say, F.Y.R.O.M..."

Their faces stayed angry. "F.Y.R.O you should say," one of them jabbed a finger into my chest. "No M..."

Former Yugoslav Republic Of... didn't make sense, but I knew better than to question this.

Giristroula and I made our way to the car as things were becoming belligerent. They followed us closer.

"Is he drunk? Does he have problems?"

We got in the car and as we drove off I thought how, just before the summer, Giristroula and I had been in Piraeus stood on the platform at the railway station. We watched as wave after wave of refugees flowed from the port and the ships towards the trains. A fast moving, continuous stream of people. We had waited and watched as three trains left, packed with so many bodies that we couldn't get on. Men had approached us to ask practical questions about how to find a certain area in Athens at the other end of the Piraeus line, or how to travel further into the country. Each interaction was friendly, though the men were clearly tired and anxious. Each of them fixed, looking and hoping for something ahead. The train ride, when we finally managed to get on, had a tangible sense of optimism amongst the migrants. Relief seemed to flow through the carriage. It depressed me as the decayed Idomeni station receded in the car's wing mirrors, with the two railway workers stood glaring at our departure, that this was where the journey led to for many of those people. And, despite the great displays of care shown by so many Greeks for the refugees on the Aegean islands and throughout Greece, it saddened me to see this other reaction they must have faced here where their journeys had stalled.

Our car was pointed south, towards Thessaloniki, but we swerved left as we were not feeling ready for Greece's second city yet. Instead, we headed to the fat three clawed cat's paw peninsula, scratching into the Aegean Sea: the Halkidiki region.

'San tin Halkidiki... then echi' – Like Halkidiki... nothing. This is what they say, and it is easy to see why they say it. Although Halkidiki was once unwanted. The government gave this area to the Greek descendants who had been forced away from their homes in Turkey during the Population Exchange of 1923, as Turkey finally released Greece from its crumbling empire. The government didn't know what to do with this groundswell of people coming to live in Greece, Greeks who had been living in Constantinople or areas of Asia Minor. Anyone who was Orthodox Christian was not welcome in Turkey after 1922 and moved in great numbers into Greece. There was an appalling genocide of Greek minorities in Turkey and then further repercussions followed when the Greeks failed with their 'Big Idea' to grab all the old ethnic Greek-inhabited areas in Turkey at the end of World War One. Prime Minister Venizelos had thought he could capitalise on the disintegrating Ottoman Empire and push for greater chunks of Turkish lands which the Greeks believed to be historically theirs, but failure meant more Greeks were forced to leave their homes and cross the border. Land by the sea in Greece wasn't wanted back then – what could you grow on it? So these newly disenfranchised people were fobbed off with large parts of Halkidiki to live on. Halkidiki is now one of the most sought-after holiday lands in the country. The Greek families wrenched from their lives in Turkey in such terrible circumstances have made their fortunes.

Giristroula and I drove on high roads looking over pine tree-guarded sea views, down Sithonia – the second leg of the Halkidiki peninsula: less built up than the first leg, Kassandra. We were heading for the coast of Platanitsi. Scorched biscuit-coloured earth and scattered gnarled olive trees sat like the top of a cake, while rocky white-icing vertical cliffs fell down into small beach bays. We stopped to scrabble down the cliff face and swam in the sea, looking straight along the turquoise waters to Mount Athos. The mountains burnished on the blue sky, distinct and excluded over on Halkidiki's final third leg. When Alexander the Great died, his architect Dinocrates of Rhodes suggested the entire mountain should be carved into a statue of Alexander holding a small city in one hand, the other hand pouring a river into the sea from a gigantic pitcher. Sounds trippily crazy. Shame they never did it. It's a land for monks now.

The monasteries on Athos famously don't allow women onto their grounds. The monks claim this is due to it being the Virgin Mary's garden and how she doesn't want other women to share it. The story is that the Virgin was in a boat on her way to Cyprus to see the recently resurrected Lazarus when a storm blew her onto Mount Athos's coast. The Virgin Mary was so overwhelmed by its beauty she asked her son for it all for herself. I personally prefer the earthier version from Greek mythology of Mount Athos being a huge rock that Poseidon threw at one of his enemies, landing with a clatter into the sea. We thought of trying to get over there ourselves, with Giristroula copying the few spirited sisters who had landed on Mount Athos disguised as men, sometimes disguised as sailors, in an attempt to observe and mix with the monks. But then we thought how around here it's not really the places for putting more clothes *on*.

The beach of Kavourotrypes was settled in the '60s and '70s by the hippy movement. A haven for nudity and free love. On rhe beach, we ran into Giristroula's old violin teacher on the beach. An old straggly wild-haired kook, the maverick of the Thessaloniki State Conservatoire. He told us tales of finding himself in his youth in this paradise of nonconformity and naturism. He still returns every year, but things change. *"Brosta pane ta frikia… keh piso i ergolavi"* – First come the hippies… and then the civil engineers follow. So now families crowd under stripy umbrellas, games of racquets slap and clack, a beach bar runs with a thudding generator due to the lack of any electricity here. Giristroula's violin teacher and the rest of the hippies have been pushed, with resentful faces, to the very edge of the beach. Or they have moved further along to the small hidden beaches under the cliffs where nudity and, to my English fastidious discomfort, quite obvious free love in the shallow sea caves still happily existed.

The Greeks of our party – Giristroula and some of her friends who she had met up with – took part in all the naked misrule down on the beach. I sat up on top, reading under the trees, resolutely buttoned up. As much as I might have thought I'd become Greek over my years here, the transformation wasn't nearly complete.

We entered Thessaloniki creeping through the traffic along the curving sea front. The White Tower of the town stood a smirking distant figure at the far end of the choked promenade.

We turned off the front and battled up the climbing streets towards the old upper town, Ano Poli. This is where our Thessaloniki days were to be spent: lounging with the old men, cigarette smoke rising to the ceiling, *koboloi* worry-beads swinging unceasingly in the heavy air of the perfectly ramshackle Taverna Makedoniko. We listened to the Thessalonikians talking with their heavy 'L' sound accents. *"Eh Malllaka, halllara…"*

Once upon a time the people in this crossroad of a city would have swapped between six or seven different languages. All gone now. The 50,000 Jews of the city before World War Two all gone too. More Greek Jews were killed, proportionately, in the Holocaust than any other nation. Five hundred years of Jewish life in Thessaloniki completely wiped out. The Greeks, of course, led the few attempts at uprisings and resistance at Auschwitz: once getting beyond the camp's wires and fences and singing the Greek national anthem as they ran for the woods in their brief moments of freedom before being gunned down. But I also heard that the Greek Jews in Auschwitz died in large numbers before they ever reached the gas chambers. All the prisoners in Auschwitz knew the water supply was contaminated, but the ever-thirsty Greeks just couldn't stop themselves drinking it.

Back in modern day Thessaloniki, Giristroula and I late-breakfasted on the Thessalonikian morning staple of cream-filled pastry *bougatsa* and chocolate milk. We ate warm *koulouria* rings of bread coated in sesame seeds while we sat outside the ancient Roman market with the heat kindling the streets around us. Thessaloniki is a city of food. Greece's heart and its belly. We were here, however, for a wedding.

Giannis picked me up in his battered car at the corner of the street, opposite the remains of the old Ottoman fort that had once been the infamous Yedi Kule prison high above the city. We drove through the old stone city gates into Ano Poli and down the twisted streets to the city below. We were running late. My heavy bull-like driver was sweating and bellowing at every other car on the street, pounding at the horn, cursing every piece of bad luck he'd ever had in his life from the very day he was born. We were late to attend the dressing of the groom. Giannis burst through the door of the hotel room, loudly proclaiming his arrival. I followed behind. It was a large room full of devoted Orthodox Christians. Music was being played somewhere. And everyone had the most prodigious beard. Giristroula, while studying music at the conservatoire in Thessaloniki, years ago, had in her first year of studies made friends with a fellow violinist, who turned out to be a dedicated Orthodox Christian and so now here I was, in a noisy room full of them.

The great tradition before a Greek wedding is for all the men of the party to gather and for each person to put different items of clothes on the groom, as he pretends to resist, before everyone makes their way to the ceremony. Coming late, Giannis and I were left with just a sock each. The wedding was due to start in less than an hour, but the bottles of tsipouro were being passed around over our heads, the groom glugging deeply, wiping at his flushed face and alcohol-soaked beard with the back of his hand. There was a problem with his cuffs. Should he wear cufflinks or go with the buttons? I watched as ten large, hirsute Greek men crowded over the shirt and fussed and fiddled and flapped and waved hands at each other. Every one of these big heavy men with a heated point of view on the cuff situation.

"Ten Greeks... Twenty different opinions!" someone said to me, laughing, nudging me hard in the ribs, pointing at the chaos in front of us. Someone else then started cutting at the tiny buttons with a huge glinting knife. I decided to sit down and have another tsipouro.

Finally, and very late, we left to make our way to the church. Everyone singing the traditional song as the groom took the lead down the road to the ceremony.

"Simera ga, simera gamos ginetai
s'oraio perivoli, s'oraio perivoli
Simera apo, simera apohorizetai
i mana apo tin kori, i mana apo tin kori
Gabre ti ny, gabre ti nyfi n'agapas
Na min tin emaloneis, na min tin emaloneis
San to vasi, san to vasiliko stin gi
na tine kamaroneis, na tine kamaroneis..."

"Today there's a wedding
In a beautiful garden
Today the bride leaves the mother
Groom, love the bride
And don't be bad to her
Treat her like basil in the soil..."

Moni Vlatadon is one of the oldest churches in northern Greece. The only one to still carry out Byzantine services in Thessaloniki. It is high in the old town, by the Great Gate, with the city spread beneath. Peacocks strutting about in the courtyard. One of the Beards clasped me by the shoulder as I looked out on the 14th century terrace towards the sea and the vague hazy gleam of Mount Olympus beyond.

"We Christians make sure we get the best views, eh?"

Another Beard led me inside. The paintings and frescos on the walls and columns and arches, put up in the Byzantine reign, had been attacked by the occupying Turks as the Ottoman Empire swept over Thessaloniki. All the biblical paintings and the depictions of Christ and the apostles had been hacked with knives and swords and thousands of small chipped holes litter the walls, scoring the saintly faces, as if dotted by rapid machine gun fire. It was both a fantastic and faintly unsettling sight. The Beard showed me a small worn stone step in the church, where he told me the apostle St Paul preached to the people of Thessaloniki. Before I could make a query about this, the wedding party entered the church.

Hundreds of candles hung, illuminating four elaborate priests dressed in gold, jewels and brocade who were stood in front of a decorated altar. A group of chanticleers sang low droning Byzantine songs. Packed guests crowded in the formidable heat. The embellished priests began reciting flowing ancient texts. At first the best man's duty appeared to be nothing more than standing behind the couple waving a fan, as time moved inordinately slowly in the thick heat. Then the priests placed two garlanded crowns on the couples' heads and the best man found his role, changing these over and over on top of the groom and bride, twisting and twirling his arms while the priest rubbed the gold wedding rings on their foreheads.

The intense singing hum filling the church grew louder, more ominous. The guests stood together, rapt, hands to their mouths, watching the service... And then suddenly they just broke-off, and left to go outside to have a chat. Outside the church, it was a hub of chatter and laughter with people catching up after years. Old women preparing the *boubounieres* – tied lace bags that everyone was to be given as they left the wedding, full of almond sugar-coated sweets. Then the guests returned into the church to gaze, enraptured again, at the long, protracted, hymeneal service. Back and forth they traipsed. In and out, in and out.

Keen interest picked up in the crowd at one point as one old priest – curly beard to his navel, white kalimavkion hat resting over his eyes – began the traditional warning to the bride "*I the gyni na fovate ton antra*" – the woman must be frightened of her husband... The hundred-strong congregation elongated their necks, craning to see if the bride would follow the modern update on the tradition... and all settled back again, smiling, pleased to see the bride did indeed stamp on her husband's foot. The priest ignored this, continuing with his toneless demand that she obey and respect out of fear of her husband.

And then it was over. After what had felt like hours, and as the sonorous singing continued from the candle-lit group in the corner of the dark flickering church, we piled out of the Vlatadon monastery. The groom was grabbed and thrown into the sky over and over again. Cars left, blaring horns, arms out of the windows holding lit flares, as we descended into the centre of Thessaloniki.

The wedding crowd spilled into the narrow cobbled streets of the Ladadika area down near the port gates, the old Jewish area and the old red light district, where all the bars are now in what were once Thessaloniki's ancient olive oil warehouses. The drinking and dancing carried on until well into the middle of the next day.

I found myself sat out on the street with a man called Giorgos. A portly man, his round head haloed by hair. Giorgos told me he had trained for years to be a monk, before falling for the girl he married and giving it all up for love. As another bottle was drained, Giorgos told me how at Mount Athos a monk he knew had stood on the rocks one day and was looking out at the sea. From the depths, an arm appeared holding a shining silver ikon.

"We both stared at the ikon," Giorgos said to me. "We didn't know what to do. And then I watched as my friend started walking out to collect this offering. I saw him walk out over the waves to take it as clearly as I see you..."

I looked at Giorgos. He looked back at me impassively, blinking once or twice. I looked at the drink in my hand. Then back at Giorgos again. I looked about me, at the city of Thessaloniki and the night-time ballet of life going on all around. I looked up at the Greek sky, the stars shining white as bones on the black cloth night. I thought of the magic that Greece always has somewhere deep within it. I looked back at Giorgos. And I almost let myself believe it all to be true.

Part 4
North By Northwest Greece

Alexander the Great aimed for the Ends of the World and the Great Outer Sea. Giristroula and I were a little less ambitious. We had got as far as the Aegean seacoast of Central Macedonia and the ruins of Ancient Stagira where Alexander's tutor, Aristotle lays buried in his broken tomb looking out over the sea. But time had run out for us. Now we had to turn and head back across the country. Homeward bound, back from north to northwest Greece. We vowed to return to the north again one day, as we rolled into the first town on our journey back home, Pella.

All Greeks have a name day – an *onomastiki yiorti* – when they celebrate the saint of the same name as theirs and are visited at home by friends and family, who arrive with eager faces expecting to be treated. It's a bigger occasion than a birthday. Today was the 30th of August – the name day for all Alexanders. *My* name is Alexander. Pella is the town where Alexander the Great was born. This all appeared meaningful in some vague way, as the car drove into the unexpectedly plain-looking home town of *Megas Alexandros*.

With disappointed faces, Giristroula and I crawled through Pella looking for traces of Alexander. We walked the preserved columns and stone floors and passages and broken rooms of his old city, laid out across stone-pitted acres of ground, which was once the largest and most prosperous in northern Greece. And then we returned to the new town and called in on a rather inglorious-looking grill house for souvlakis. As the skewers of meat were slowly turned on the coals, just to make conversation, I told the people working there my name, and the – very – small coincidence of being here on this day. The old lady of the restaurant lit up.

"*Hronia polla!*" she said, throwing her arms up in the air and tottering round the counter, grabbing at my face to kiss it.

The cook caught on and came running at full pelt from the kitchen at the back to shake my hand.

"I'm Alexander too!"

He hugged me close, jiggling me up and down. The other customers patted my back, offered me good wishes. I told them it was only a name. The other Alexander opened a box of Turkish Delight and insisted on me taking a few pieces and stood grinning at me. I smiled back. He told me once again that he too was called Alexander, pointing to himself in case I hadn't quite got it.

The town of Alexandreia had previously been known as Gidas, only changing its name in the 1950s when the state demanded its Turkish name was replaced with a marker of its near-by regal connection. The locals – no fans of change, even if it is change they are too young to remember – still stubbornly called it by its old name. It was an unattractive, large-looking town, built on a grid of streets that pretended to lead somewhere, but didn't. On the main road, driving alongside the town, I noticed a large municipal building set behind a long dirty grey wall. An old factory or a school perhaps. But then, in its grounds, I saw tents pitched. Women in long coats and hijabs. Kids looking out through the railing.

We parked up and I walked over. There was a police guard on the gate. I asked him if this was a refugee camp. Having seen the site of the largest makeshift camp in Europe in Idomeni a few days ago, I wondered if this was perhaps where some of the inhabitants had been moved to? The policeman offered no response. I asked him if it was ok for me to be here. He shrugged. Happy to give the impression he spoke no English. A blonde pair, a man and woman in matching blue t-shirts walked past. I asked them if this was a camp for the refugees. They were volunteers from Sweden. They told me that, yes, this was one of the largest official camps in Greece where many of the displaced refugees from Idomeni had been placed. There were 25 camps like this one around the country. I looked past them at a long line of women in bright dresses, dirty-looking now, queuing outside one of the broken-down outhouses on the complex. Two women came out of the dark doorless entrance, carrying bottles of water.

"Are things going ok here?" I asked.

"No," they both said, as one. "There is no organisation. There is nothing. Sometimes food arrives, sometimes it doesn't. Nobody knows what's happening. Nobody has any idea here."

The previously silent police guard stepped forward.

"Why are you asking questions?"

He stood between me and the volunteers, blocked the entrance to the camp.

"Why are you asking questions?" he repeated and prodded hard at my shoulder. I got the message and walked away, back to the car, catching as I left a last, flicking view of the camp through the railings. A child sat, playing on its own in a dull patch of dry mud, blowing listlessly on a plastic whistle which made no noise.

Giristroula and I headed south. Briefly leaving the state of Macedonia, crossing the borderland shared with Thessaly. Perhaps because the land had become flatter than anything we'd seen for a long time, the sight of Mount Olympus was more of a shock and looked even higher than expected. It seemed to just leap from the ground, as if spat out from the sun-boiled land. It was preposterous something so big could just appear so secretly and quietly. We had tackled Olympus a few years earlier, when I proposed to Giristroula at the very top and joined her in this Greek world that I was now happily tangled in. We had climbed its eastern side then, from the popular starting-point town of Litchoro, so this time we went west to the more forgotten side, to the town of Dion.

Dion was another significant ancient city, and a dedicated sanctuary to Zeus and the Gods. Alexander and his father King Philip held huge festivals here at the foot of the mountain, making momentous sacrifices for their successful travels conquering unknown lands. Giristroula and I walked the exhumed ancient roads, between the old columns. I threw a coin, our own small dedication, into one of the now overgrown, rather weed-run shrines as booming thunder rumbled menacingly over Zeus's mountain-top home behind us. We still had a long way to get back to *our* home. I felt it was wise to make some sort of offering to the gods. We walked a way up Olympus in thick, heavy air and took a swim in a quiet pool under a waterfall, but the sky darkened further and soon we were scurrying back down and out onto the road again.

We followed the range, the mountain tops rippling alongside us like the back of a huge serpent. The sky glowing bright silver grey. Flashes of lightning high above.

Vergina was King Philip's town. Having been disappointed by Alexander's town, and having learnt my lesson to keep my middle name, Philip, quiet here we arrived expecting little. We drove in, giving little "told you so" nods to one another as the fairly prosaic, colourless town emerged. We pulled up at the museum for the tomb of Philip. It appeared to be a well-manicured hill. The sun had battled out from between the clouds, the sky a deep blue colour over the grass dome. An old stone football stadium-style tunnel led into the belly of the hill. Puzzled, we shrugged to each other and walked into the dark… Philip's tomb burst back at us out of the darkness. We were jolted in astonishment, like being on the end of a falling rope. Unlike many ancient archaeological places I'd been to, I didn't have to stare at a pile of stones or use my imagination as to what might have been here or how it might have looked like, millennia ago. Philip's tomb was complete, standing proud and unaffected, staring straight back at me. To cover the original excavations, a hill was built over this museum to leave Philip's tombs as they had been made originally: underground. Inside, in the new large cool dark antechambers, the pale-coloured, decorated stone tombs of Philip and Alexander's son stood tall, unlooted, unbroken, entire and intact. The museum didn't have twisted old coins and bits of metal that once could have perhaps been a sword handle or a spear head. There were great finds: graves and paintings, and there, under bright spotlights, rested the actual golden box that held Philip's bones. The dazzling gold crowns Philip and his wife were buried in. Philip's own armour laid out, 2,500 years old. All quite unreal.

After Philip's final resting place, we headed towards Veria in the evening and stood in the town's square in the dying orange sun. The kids ran and played, the old people drank and gossiped. As in every town square in Greece, usually centred round one plane tree, this will go on until late: 11pm, midnight, 1am. There will be school and work the next day of course, but Greeks always seem to think that if they don't acknowledge that it's late, if they don't admit that time is passing, then perhaps it won't.

The Via Egnatia – an essential Roman road, linking the western coast of Greece to the Byzantine capital of Constantinople. Julius Caesar marched his army down this road. Marc Anthony chased Brutus along it after Caesar's murder. Richard the Lionheart crusaded down it towards Asia. And now Giristroula and I were following it, in its modern form anyway: the E90 motorway.

This modern road follows the line of the ancient road, still visible in some parts in the undergrowth to the side of the motorway, all along northern Greece, all the way into Turkey. We were on it now, but heading west. The road was quiet, as so many of the modern new-build roads in Greece seemed to be. There is often nothing for miles, outside of the cities at least. Here there were no cars, just long stretches of dazzling grey. My interest picked up every time I saw a rare vehicle coming in the other direction, like someone floating on a raft out in the middle of a dead ocean spotting a seabird flying overhead. There were high rocks all around us though. The rocks grew higher and more whipped-cream like. Surreal, high, twisting cliffs. But no adequate preparation at all for what we were about to see, as we turned off to the south, dipping back into the state of Thessaly and onto the edges of the Thessaly plain.

The Meteora. Churches suspended in the air. Monasteries built on enormous, bent, twisted cylinders of stone rising straight up. Giant columns of red rocks, 1,800 feet high, and other scraped pillars of white stone curling to the sky. Springing up from the flat plain like gigantic mushrooms.

A long, turning road took us up to the top of one these columns. From here we could see across the whole sweep of this quite insane landscape. Looking along left to right, we counted the large stone monasteries on top of their rock spikes, blending in with the tops so it's hard to see where rangy rock mountain ends and monastery begins. Six big monasteries, built around the 15th and 16th centuries as the march of the Ottoman Empire flooded these plains from the east to the Pindos mountains, where our northern tour had started. The monks, fearful of the Turkish threat, purposefully built their homes up in these most impossible-to-access areas. Until recently the only way to reach the monasteries was via a rope and winch, hauling goods and people all the way up to the tops. A monk, when asked when they replaced the ropes replied, in good, faithful 'God-has-the-answer style': "When they break."

Giristroula and I approached one of the monasteries and climbed up the steps to a huge wooden door. The day was finishing, and most of the crowds had dispersed – just a huddle of people taking photos of themselves on rocks bulging out over the long drops down to the town of Kalambaka below and a minibus of Asian men being ferried back and forth, up and down the road, in a panicky attempt to see all six monasteries in the short time left. We looked up at Moni Varlaam. The second largest of the monasteries on the Meteora. It was shut, but I had heard tales that the monks would take travellers in to stay. I hammered on the door. Nothing. I hammered longer. Still nothing. Eventually the door, with its Godly scenes painted round the frame, was opened a crack. An old, thick-set, heavy-bearded monk peered at us through the crack.

"*Ya sas*," I said.

No reply.

"Can we come in?" I asked.

The monk appeared unhappy. "Well... that is... difficult," he said.

The door opened slightly wider.

"Yes, it is difficult," he repeated eyeing me closely, up and down, and rubbing at his beard.

I could see the courtyard running round in a square, doors leading off, a central chapel and, inside, bizarre frescoes of a priest blessing coffins of skeletons. It made me want to stay here even more. I looked imploringly at the monk.

"Is it possible to stay the night here?" I asked.

"Oh. This is *very* difficult. We are... um... having redecorations," he said, throwing a hand back towards solid brick edifices that clearly hadn't changed for centuries and wouldn't be changing for centuries more.

"We don't mind," I said. "We're happy with anything. Really."

"Well... Where are you from?" he asked me quickly, a finger pointed at my chin.

"England," I said "But she's from Greece," I added, but it was too late.

"Oh no, we have no place for you, no. I'm sorry," he ushered us, flapping his hands, back away from the door.

He stopped. "Are you Orthodox?" he asked Giristroula but before she had time to reply – her hesitation telling him all he needed to know – we were pushed from the step.

"*O Theos mazi sas*," – May God bless you – the monk's final words behind the thumped closed door as the locks were turned.

Later, as we sat in an old tavern, I was told the best answer I could have given was to say I was Russian. "Then they would have *definitely* let you in."

Under a fast unfolding darkness, we realised we had no choice but to head back down again the winding road from the top of Meteora to the plain below. The gigantic rock formations around us were throwing dark shapes on the blackening sky as we descended. Then, on the side of the road, in the gloom, we saw a younger monk holding his robes high up over his knees stalking up the angled road: his upper body bobbing back and forth as he took long strides up the climb. Giristroula stopped the car and got out to greet him and asked if he knew anywhere where we could stay. The monk looked at anything he could rather than at Giristroula as she spoke to him. Twisting his head this way and that: looking at a tree, some boulders that had fallen onto the road, looking down over   the vast view back down onto the plains, the huge sky above us. When she had finished talking, he leaned his long neck through the window into the car to reply to me.

"I'm sorry. There is nowhere," he said. "Maybe you can stay with us. But not today. Another day... *O Theos mazi sas*," he touched me on the forehead and smiled.

The monk continued on up the mountain – throwing his head upwards, to the emerging moon as Giristroula said goodnight to him. It seemed the monk, this high up, this close to God, didn't want to run any risk of being caught even glancing at a woman.

We were homeless for the night. We drove on without really knowing where to go, back on the old Roman road, back heading west. Back high up into the Pindos mountains, through the Katara pass – *katara* meaning 'curse' in Greek, and all Greeks know this bit of road as one of the most dangerous in Greece.

We drove hanging 1,500 metres up, in the air in the black night. Eventually the town of Metsovo emerged. It was Alpine cold, even in this summer night. We were so high up and the atmosphere was so clear. The town looked Alpine too: wood panelled villas, carvings, stone houses, chalets. It seemed designed for rich tourists and the skiing season. We were too late for much to be open. The loud, spoilt, well-off-looking Metsovo kids pushed us out of the way as we entered a tavern. The old owner told us with a great sadness he had run out of *kodosouvli* – thick roasted pork slabs on a spit, the speciality of Metsovo. Instead he had *kokoretsi* – goat intestines – for us to eat. He served us up a few slices of the strong *Metsovone* cheese from here. Any sort of hotel was far too expensive for us to contemplate. Metsovo is very beautiful, but it was not for us. Like a smiling stranger shaking her head and waving a hand for us to keep moving along and not to bother her.

There was nothing for us to do but carry on driving. We passed through the remote wooded mountain area of Tzoumerka, stopping at the old stone village of Kalarites. We sat in an old wood tavern, with no rooms here for us either. The people of Tzoumerka were all walking around with *glitses* – long wooden walking sticks with a sort-of duck's head handle. They rested their sticks over their shoulders with their arms draped over it, as if hanging on their own crucifixes.

No one ever seemed to break into a smile in Tzoumerka. I also noticed that many of the residents weren't speaking Greek. I asked what language it was, and was surprised to learn they were speaking Vlach. These were descendants of the Vlach nomad shepherds I had previously caught glimpse of on the slopes of Mount Gamila. They no longer wandered the northern Greek lands but were settled in this village. They recommended we try the next village along, Syrrako. So Giristroula and I took a plunging route on foot down a steep valley, groping about blindly in the dark and then up thickly cut steps on the opposite hillside only to find Syrrako's stone-faced houses had no place for us either. Unwanted, off-course, vagabond and destitute, we returned to Kalarites, two hours after leaving, tired and thirsty. Everything was closed now.

Dawn was breaking along the coast road towards Parga. We had driven through the night. Idling through the middle of northern Greece, nowhere to go but around and around. There was an overpowering smell of pine and lavender in the early morning air all along the western road by the sea. The first rays of the sun pierced the wooded fields, waking and opening everything up. The disc of the new day's sun shining through the trees. It could have been mistaken for a fat orange hanging off the branch. The sluggish sea, the Ionian now, to our left was slow to get started this morning.

In our aimless driving during the night we had meandered along small roads far south, not knowing where to go, frequently lost. But at some point we had hit the far west point of the Greek mainland and the coast. Turning right at the sea edge, we were now driving up northwards again. The ghostly shapes of the islands of Paxos and, beyond, our home of Corfu could be seen out in their bed of still blue sea. To our right were the large slumbering animal-shaped mountains we had wandered up on our very first day travelling northern Greece. By the time we reached Igoumenitsa the boat to Corfu should be running.

The town of Parga was still asleep. A beautiful town with small houses tumbling down amphitheatre-like hills to the sea, followed over by the rays of the sun that were rising up, groping their fingers over the hilltops. Parga looked more like a town on an island than on the mainland. When it woke up, it would be crowded with holiday makers so we took the opportunity to walk the quiet

Venetian-style small lanes up to the battered castle overlooking the town. Ali Pasha, the Turkish-sponsored lord of northern Greece in the early 19th century, whose bloody reign had haunted us throughout our journey here, was the last to live in Parga's castle. Giving it its great baths and harems.

Giristroula and I stood on the battlements and looked down onto the town – the Bride of Epirus – still fashionable for its gratified living today: hotels, jewellery shops, up-market tavernas. The curve of Parga's sandy beach was making the most of its moment of peace with hundreds of beach umbrellas resting, furled up like sleeping seabirds.

We walked around the higgledy, old Italian-style houses, all bunched together and pastel-coloured. Past the soon-to-be-thrown-open shops and travel agencies with posters in the window and boards waiting to be put out on the streets advertising trips: the Meteora, the Prespes Lakes, the Zagoria villages, the Acheron River. Like a flicked photo album of all the memories of our journey.

Giristroula and I walked out onto the beach and stood looking out towards the open sea and the rippling cloth of silver-blue and the tiny island of the Virgin Mary a short swim away, with its hunkered-down gleaming white church surrounded by trees. And then we turned our backs on it all, and looked inland instead, to where our travels in the north of Greece had taken us. We stared at the hills and the rolling ground, reflecting on the journey now we'd reached the very end with nowhere further left to go. The sea that would soon take us away lapped in and out on the beach behind us, sighing to itself.

Chapter 5
Thrace

The White Arrivers

We arrived in Xanthi as the worst winter storms in over 50 years hit the Balkans. Blizzards, blocked roads, violent flurries of thick snow throughout the whole of northern Greece. A church bell chimed in the darkened sky, splattered with snow, as we crawled in. And then, from somewhere on the hills over Xanthi, barely visible from our newly found, unheated rooms in an ancient house in a crumbling part of the city, the unexpected sound of a mosque's call to prayer.

Next day, Giristroula and I walked out on the streets, blindingly white with thick snow under bright silver-grey skies, to see what the town of Xanthi looked like. We walked side-by-side along with headscarfed Muslim women, bent double into the wind-angled snow. The town was understandably quiet, but remarkably the old *salepi* seller was standing in the square with his wheelbarrow and a large battered urn sitting on top, holding the hot thick flour-based drink that is popular in the winter months in these northern parts of Greece. He looked a miserable lone figure, snow piling up on his black eastern *karakul* hat. Giristroula and I darted into baker's and grocer's shops to avoid the weather and heard Turkish voices behind the counters and amongst the customers. Tins and products we didn't recognise with Turkish labels. Other voices too: half Turkish, half Slavic. Women in veils, but with bright blue eyes and strands of blonde hair falling through. We were a little unsure of ourselves here, not knowing what to expect in this province of Thrace in the remote northeastern part of Greece not often visited by outsiders, but already it seemed a special place. Quite unlike anywhere else.

Kapnos City

We were in this far region of Greece as Giristroula was researching schools throughout the country for a book she was writing. We had left the warm, rich fields of Corfu for a few months and swapped them for these far-flung lands of Thrace. It was hard to believe they were part of the same country.

The snows faded and the skies over the city became open and blue. The mountains to the north of Xanthi were suddenly startlingly clear, and close. The Rodopi mountains flowed right to the very edge of the town, as if the rumbling landslide of rocks had pulled up just short of the backdoor of the very first house in the Old Town.

The Old Town was our new neighbourhood. It revealed itself, after the snows, to be a remarkable village within the city: narrow tilting alleys of museum-piece pastel-coloured Ottoman houses; buildings that looked like stage props but were still lived in; Byzantine churches; Christian frescoes. All overlooked by the white, tall, towers of mosques built higher up on the hills. And then, on the far east end of Xanthi, piled up next to the Kosynthos river where we had our rooms, smaller box-ish houses, outside of which stone stairs climbed to wonky wooden balconies and roofs. Beautiful in their own dilapidated way, these houses must have been built for the workers in the tobacco industry.

Xanthi became rich on tobacco in the 17th century. It is still grown now, out on the hills and fields beyond the city. For centuries, tobacco was a huge industry and made many Xanthians rich. This was clear to see as we walked through the Old Town getting closer to the centre of the city and the clock-tower square. The houses turned into hefty neo-classical mansions: yellows and pinks, sculptured balconies held up by vast wooden beams. Impressive stone villas for the owners of the tobacco warehouses. Their luxury lives, 200 years ago, remaining in heavy stone, ornate doors and iron-work windows. The grand old warehouses remained too, on Odos Kapnergaton – literally Tobacco Workers Street – handsome sandstone buildings, but most of them now empty and broken-down and decrepit. In London these warehouses would have been turned into expensive hipster flats and studios. In Xanthi they were languishing like once majestic elephant graveyard carcasses. And all the while, as we walked around, I was aware of those mountains just over my shoulder, on the very edge of town. If I turned round quickly, northwards, to face them, I felt sure they'd edged closer. The range suddenly frozen, as if in some game of musical statues.

Thracian Exile

Exploring Xanthi at night, we had a fruitless search for a *tsipourathiko*. With northern Greece being the heartland for tsipouro, I had expected the city to be lined with these sort of bars. As we watched the young students from the university filling the streets, there also seemed no tradition of Greek folk music or the old underground sounds of rebetiko either. Another big surprise as Xanthi is the birth place of Manos Hadjidakis, the magician of Greek melodies. The house Hadjidakis was born in had been restored and was now an arts centre, but it never seemed to be open. Giristroula and I took a place at 'Zefyros', a tavern opposite Hadjidakis's old house with a big print of his famous 'Street of Dreams' record sleeve and caricatures of Hadjidakis's plump face on the walls. His music faintly playing in the background. The city was alive, the tavernas and bars were all neat and tasteful, but the old culture of Greece seemed somehow missing amongst the cleaned-up stone buildings. But people seemed to be happy. Happy at least to be able to finally come out from their houses after the snows and walk around and chat. People had time for us, wanted to talk, wanted to help.

We had first arrived in the city in the undignified state of being towed as we sat in the hoisted-up car, on the back of an old pick-up truck: our car having been defeated by the bad weather as we travelled in, just outside of Thrace. The garage owner insisted on driving us to where we were staying, even though the streets of the old town of Xanthi are old and small and difficult to tackle. His van stalled on the climb to our house and slid back down the slope, crashing with a sickening blow into a wall. Our things tumbled out of the back onto the road, his light was smashed and the bumper hanging off. The garage owner seemed far more concerned, however, with hoisting our bags up on his shoulder to help walk us up to our door. Looking back at his prone, shattered vehicle he shrugged "*Ah then pirazi...* " – it doesn't matter. He nodded upwards. "This is a difficult climb for you. I hope you'll be okay..."

Later he called by again, to find out how we were doing, if we were eating well. He took us, in the patched up van, to his favourite butcher's. As we talked, it transpired the garage owner called himself a Turk, even though he, his father and his father's father had all been born here in Greece. We met his friend the butcher. The butcher told us *he* was a Pomak. His ancestral roots were a tribe found only in this part of Greece and a few pockets over the mountains in Bulgaria. He too was a Muslim, and spoke Pomak, and Turkish, but spoke Greek to us and his other non-Muslim customers. The meat was given to us for free.

"You are friends of my friend, so you are now my friends," said the Pomak. To the English. And the Greek. About his friend, the Turk. Who had 'Greek' written in his passport.

Giristroula's parents had stayed in Xanthi, years ago. They had told me a story of how while on holiday here they had sat on a bench and chatted, briefly, just passing the time of day, to an elderly woman.

"You're not from Xanthi?" said the old lady "Well, where will you sleep? It's getting dark..." she started to fret.

They told her it was okay, they were staying in a hotel. But she had trouble understanding this.

"A hotel?" said the woman they had met only moments ago. "But why didn't you tell me before? You should have stayed at *my* house."

Giristroula's parents told me they had to physically restrain the old woman from going back to clear the floor of her front room.

Market Days

On Saturdays, the bazaar comes to Xanthi. Filling the whole of Emporio Square, bright stalls running as far as you can see. Spices, fruits, wines, clothes. Tat you don't want, fresh foods and products you do. The villagers from the surrounding areas all descend from the mountains into the town, packing out the cafés. Chatting, gossiping, spilling out of bakeries eating bougatsa pastries – not with cream as elsewhere in Greece, but with meat. The bazaar market traders were different from others you find in Greece. They tried their best to lure us into buying their goods, unlike the usual proud Greek shop owner who never stoops or demeans themselves by trying to appeal to customers. "Either you buy, or you don't buy. What do I care?" is the usual response in Greek shops when you try to haggle or show any indecision about buying something. Even if the shopkeeper has no custom whatsoever and you would think should be desperate for any kind of trade. Here in Xanthi, the market merchants vied with each other to attract the customers' attention. Turkish Delight was handed out to lure you in and, almost uniquely again in Greece, there were expressions of gratitude. "*Agapi mou!*" and "*Omorfi!*" hollered out from hundreds of stalls.

I saw one smiling stall owner tell a Romani gypsy girl in a dirty torn dress, with skin the colour of a deep varnished table and brittle, electric shock, blue-black hair, that she could take one of the Eastern sweets the woman was selling. In a flash the girl took handfuls.

"*Ochi! Ochi! Ochi!*" cried the stallholder. "*Ena! Ena!*" – One! One!

The gypsy girl, quicker the eye could see, had hidden the sweets in every single hiding place she had on her. The market holder raced round to the front of her stall.

"*Tha fas xilo!*" she said - the common cry to threaten naughty kids with a whacking - You'll eat wood!

Cherub faced gypsy boys walked along, seven or eight-year-olds, smoking long cigarettes, trying to look tough. One dangling a catapult. The Roma are Muslim here in Thrace, unlike in the rest of Greece. We followed them, as they meandered past spice shops, silk shops, and shops selling football shirts – all Galatasaray or Fenerbahçe or Beşiktaş from the Turkish league, rather than the usual Olympiakos or Panathinaikos or PAOK Salonica. We went into a grill house and ordered souvlakis and gyros. The man behind the counter rather sweetly checked first that we were okay to eat pork. We sat and ate and watched the Saturday crowds pass.

The Broken Journey East

We had been waiting on Xanthi station platform for a long time.

"No, not here," said the station master. "You shouldn't wait for a train here. The line… it's… er… it's broken. Trains are late."

"How late?" I asked him.

"Six months."

So we piled onto the replacement bus and headed out into the surrounding countryside. Mountains dominant on one side, a flat plain on the other, with tall grasses and the odd lone minaret rising over clumps of trees. The plain spread towards the shining waters of the Nestos Delta in the distance.

Giristroula and I got off the bus at Komotini. A large town set around a long, busy square. Komotini has the highest proportion of Turkish people in the country, around fifty per cent of the population. Although the Greek government does not recognise them as Turkish, instead they are formally called 'Greek Muslims'. The old town of Komotini was remarkable for the old, squat, Ottoman stores and workshops. Most of them carrying Turkish names. Or a comical Greek and Turk mix, like the sign for the barber 'Ali Christos'. The official street signs also had something I hadn't seen in Greece before: under each road name – 'Odos Smyrni', 'Odos Aristotle' etc. – there was a description of what or who the road was named after. They mainly seemed designed to highlight the significance of Greece and Greek history:

'This road is named after Smyrni, a great ancient Greek city in Asia Minor, now called Izmir.' Or *'Aristotle: a great Greek philosopher and thinker.'*

Were these subtle messages designed for the minority population? It all seemed unnecessary if they were. The Greeks and the Turkish – the Orthodox and the Muslims – all seemed to get on here in perfect harmony. Here, where perhaps tension *should* feel heightened, there was none of the anti-Turkish sentiment you hear in other parts of Greece… parts of Greece that are much further from the border and these mixed lives that have existed here for centuries. I was told that it is only people who were not from this area that ever caused any trouble between the different groups here. "The pot is always stirred from the *outside*" as one resident of Komotoni put it.

Komotini has two impressive central mosques. Giristroula and I walked around the, more impressive, newer one. We were followed by a man making sure our shoes were off at all times. I asked him if he was Turkish.

"Pomak."

"You language is more Slavic, is that right?" I asked him.

"Bulgarian."

"So you don't speak any Turkish?"

He shook his head. This was strange, I thought, in this most Turkish of Greek towns.

"But the graves here," I said, pointing. "They're all inscribed in Turkish."

He shrugged. "We are all Muslims. But I don't speak Turkish."

I asked him if he feels Greek or Pomak.

"Both." He scratched his beard and thought about it and smiled a dirty grin "It depends who asks..."

I said goodbye and thanked him in Greek. And then asked how to thank him in Pomak.

"Like the Turkish," he said. "*Teşekkürler.*"

Things in Thrace were just getting more and more confusing.

Giristroula and I walked back to the train station, to wait for the ghost train, which ended up being someone's old van, to take us back to Xanthi. We passed the large park with its towering war memorial, complete with a gigantic hanging iron sword. Much blood was spilt to take and hang onto these lands. The Greek state clearly didn't want this forgotten; even if the concept and the convictions are blurred and lost in the actual day-to-day living within these communities of Greeks, and Greeks with Turkish roots, or the fully ethnic Turkish – the Turkish people who were allowed to stay when the Ottoman Empire finally fell. During the Population Exchange of 1923, when Greeks in Turkey and Turks in Greece were swapped, moving around two million people from homes that had been passed down through the generations across the borders on both sides, Turkish people living in this area of Thrace were the only ones allowed to stay. The Turkish who now have to officially label themselves with this strange name of 'Greek Muslim.'

We rattled in the van along the plant-lined roads back towards Xanthi, where the communities of northeastern Greece are confused even further there by the large numbers of Pomaks, with their connection to Bulgaria across the mountains to the north, living within this ancient, beautifully scrambled, city. It was a riddle of peoples and belongings that even the locals can't explain. But it all seemed to work, in its mysterious way.

An Education

Giristroula was conducting research here in Thrace, working in a school in the centre of Xanthi. Each day the unusualness of this world revealed itself further. Giristroula's school was a mixed school, but only 20 years ago most of the 'Muslim' students – 'Muslim' the official term for Pomaks and Roma as well as Turkish – were taught solely in Muslim-only schools. Still today there are a few of these 'Minority Schools' in the town, one provided by the state and the others privately. The private 'Minority Schools' are suspected of being funded by Turkey and some say they promote a feeling of closeness towards Turkey. While pretty much all the ethnic Turks and Pomaks I spoke to identified themselves as Greek citizens, still a strange feeling of disassociation can exist.

But not in the playground. A roughly half-and-half split between Greeks and Muslims in Giristroula's classes meant students were switching between Greek, Turkish and Pomak as they shouted to each other in the playgrounds. Girls playing singing and skipping games in Turkish, then a dance in Greek. Boys playing football yelling to their cousins in Pomak, then to their friends in Greek. It was perfectly natural and made a great scene. I was told the staff room was different though.

"I was never racist," said one teacher to Giristroula "They've *made* me racist."

This teacher claimed that many of the Muslim children need special help as there is rumour of interbreeding in the communities up in the mountain areas. She railed against the extra benefits Muslims get.

"They can get to university with very low scores. They get preferential treatment. The teachers here will soon all be Muslim and no Greek will ever be taught. You'll see! All the parents only speak to me in Turkish as it is... It's just not right. And..." she finished, wagging a meaty finger in the air. "Have you *seen* how good the cars they drive are?"

I was disappointed to hear all this, having previously been impressed at the lack of prejudice or conflict up here in these mixed areas. Giristroula told me, though, that this teacher who had ranted all this at her was a Greek raised in Germany and had only returned to her family ancestral town later in life. Perhaps she was just one those stirrers from outside of the pot.

Giristroula got on well with the students. They wanted to show her games and songs she didn't know from elsewhere in Greece. And they had some great names amongst all the usual Greek names of Maria, Kostas and Nikos.

"*Binnur* – it means 'A thousand roses.'"

"*Sudem-Miftah* – it's... er... what's the place called when you die?"

"Paradise?"

"Yes, that place. My name is 'The key to Paradise...'"

I wandered around Xanthi while Giristroula was teaching. An afternoon call to prayer drew me in to one of the mosques in the new town. Everything was quiet in the dark main hall. Prayer mats were rolled out down, *misbahah* prayer beads left, ready for action, along the wall. Upstairs, however, were hidden voices: a lesson was going on. Young sweet-sounding kids were struggling through the Koran. Reading in Arabic, getting it wrong, asking questions in Greek, being barked at by an exceptionally bad-tempered teacher in Turkish. There was confusion and he repeatedly banged on the desks in frustration. It sounded a frightening learning experience to listen in on, and I slipped away back into the open sunlit day unobserved.

Giristroula and I went out one night with the teachers from her school. As we sat and ate, one of the teachers told me that the curious Slavic/Turkish hybrid language that the Pomaks use is not a written language; it is only an oral language. The few Turkish words that slip in came from the trade conducted during the Ottoman Empire, so the Pomak, for expedience, when buying and selling with the Turks adopted their numbers and certain bartering words and phrases. Hence the "Teşekkürler"s for thanks. It felt strange to me, however, that the adult Greeks I met could speak absolutely no Pomak at all. I said to the teachers around the table, how could they not have picked up something, hearing Pomak every day growing up here? This didn't go down well. They didn't see it as curious at all. Some said, defensively, that most Pomaks went to the Muslim schools not their schools. Still, it seemed odd to me, a refusal almost. It must have been more difficult *not* to learn some of the language than to learn it.

Into Deep Thrace

Our car was finally repaired. Giristroula and I drove out of the city to where the Nestos River snaked down from Bulgaria, flowing towards the Aegean Sea, cutting through northeast Greece and slicing between the Greek states of Macedonia and Thrace. Down on the bank of the ice-cold river on the Thrace side, huge Macedonian cliffs rose above us. We turned and climbed up from the dark riverbed, which would be flooded in a few weeks when the snows higher up melted, into sun-lit Thrace mountains. We followed a railway line that cut into the cliffs, disappearing into tunnels below us and walked on over the rocky path, taking in the views across the Nestos Straight and the deep forested ravines.

Further south, Lake Vistonida was full of balancing flamingos. As we approached the pink birds with their purple underwings, spindly legs, stupidly long thin neck, they got the jitters and suddenly took flight. The sky filled with pinks and purples as the birds moved away in one huge flock to settle further into the middle of the lake. Out floating in the lake too was the church of Agios Nikolaos. We were lured over the narrow walkway to the white-towered church, all alone out in its vast churchyard of water, by the sound of religious song coming from somewhere within. I opened up the doors to see deep orange sunlight falling over the dark, dusty, empty pews. No one in attendance, just four old Orthodox priests on their own, pressed together at the small lectern, like four huddled old black crows leaning together, singing a Byzantine harmony.

This lake was where Hercules tamed the wild horses for the eighth of his 12 Labours. There are still wild horses around here, and wild cats and brown bears somewhere in the mountains on the horizon. A huge congregation of nature. We continued down to where this large fresh water lake turns salty, and then finally meets the sea. The modern town of Abdera, on the sea, looks utterly undistinguished, but it holds inside it the remains of a great ancient city. The city was built in tribute to Hercules's friend Abderus, who was given Hercules's wild horses to look after while Hercules completed his other Labours. Unfortunately, not being a Herculean hero himself, he was soon eaten by them. Giristroula and I walked the ancient walls of the old city built high up on bluffs on the very south edge of Thrace, looking straight out to sea and to the island of Thasos. I stood and stared and tried to meditate on the big things in life as seemed appropriate in this city that produced several great philosophers of Classical time. Democritus – the Laughing Philosopher – came from Abdera. I liked the sound of him: living to well over 100 and travelling widely throughout Greece to fully understand the country and its people, and mocking the Greek human foibles as he went.

Giristroula and I headed back to Xanthi on the empty roads. Golden, tall grass-fringes, with marshy fields all around us under a huge, sun-smeared, glassy sky. We pulled over to take it all in. A silhouetted lone farmer stood up on a horse and cart in the distance. An eagle sat just a few feet away on a low branch of a tree staring severely through our open passenger window. Thrace's emptiness and remoteness felt perfect. On our way back into the centre of the town, though, Greek life soon reminded us of itself. You can only ever be away from it for so long. A man sat in his car at a red light, the only car waiting. He thumped repeatedly at his horn, honking at the fully automated traffic sign, again and again. Until it finally turned green for him.

Edgelands

Heading into the north of Thrace, towards Bulgaria, we came into a hidden, seclusive area: the Pomakohoria. Collections of villages, scattered like seeds across bare rolling mountainous lands. The towns themselves are often fairly unattractive, the lone arresting site being the substantial mosques sat in the centres. But there was a strange singular feeling surrounding these mountain villages as we drove around.

We stared down from the high snakey road on the hills above, and then free-wheeled into a Pomakohori village. The broken old farmers' houses were held together only by a hundred years of habit, so it seemed. They stood in glorious contrast to the short blocky new home. They have a unique Thracian look: bulging large stone brick boxes sticking out from the thick stone walls, a storey up, where enormous fireplaces inside heat the rooms. The Muslim residents' styles on the streets were resolutely old fashioned too. The men were wearing fez, the old women wrapped in scarfs were sat knitting in cafés. All along the roads, between the villages, were dotted fountains. This being an extension of the Greek tradition of erecting a shrine where someone had been killed, or where some miracle is supposed to have occurred. There are so many of these shrines throughout Greece, I always wondered if there *really* could have been that many road accidents or religious apparitions? In Thrace they go one step further though, and the Muslim community erect a fountain to the dead and dig down to tap into the water and families build impressively elaborate brick edifices.

We passed villages with names such as Medusa and Kedavros – the centaur. Names that must have been changed from Bulgarian or Turkish to dramatic, faintly ludicrous, historic Greek names. Names you would never see anywhere else. I'm sure the older timers here wouldn't ever use these names for their villages. There was a silence embedded deep into the very heart of the Pomakohoria.

Crazily, on an almost impossible dirt road winding high up on the side of a plunging drop, someone was running a large stone taverna. We felt we had to pay it a visit.

Crouching through the ancient wooden door, we entered this Pomak inn. Black wood, fireplaces, mud walls, the room divided with screens of sticks, rough shepherd rugs on the walls and trinkets everywhere. The elderly owner's grandmother's Pomak wedding dress was hung up proudly: bright reds and greens, high frilled collar, long sleeves, jewelled belt. The son, with bright blue eyes, blonde beard and powerfully built, wearing an old collarless shirt and an ancient thick, itchy, woollen waistcoat came to ask what we would like his mother to cook. He pulled up a chair, clasping me by the shoulder with his heavy hand and knocking all the wind out of me, and sat and ate some of our bread as we decided. When our plates of meat arrived, he sat down again, not asking, helping himself to some of our food, taking some of somebody else's off another table, giving it to me to try. I asked him questions about the Pomakohoria. He gazed into the middle distance, chewing, and didn't reply. I waited, but he didn't speak so I turned to my meatball dinner. I tried asking him another. He chewed and ruminated some more. Minutes passed, but nothing was forthcoming. I gave it one last go, asking him how life was for him and his family so far out here to the east. He finally started to talk.

The Pomaks feel abandoned by everyone, he said. The Greeks overlook them, seeing them as an inconvenience best ignored. The Turks took advantage of this, offered them good land when the Greeks would give them nothing and so, to all intents, the Greeks lost the Pomaks. But the Turks clashed with them too, not wanting them to hold any traditions of their own.

"The Pomak people fought bravely for Greece in these lands during the war," Jamaal, the old tavern owner who had heard us talking to his son and had come over to sit down and speak to us. "And now Greece just forgets us."

One of Giristroula's teachers had invited us to her house back in Xanthi. Her name, appropriately enough, was Xanthippe. There is a legend in the hills above Xanthi town that there was a Xanthippe who was the lover of a local boy Xanthos. When Xanthos died tragically young, Xanthippe turned herself in her sorrow into a bird and she now accompanies lovers she spots walking over the hills and rivers and sings them songs. Our modern day Xanthippe, however, lived in a chaotic house with her kids and parents. Her father had been a salesman and every day he had driven round the Pomakohoria trying to sell his wares. He told me that, 20 years ago, there were barriers up outside every village in the Pomakohoria. He needed a special pass to enter or leave the villages.

"Was this to keep the Pomaks in, or the Greeks out?" I asked.

"Both," he replied. "There was... suspicion. You know, there was the Cold War. No one really understood who the Pomak people were. I was okay though," he added in the usual Greek self-effacing way. "They all loved me..."

Barriers and walls within Greece, keeping people away from each other. It all seemed hardly believable, and very sad.

Orpheus's Kingdom

A commonly heard, disagreeable, statement in Greece is how the Greek dictator, Giorgos Papadopoulos, 50 years back, *did* do one good thing: he built good roads in the country. Giristroula was now researching for a few weeks in the village of Stavroupoli. I accompanied her to the school and heard in the staffroom something altogether stronger.

"There used to be a grand mosque in the main square in Xanthi you know," said one of the teachers. "Behind where the clock tower is now. Papadopoulos did one good thing... he pulled that mosque down."

Stavroupoli had a different feel from what I had grown accustomed to in Thrace. It had no real Muslim population. Giristroula said there were only two Muslims in the whole school. The village had very little work and people were leaving in large numbers. Three students had left the school just in the last few weeks as their families had moved away. No one spoke English as I sat and chatted to the koboloi twirling old farmers, a retired butcher, an old shoemaker in the kafeneo in the village square. But quite a few spoke German. Alongside Athens, Germany was the destination for the people leaving the Thracian villages. Even the old men in their 70s and 80s had learnt the language, just in case. Places like Stavroupoli had once had their own thriving industries and communities. Now they were all dying. What would finally happen to these places in the next few decades?

In the afternoon, after school, Giristroula and I headed north, towards the Bulgarian border. We were close to the border, just as when we were travelling up in the Pomakohoria, but this time further east, and there was now a 2,000-metre mountain range between us and Bulgaria. Plus the vast Haidou forest.

After 1945, this area was an Iron Curtain border. An easier crossing point into the West than going via Berlin. For a time this land and the forests teemed with soldiers, spies, fugitives.

We parked at the tiny village of Livaditis, perched remotely on a mountain peak. An old man with no teeth, in falling down dungarees, carrying a large dead fox in one hand up the road towards a bin told us he would watch our car for us, even though he appeared to be the only person on the whole mountainside. Giristroula and I walked into the forest. The snow from earlier in the winter still lay, thick and compacted. We saw no other human foot prints, but instead the exciting, slightly worrying, prints of large round heavy paws. A bear? Then the tread of large dogs. Were these wolves' prints? We walked, slightly agitated, along the two-kilometre path, then took a long, plunging climb down through thickly bunched, tall, beech trees. The snow thinning to lie in patches as we scrambled. Eventually we reached a waterfall, in what felt the middle of nowhere. The tallest waterfall in the Balkans. Until recently the 40-metre fall must have been frozen solid. Now, however, we the water slid through the cracked ice, the tumbling falls making a rolling musical sound.

Orpheus, the mythical musician of ancient Greece, was born from Thracian roots. His father was a Thracian king. Orpheus made the rivers and the rocks dance with his music. Zeus eventually killed him for revealing the mysteries and magic of music to men. Either that, or the story goes that Orpheus was so distraught at being unable to bring his beloved wife back from the dead when he travelled down to Hades to rescue her, he spurned all the advances of the Thracian women. In his grief all he could do was play his music and transfer his affections towards the local young boys to *enjoy their brief springtime...* so the enraged local women tore him to pieces. They had tried throwing stones at him, but his music was so beautiful the stones refused to hit him. The deserted forest around us, singing to the sound of the waterfall seemed entirely appropriate. The ice hanging high up on the top of the falls cracked with a gunshot sound, echoing off the towering rocks all around us, and fell with the booming sound of an orchestra's bass drum.

Beyond Stavroupoli there are two clearly defined mountains that loom higher than the rest of the large range. King Haemus of Thrace was very proud of his wife, Queen Rodopi. So proud he even boasted she was more beautiful than Hera, Zeus's wife. Big mistake. They now sit, in Zeus's vengeful metamorphosed state, as these huge snowy twin peaks. They stared down on Giristroula and me as we travelled up a vertiginously climbing road. A thousand metres up, we could see way below us the coiling Nestos river tracing like a slug's silver trail through the rough Thrace landscape. In the distance the mountains of the Bulgarian border, where Greek rebels were holed up during the civil war. The other way was the sea and the island of Samothrace, where legendary trance parties and summers of hallucinatory drugs and naked dancing take place every year. Mount Athos, the residence of Greece's hermetic monks, could even be glimpsed far off ahead of us, towards Halkidiki and the body of mainland Greece. I could picture regular Greek life going on over there, off towards Thessaloniki with all the industry and expositions at a pace and in a manner quite enormously removed from these silent Thracian hills.

A Smell of Summer

Tsiknopempti day is a Thursday before Lent where the whole of Greece is out grilling and eating meat so that, before the coming 40 days of fasting, they've made sure they've fully sated themselves of flesh. Every garden and terrace and balcony has a long trail of smoke rising from it, like a waving grey flag high in the air. Xanthi had gone suitably crazy for this grilling day. I saw stalls selling meat everywhere, not just outside the tavernas but tobacconists and shoe shops and fruit sellers and furniture stores had all given up their usual trade for the day and were outside setting up fires, turning great skewers of lamb.

The Xanthians were lucky that this day had also coincided with '*Alkyonides*' – the strange 15 or so days of good weather that Greece always gets in late January or February. Where the phrase 'Halcyon Days' comes from. Alkyonides are kingfisher birds which need two weeks of good weather to hatch their eggs. According to legend, these birds were created because of another boastful couple who were turned by Zeus, again, of course, into birds who as a punishment have to lay their eggs in wintertime. Although this time Zeus felt a tinge of sorrow for the wife and ordered the winds to drop and for the sun to shine every year for her 15 days of labour.

"*O Flevaris ki an flevisi kalokeri tha mirisi...*" the Greeks say – as soon as February starts, it smells like summer…

Giristroula and I sat outside the hunkered red brick Agia Sophia church in the centre of Xanthi, in the sun and ate steaks. A fat man sat next to me punched at his breastbone, letting out a long quivering belch. Then, for afters, we all headed down Tsaldari Street – *the* high street for Muslim shops and products – for *halva* at 'Taselaridis'. Halvas is the sweet eaten all through Greece, a crumbly nutty dense slab of dry cake, but it's usually eaten only around Kathara Theftera – Clean Monday – the Greeks' first day of Lent. In Xanthi, though, it is eaten every day, and the huge queues rolling out of this plain, slightly shabby, white interior bakery show it's eaten *a lot* every day here. This is, of course, as with most things round these parts, due to the closeness of Turkey. Halvas came to Greece with the arrival of the Ottomans. Turks love halva, perhaps almost as much as, so it is stereotypically said, they dislike the Greeks. There is even a saying "*Romeikos kavgas Turkikos halvas!*" – when Greeks fight between themselves, it is halvas to the Turks!

We ate huge slices of halva and had strong coffee brought to us on a big brass tray looking like the skeleton of a bell, hanging from the hand of the man serving our table. The eastern coffee cups suspended in mid-air. We sat and played *tavli* as the late afternoon slipped away.

East from Xanthi

Alexandroupoli had the things that were missing from Xanthi. It's a city built on the sea front, a port city. There were good looking places to drink tsipouro, to go with all the fish caught here, and old-fashioned taverns advertising rebetiko nights. People also appeared to choose to cycle around the city, almost unheard of in Greece. There was a good feeling in the city. The sea front was plain though, just concrete flats and a long grim beach, only saved by the lighthouse standing tall looking out to the floating tall jagged rocks of Samothraki across the water.

There were also two Turkish soldiers here. Two soldiers who had fled over the border in the last week and had been on the run, having been accused of leading a plot to assassinate Turkish president Recep Tayyip Erdoğan. They had now given themselves up and were seeking asylum in Alexandroupoli. Turkey had taken this badly. War ships were crossing Greek waters daily, planes flying over Greek lands. Greek tanks were visible on the edges of Alexandroupoli and the usual insouciant feeling in the army camps, as young 18-year-olds lope and loaf their way through their compulsory service, was missing. Things felt tense.

Giristroula and I drove out to the vast expanse of the Evros Delta. The Evros river is the line between Greece and Turkey. Under the huge skies we stopped and breathed in lungfuls of pure air. As the sun started to fall, the sound of the beat of the flamingos' wings marked their return. There is no animosity or jaundiced eyes for them. The flamingos fly to the Turkish side of the delta to eat, with Turkish cuisine obviously more appealing, and then return to Greece each night to sleep.

Heading backwards, by the sea, in the small village of Makris, Giristroula and I took a walk along the cliffs and found a broad rough cave staring out above the beach. Large rock boulders sat outside, as if thrown from the sky. We pushed a little way in, but the cold and the sudden deep darkness felt unpleasantly oppressive and we quickly forced our way back out again. A waitress in a local café said this was the cave of Polyphemus, the giant Cyclops who imprisoned Odysseus and his men. The Cyclops was finally blinded by Odysseus and sat on the sea shore that had lapped before of us, bathing his weeping eye. The waitress told us a later tale of two local fishermen who had entered this cave. The fishermen thought they'd been in the cave for just an hour or so, but when they emerged from the darkness worried wives and townspeople were all gathered outside waiting for them. They'd been in there for days.

Giristroula and I drove the broken backroads towards home, through the disorientating Thrace countryside, with the sun in our eyes leaking a copper colour over a sky streaked with clouds. Time could still almost be an abstract concept around here.

One Way Rome, the Other Way Mecca

It felt like we were following a thread of minarets, leading us out to the east. The long ancient old Roman road – Egnatia Odos – took us into deepest Thrace. Mosques lined the road, agricultural fields flowed away on both sides: a reminder that under the Ottoman Empire, Thrace was known as the 'bread basket of Constantinople'. Our first stop was Soufli where Giristroula's father had done one of his years of compulsory military service. We stopped in vague homage to him. The town was dull: new architecture set along a couple of main roads, not even a square as with most Greek towns. Soufli was famous for centuries for being a great producer of silk due to the mulberry bushes growing on all the hills around the town. There are now just a couple of silk museums in the few old buildings left. The owner of one told us, with a sort of wretched hope, that she felt that silk production would come back. That the town would rise again.

"The EU paid us to replace the mulberry bushes with other crops. They said it would be more profitable. So no one makes silk now. Nothing, all the way until you reach the Far East... But lately they've realised their mistake and have been asking us to put the mulberry bushes *back*..." she said, shaking her head at the madness.

Giristroula and I walked around the town, approached a couple of men who were stood in a pool of sunlight, idly chatting by the railway track in the centre of the town. We asked them what Soufli had to offer.

"*Tipota*" – not much.

I asked them if there was a Muslim culture here at all.

"They're all up there" said one, waving a hand to the raised land above the town. He pulled a face "Leave them up there…"

We told them we were heading as far to the east as we could go in Thrace, towards the Turkish border. They sucked their teeth. Why do you want to go there? The Turkish are bad people, they said.

"Where are you from?" they asked Giristroula. She told them she was from the Peloponnese.

"*Oh…katavlakiotisa, eh?*" – Under the ditch eh? – the ditch being the Corinth Canal. "So *we're* the ones who'll have to do the fighting when the Turks come, eh? You can just run back home south…"

It was one of those conversations, spoken as a joke, but there was no joke there. Just disconcerting views revealed under a thin veil of hard-faced humour. The two men frowning into the sun.

We headed towards the military camp where Giristroula's father had been based. They didn't even allow us to take a look: camouflaged men in boots pouring out from the gate to move us on. So we moved on, and just a few hundred metres outside the city we hit the Evros River, the border with Turkey. The river seemed remarkably thin here, Turkey just one impressively long leap away. I stood and stared out at this new mysterious country full of supposed threat and worry. It really didn't look much different to the bare, brown, barren-looking land I was standing on.

We carried on to Didymoteicho, where old lolling homes made of wood climbed up a fat meteorite of rock in the centre of town. Castle, medieval city walls, ancient church on the top. Centuries old windows and rooms and basements carved out from the rock over on the other side. Didymoteicho was not a large town and it surprised me to find that at one point it was the capital of the whole Byzantine Empire and the birth place of two Byzantine Emperors. The immense Bayezid Mosque, built in 1420, the oldest and the largest mosque in Europe, lurked on a side road. Hidden away in this area pretty much forgotten by everyone. The mosque looked a sad prisoner, caged in wooden scaffolding, a modern protective roof over its previous grandeur, minarets broken and vulnerable to earthquakes. The mosque still stood defiant though. Having watched the Ottomans, the Bulgarians, the re-conquering Greeks and the devastation of the Second World War pass its solid, stark front, it would take more than any of that to get rid of this venerable patriarch of Thrace.

Through the real edgelands of Greece now, having gone as far east as we could. We were heading up along the Greek and Turkish border, northwards, looking for a place to cross over and enter into Turkey. For a long while there were only small Greek villages, with names of comedic lack of imagination: one even simply called Elliniko Horio – Greek Village.

At Kastanies, almost as far to the northeastern corner of Greece as you can possibly go, we found a border crossing. The road led up to a check-point. The rail crossing here, and the 'Friendship Express' train, seemingly permanently suspended. I had been told earlier that Giristroula would be fine to cross, as a Greek, but being

British I would have a lengthy wait and questions would be asked and a payment would be needed for a visa. On a sudden impulse, I turned to Giristroula and said I was going to hide in the boot of the car as we crossed the border. Giristroula stared back at me with her mouth open. I got her to stop the car, waved away her protests and as she sat shaking her head at this lunacy, I bundled myself in the back. My heart was thumping with the unnecessary danger in all this. I was smuggling myself over a border that had the world's attention on it, as volunteer Islamic State fighters from across Europe crossed one way and desperate refugees crossed the other, and all for the sake of a 25-euro day-visa. I sat, folded in the dark boot of the car and reflected on what a cheapskate fool I could so often be. I could hear voices outside. What sounded like an argument. The blood was ringing in my ears. I couldn't swallow. Then the car moved. Stopped. The sound of footsteps. The boot opened. I looked up, blinking, at a figure shadowed in the bright sunlight. It was Giristroula. She told me that we'd been turned away from driving over the border as she hadn't any proof that the car was hers. Her documents were written in Greek and the Turkish guards had wafted them away as no good without even looking at them. So, instead we trudged over the border on foot with me having had a lengthy wait, questions asked and, of course, a 25-euro day-visa bought.

Once in Turkey we were on a dead-straight road, fields either side. A farmer had planted a huge 30-foot Turkish flag in his field. The town of Edirne lay shimmering on the horizon.

We managed to flag down a lift from a Greek couple who had crossed the border. I asked them why they'd come.

"See those houses?" the driver pointed to a broken-down settlement over the fields. "That's where my family is from."

"But you're Greek?"

"Haven't you noticed you haven't crossed the river yet? This was Greek land. But the Turkish wanted this land just west of the river. I don't know why," he peered out the window with a sad look on his face. "The Turkish and the Greek government did a deal. Greece was given the island of Limnos in return. The town over there was called Rizia. Now we live in a newly built town on the Greek side. Nea Rizia." He looked over at the few spread-out houses. "I like to come back to see my home."

His wife twisted her big face round to us, beaming. "I like coming to the big city. It's the nearest city to us even though it's in a different country. Isn't that strange? And everything's so much cheaper..."

The shopping streets of Edirne were busy under good-looking old buildings as, while again not a particularly large city, we were in another Empire's former capital and Edirne was once the head of the Ottoman world. I tried to find the large covered bazaar I'd heard about. *No one* spoke English. Or Greek. This was surprising. Despite the lack of Turkish spoken in Greek Thrace, I assumed that, even for mere mercenary reasons, some Greek would be spoken here. I also counted on finding someone who spoke English. Usually complacent and overindulged, I now suddenly felt cut adrift. It was exhilarating and a little disconcerting and I knew I'd entered a completely different world, just a few miles from my new Greek home. Greece, which seemed normal, safe, even a little dull to me now. The lack of any common language meant there was no hassling in the bazaar, no haggling or pushing. We took a place at one of the many liver restaurants around the city. The Turkish appeared crazy for liver dishes and the waiter, through a ridiculous routine of sign language and dramatic mime, let me know that Edirne is *the* place for liver. Istanbul folk making the 500km trek to Edirne, there and back, just for a little taste.

There are three monumental mosques packed in close proximity, all complete with towering minarets and imposing domes. When the call to prayer started, it was an impressive sound. Far more strident than back in Xanthi. Giristroula and I stood looking up at the grandest mosque, absorbed in the Mu'ezzin's singing as he recited over and over his *adhan*. The clear strength of the Islamic faith flowing out transporting us with the sounds of devotion and ritual... and then his mobile phone went off, ringing through loud speakers and bouncing off the other marbled mosques, echoing off the falling down homes behind and off the walls of the city's hamams. We snapped quite quickly out of the reverie.

It was time to leave Eastern Thrace and head back towards the border and Greek Thrace. We crossed back over one of the several old handsome stone bridges: nine long arches spanning the Meriç River. We bounced along in a clapped-out bus down the drawn-out road towards Greece, the road behind us stretching all the way back to the Turkish capital. Moonlight jumped through the trees as we rode on towards Greece.

The Karnavali

The day before Lent is a big day in Greece. Carnival time. They say only Patra, down in the south, can rival Xanthi for a bigger carnival in the whole of Greece. Everyone talked about the Xanthi carnival, I'd heard of it back in Corfu. People in Macedonia, Epirus, Thessaloniki all travel here to see the festivities. Fancy dress shops bursting with costumes dotted the city.

A few weeks earlier, bright masked faces and lights started appearing on all the walls and lampposts. Dances broke out spontaneously in the main square with men and women in decorated costumes, traditional music and complicated steps, huge circles of dancing, violins wailing, drums banging, cheery old men raising glasses in salute from their seats in the cafés. I was expecting great things from the main event on this last day of the Apokries festivities...

The crowds on Carnival day were colossal, packing every street and bar. The procession of dressed-up dancing people and bright floats stretched back miles. Everyone drinking, having a good time.

But where were the traditional costumes? All the old-style culture that had been hinted at in the weeks' build-up? Giristroula told me that Carnival time is usually a great ribald pagan celebration, with men wearing strapped-on wooden penises and sinister painted smiling masks. Men in their traditional thick tights and pleated skirts, dancing with handkerchiefs and bells and hitting sticks, and singing songs with accompanying acted-out dance like *'Anevika Stin Piperia'* – 'I Went Up The Pepper Tree'

Me to gonato to trivoun keh to psilokopanizoun
Me tin myti tous to trivoun keh to psilokopanizoun
Me ton kolo tous to trivoun keh to psilokopanizoun
Me ton poutso tous to trivoun keh to psolokopanizoun

With their knee they grind it
With their nose they grind it
With their bum they grind it
With their dick... etc etc.

Xanthi was a lot more tame. It was a modern Mardi Gras. It must have been fun if you were involved – if you were one of the students spraying everyone with paint, or a child up on shoulders in an overdone outfit taking it all in – but it seemed a bit dull to us and so instead, Giristroula and I decided to leave it behind and climb the tallest hill above the city. We sat on the hushed sacred grounds of the Archangeliotissa monastery, high above the city, and peered, with similar censorious faces as the grand ecclesiastical building behind us, at the hordes and the parties rolling in the streets below.

At nightfall the leading float, as is tradition, was thrown into Xanthi's river. The crowds on the banks and bridges cheering and singing songs as it was set alight, flames reached high into the sky. The sky exploded with fireworks, lighting up the city. It was our last view of Xanthi.

Leaving Thrace

As I had sat chatting in my reliably miserable Greek in their kafeneo, the old men up in Stavroupoli had told me that I must come back to their town on the day after the carnival, on Clean Monday, the first day of Lent. In small villages throughout northern Greece, they give out food and drink for everyone in the village square. And in Stavroupoli, for some reason, the men of the village pile into a large ancient costume of a gigantic camel and walk the streets. At least, this is what I *understood* they told me... But we had to turn down their offer of hospitality. We had to go. A date – a new school for Giristroula – to be kept in Athens. Seven hundred kilometres to the south, and a whole different world away.

We drove west towards Kavala. People were flying kites in the fields. A key tradition on this first day of Lent in Greece, along with the drinking of ouzo and eating only octopus now all meat and fish has been given up for the forty days until Easter, is to fly a kite. We crawled along, watching the skies full of bright, battling, decorated kites. And the sad sight of a lone boy running along a muddy field with a dead trail of paper, sticks and string dragging along behind him, resolutely refusing to fly.

Our journey was a slow process, but slow was the correct speed of Thrace anyway. Maybe we were just reluctant to leave. Reluctant to get to the hurried, uncaring world of the capital of this country. A capital that doesn't seem to really understand or appreciate its remote and mysterious lands isolated up here on its distant northeast borders. A place I knew I would miss.

Chapter 6
Athens

I've come to show you the Street of Dreams
It doesn't stand out; it's just a street like all the others of Athens
It is the street where we live
Small, insignificant, sad, tyrannical, and yet infinitely kind
There is a lot of dirt, a lot of children, a lot of mothers, a lot of hope;
and a lot of silence
And everything is blanketed by a tender, unbearable sky

Keratsini, 9.30pm

It was dark down by the ports. We passed up and down the unlit roads, behind the backs of warehouses, near the sprawling shipyards and gigantic ferries of Piraeus. We were looking for an old *rakomelathiko* – a tavern that specialises in the drinking of hot raki with honey – and, this one, specialising in music. And there, suddenly, it was. All lit up: the 'Stou Tsante'.

We went in to find this Athenian rakomelathiko decorated in the style and tastes of the Aegean island of Ikaria, the island of Giristroula's and my wedding party. This bar was Ikarian as this part of Athens was where many Ikarians had settled. Drawn from their slow, sweet, island lives due to the need for work and the promise of money, but then cursed to face the unknown stresses and struggles of life in the heaving capital. The Ikarians had tried to preserve their old island life here, built tavernas just like back home. There are many similar areas in Athens, where people who had moved from the islands looked back to their old worlds. Anafiotika, right in the centre, crawling up the slopes of the Acropolis is named after the island of Anafi in the Cyclades. The Cycladian workmen had come over to build up Athens as it grew and expanded, but built their houses in *exactly* the same distinct island styles from back home: white walls and colourful climbing flowers, all still there today. There are Athens areas named after the old cities in modern-day Turkey, all prefixed with '*Nea*' – new. Cities in Turkey that the Greeks had left in a panicked hurry, with their bundled possessions, in the 1922 Population Exchange: Nea Chalkidona, Nea Ionia, Nea Filadelfeia… And perhaps most significantly of all, for these exiles in their own country, the neighbourhood of Neos Kosmos – New World.

In the corner of our Ikarian rakomelathiko bar in Keratsini, Elena Falirea and a crowd of bouzouki players, guitarists and violin scrappers were all setting up. Elena is the daughter of Tasos Falireas, the historian of Greek rebetiko music who helped bring the old outsider, rebellious, music out of its forgotten state after the Greek dictatorship banned it, even banning the bouzouki, to be an important cultural touchstone for Greece again. Elena herself was a fixture now on the Greek state radio, ERT, playing crackling old rebetiko records every weekend morning. Giristroula and I took a seat in the rakomeladiko and listened to these dark-hearted Greek songs played live, in their proper setting, as most rebetiko music first originated here in these port areas back in the 1920s and '30s. These songs, that seemed to have soundtracked my whole time living in Greece, following me round the country like shadows, are full of the hard life that went on in these tough old streets: poverty, drug intoxication, migration, endless tales of lost love, infatuation, pain. Songs wrapped in a defiant hopelessness.

The great originators of rebetiko, like the hard-living, sexually seductive but forever broken-hearted singer Roza Eskenazi or the bouzouki magician Vasilis Tsitsanis, came to live and make their music around the Athens port. They brought with them the sounds and rhythms of the East.

Markos Vamvakaris, the patriarch of rebetiko with his deep, shredded voice sounding like a group of builders pissing freely into a metal bucket, fled from his island of Syros in the Aegean to Athens to work in the pits of the port. On hearing and being mesmerised by the sound of bouzoukis coming out of one of the sweating, teaming Pireaus sawdust taverns he passed, Vamvakaris vowed to learn the instrument within six months or cut off his own hand. He went on to become the Godfather of the whole scene.

Rebetiko is more than music, it's a state of mind. It has its own moral code. Rough, urban, always accompanied by glugged glasses of alcohol, swearing, koboloi beads clacked between fingers, hats, moustaches, truculence, pugnacity. The players here in 'Stou Tsante' played long into the night. The air was heavy with smoke, drink, songs. An old man who'd been sat eating at a table pushed his chair back and came forward and picked up a bouzouki and played it with incredible skill. I found out later he was Kostas Kalafatis, a famed rebetiko player who had come to Athens that day to appear on Elena's radio show the next morning.

The greatest ever player of the bouzouki was Manolis Hiotis. Hiotis was a virtuoso on the instrument. His family had an infamous café where the streets Zinonos and Keramikou meet, just under the grimly alive Omonoia Square in central Athens. This café was where all the rebetiko players hung out in the '20s and '30s, where Hiotis learnt his trade, and where he saw his father killed in a brawl.

Hiotis went on to become a star of this anti-authority workingman's outsider music, changing the sounds to create a newer more accessible form: *laiki* music. He starred in films, toured America. Jimi Hendrix was even a fan. Once, on being told that he was the greatest guitarist ever, Hendrix replied "You only think I'm the best in the world because you haven't heard the Greek guy, Hiotis. When you listen to Hiotis playing, *then* you'll know who the best is..."

Aristotle Onassis took along his friend Prince Rainier of Monaco and wife Grace Kelly to a Hiotis show in Athens. Afterwards Grace Kelly asked how the bouzouki and the electric guitar differed. Hiotis looked at her as if was dealing with a fool. He replied, through Onassis, saying "Tell her the strings of an electric guitar are vibrated by electricity... the strings of a bouzouki *by the soul!*"

Elena and Kostas and the band of rebetiko players carried on in our taverna, playing the tortured songs long into the dark Nea Ikarian night. I told them how much I like this music. They smiled and nodded with a detached gratitude and carried on playing.

"Where are you from?" one shouted over the music.

"London," I replied.

Glasses were raised in my direction in salute. "*Kalos eerthes...*" – welcome. The music continued. Glasses and bottles had built up all over the tables. Elena told us that she usually just goes straight from here to the ERT radio studios in the Agia Paraskevi suburb in the east of the city and straight on air to do her live show. I didn't have that kind of stamina though, and so we said our goodbyes and thanks and staggered out to face the dark port front, sometime around 3am.

I thought of the black-suited rebetiko players here all those years ago. Moving from tavern to hash den, instruments under their arms, hats pulled over eyes, ducking down, avoiding the police.

Next morning I turned on ERT radio, Elena was doing her show. I was slumped over a Greek coffee. Kostas joined her on air. Rebetiko was played and they chatted between songs.

"This music is not just for the Greeks. It means something to all people, everywhere. I see this all the time, I see it everywhere I go and play rebetiko. You know, I'm told it even touches people from London..."

Ampelokipoi, 7.30pm

The pavements were thronged with people. All the traffic had stopped. The streets were crowded and green.

"*Zito o Panathinaikos!*" – Viva Panathinaikos!

"*Panathinaike, megale keh trane!*" – Panathinaikos, great and mighty!

I was on my way to the Athens football derby. Panathinaikos v Olympiakos – the 'Derby of the Eternal Enemies' – at the Apostolos Nikolaidis Stadium on the main Alexandras Avenue, not far north from Athens centre. The stadium was smaller in size than I'd thought; the crowd louder, more fervent and fanatical than I'd ever imagined. Most of Greek football supporters follow one of these sides, Olympiakos or Panathinaikos, apart from those up north in Greece's second city of Thessaloniki who, of course, hate them both. Between them they'd won 64 of the league titles during the 90 years the Greek league had been running. My father-in-law was a *gavros* – the name of a small fish but also the nickname for Olympiakos supporters – so I'd felt it was my duty to take on his team. I'd been to Olympiakos's ground, down in the port town of Piraeus but which is really part of the mass Athens sprawl, to watch Olympiakos's European game against Turkish side Besiktas. I hadn't been able to buy a ticket, but neither had any of the Turks. In fear of the likely violence that could have erupted, all Turks had been banned from going to the game. All Greeks banned from going to Istanbul too. The Olympiakos fans had been banned from this game I was currently walking towards as well. There would be no fans at all of one of the teams at the great Athens derby. Hooliganism and fighting between both sets of fans has always accompanied these games; only 10 years ago a 22 year-old Panathinaikos fan was stabbed to death here. I wondered, with apprehension, what I was going to find on this warm Athens evening, as the sky streaked fantastic pink and purples over the green Panathinaikos stands.

The stalls outside of the ground were selling forests of green and white Panathinaikos flags and scarfs, plus, I noted with smile, souvlaki, feta, olives. I saw a heavy-set man skulking around. I'd seen him before, leading the rowdy crowds outside Olympiakos's ground, which had been itself a riot of red and white. He had a loathsome criminal's face and he leered it into mine.

"Eh! Olympiakos man!"

He remembered me.

"We will win today, eh? He slapped me on the top of my head two, three, four times. "We will win! We will win! We will win!" Then he stopped dead. "Eh, but why you here?" He glared at me, pushed his finger into my chest. "You *are* Olympiakos, aren't you?"

I thought of asking him why he was here too, but it seemed obvious. The riot police were outside, helmets on, arms linked, shields up. Armoured vehicles blocking roads. Many Panathinaikos fans were stood outside looking for trouble, hoping their dreams of a punch-up with their rivals wouldn't be ruined. The sneaking Olympiakos fans milling around, like my friend here, looking not to disappoint. I took a place in a crowded bar opposite the ground. Directly opposite the infamous Gate 13. Gate 13 is where the 'Ultras' of Panathinaikos crowd on the stands. *'Thyra 13'* is graffitied onto walls and bridges and houses and bins and benches and trees over the whole of Greece. I even saw it tagged on a rock on the very top of Mount Olympus when I'd slogged my way up there expecting a world of untouched nature. Olympiakos have their own famous gate too – Thyra 7 – also painted on every available space all over the country. There had been a terrible tragedy at Gate 7 in the 1980s when 21 supporters were crushed to death.

I stood in the 'Green Bar' at the Leoforos Stadium, watching the game on a small tv in the corner. I noticed that the heaving sea of Panathinaikos fans around me weren't actually paying much attention to the game on the flickering set though. They were all turned the other way. Facing the stadium.

"What's everyone looking at?" I asked the man next to me.

"We're watching that gate," he nodded towards the steel doors of Gate 13. "At some point during the game, someone usually manages to pull those gates open. We're hoping we can all get in there…"

The game continued. Panathinaikos scored. A huge roar from the ground swept into the bar like a wave, but the fans here carried on with their twisting heads and narrow-eyed scrutiny of the gates of the ground. I asked the man how long he'd been coming to Panathinaikos games.

"My father carried me in there when I was a baby… But it's not like it was. It's like a church in there now," he said, nodding towards the stadium.

The stadium I could see with green smoke pouring over the top, the cannon-like sound of the seats being pummelled, the boom of flares and fireworks, the relentless chanting.

"Like a church now," he repeated sadly, shaking his head.

"My father-in-law is an Olympiakos fan," I said, cheerfully.

"Sshhh," this big man said, crouching slightly, looking around him. "Don't say that in here…"

Suddenly there was action. The crowd of the bar all lurched up as one and started to surge out. I could see, after a few practice attempts where the supporters had been chased away by security, they'd finally succeeded. They'd ripped open the gates of Gate 13. The crowds were pouring in.

"Come on," my new Panathinaikos friend grabbed at me "Let's go…"

I hesitated. "Is it safe?" I asked.

The man stopped. Let out a belly-rattling laugh.

"Look at that stadium. Just look at it. Look how old it is. Look how falling-apart it is… Of course it's not safe! Now come on, we've got to get in there before it's too late…"

We battled our way down the tunnel, the bodies piling together, the crush getting dangerous. I started thinking of Hillsborough and really couldn't understand why I'd put myself in this situation. And then, just as I felt stuck in the scrum, neither able to get forward or back, two hands grabbed at me and lifted me up, out of the tunnel onto the stands. It was the bear-like Panathinaikos fan, beaming, looking around him at the loudest, most manic crowd I had seen in my life.

He smiled at me. "It's good, eh?"

The whole stadium was pounding up and down on their seats. Everyone, without exception, was jumping, flags billowing along the stands, the chants were deafening. Down by the cages at the front of the pitch, Panathinaikos fans, in the absence of Olympiakos fans to fight, were fighting with each other. Bunches of men punching and kicking and throwing broken seats at the each other. Smoke and flares and instruments and an enormous smell of alcohol. It was like some film scene from the camps of those getting ready for the Battle of Agincourt.

The game itself was not really of high quality. The players seemed cowed by the noise around them. No one seemed to want to play the ball out wide as no one wanted to go near the edges of the pitch close to the supporters. The Panathinaikos football songs rang out. In typical Greek fashion they were almost poetic, romantic...

"Panathinaikos I follow you... for me you are a sickness..."

Some were almost like rebetiko songs:

"It's a magical weed. Like hashish. Give me a little bit to taste. To dream of my Panathinaikos and to shout up as far as God. 'My Panathinaikos, I love you!'"

Panathinaikos won the game. An impressive victory. Olympiakos had been the Greek champions for the last six years, and were currently completely dominating Greek football.

Originally Olympiakos were the working-class team of the city. Formed in the port area and supported by the poor, rather than well-heeled Panathinaikos supporters of central Athens. Nowadays though, they are owned by a billionaire ship owner and the fans of both clubs come pretty much from the same varied classes. The other big team of Athens, AEK, are different though. Their fans are on the left and proudly anti-fascist. Their team, with their Byzantine double-headed eagle badge, have their origins back with the Greeks in Constantinople. They played their games in the vast Olympic stadium and threw it open for all refugees to come in for free. 'The Mother Of All Refugees' read the banner that ran across the stands. Another team in Athens with roots in the old Asia Minor is Panionios. They are based in the suburb of Nea Smyrni, but Nea Smyrni is rich. These were the refugees that got out of Turkey before the great fire of Smyrna in 1922: the haunting tragedy where the Turks, in revenge for Greek armies pushing into Turkey, burnt the Greek areas in the town of Smyrna for nine days. People crammed on the waterfront waiting for any clapped-out boats that could take them away to Greece. Similar to the refugees of today, and similarly to today, so many just didn't make it.

The history of Greece, the history of Athens, joyful or terrible, the politics, the nuances, the pain, the sense of identity, it all flows even through Greece's football, just as it does through every single aspect of Greek life.

As we left the match, the crowds piling over each other, songs still ringing out, I asked my new friend if he was happy Panathinaikos had won. He shrugged.

"Yes... of course. But it's already decided who will win the championship. It has always been decided. In 20 years Olympiakos have won 18. It's all blackmail, it's all corrupt. Bombs are sent to referees in the post. It's like the football league in Chile or something like that... So, of course, you may ask the question why do I still go..." he said, laughing out loud.

"Why do you still go?" I asked him.

He stopped, scratched at his chin and thought, before giving a rueful smile. "I don't know!"

We both looked at the ocean of green flowing away down Leoforos Alexandras.

"But who could ever leave all of this?"

Iera Odos, 11am

The Sacred Way, originally made by the feet of devout pagans on their way to Eleusis. This holy road is now a multi-lane anonymous highway cutting through central Athens. They still give it its religious name, Iera Odos, but it seems a sacrilege really, set as it is amongst the petrol stations, the furniture depots, the 'Pet City' superstores. Giristroula and I set off to walk it one early summer day, just as those ancient walkers would go: leading away from the city and aiming for the mystical site of Eleusis. At first though, we were hounded by a priest as we walked through the suburb of Egaleo. I spotted him coming out of a betting shop and he beckoned me over and brought out some religious literature from under his dirty black cassock. He placed cards, featuring various saints and Orthodox iconography, in my hand.

"Ah… I'm not Orthodox," I half-apologised to him. "I'm English."

"*Ise Anglicanos?*" – you're Anglican? – he asked, and pointed a finger straight under my chin. He smelt strongly of alcohol, his beard had white strings of spit in it.

"*Then pirazi*" – It doesn't matter – he shrugged. "This is still good for you. It's all the same God…"

He closed my hand round his pamphlets. I didn't want any of this rubbish, but smiled and thanked him.

"Ten euros," he said, holding out a demanding hand.

The street opened wide as we carry on towards Eleusis. Hot concrete, deserted, no people, just cars blurring past and a punishing sun high above. We were chased by two mad stray dogs and decided to abandon the pilgrimage by foot.

Next day we were in a car heading down the Iera Odos again. As we went further and further along the fume-filled street, the Holy Road at last thinned out. The trees started to close in around us, the buildings of Athens disappeared, turning slowly into parkland and woods. The road became more tranquil and benign. The Daphni Monastery appeared: a masterpiece of Byzantine architecture, with its orange brick domes and dazzling gold mosaics inside and the terrible figure of Christ looking down severely on his creatures from the ceiling. It sits across the road from the famous Daphni madhouse. "*Ise gia to Daphni!*" – You are for Daphni! – I often heard exasperated old women shouting at their husbands in the streets. Giristroula and I were again thrown on to another frantically busy road, but as we finally approached Eleusis, the Iera Odos reappeared once more. We turned onto it, just a residential road getting smaller and smaller until it reached its end. A cul-de-sac. A cul-de-sac leading right into the unique divinity of ancient Eleusis.

A thousand years before Christ, the sanctuary of Eleusis was dedicated to the Goddesses Demeter and her daughter Persephone. This was where Persephone had been snatched, kidnapped by Hades, king of the underworld, and taken down into his world of death. But when she was rescued and brought back to her mother, Demeter in her gratitude gave the world fertility and growth and crops. In celebration of the two Gods and their gift of cultivation to the world, the ancient Greeks would gather here and perform the most extraordinary rites and celebrations. The 'Mysteries of Eleusis.'

Modern day Eleusis was now a massive industrial centre for Athens. A desolation of quarries and cement works and factories and petrol refineries. Ugly and unhealthy. What had they done to this place? The ancient site seemed mainly forgotten, overlooked and ignored by tourists normally so randy for the old civilisation's treasures. But we were here. We had checked before starting our pilgrimage to make sure that the site didn't shut until 8pm and we walked confidently up to the gates. There was a heavy, official, metal board with the opening and closing times embossed in thick letters... and covering the 8pm closing time was a ratty scrap of torn paper, hurriedly sellotaped up, with a '3pm' scrawled on it. It was now 3.05pm. The place was firmly locked up. The wife of the man on the gate had obviously made his favourite meatballs for lunch. Or perhaps an interesting game of backgammon was taking place in one of the many cafés lining the roads, running alongside the old sanctuary of Eleusis. Whatever the reason, the site was definitely closed.

Having come all the way here, all the way down the Sacred Way, we weren't going to let locked gates stop us. Giristroula and I walked around the perimeter, found a low part of wall at the back of the site, and hurdled the fence into Eleusis's mystical grounds. Dropping down into the arena of columns and steps and altars, where the bizarre initiation sacrifices and practices took place for perhaps more than 2,000 years. This was a place so secret and protected back in ancient times that no one ever dared reveal the rites that were performed at Eleusis. The strange ceremonies that were carried out to make the ancients feel better, happier. Life would be unliveable for the Greeks if Eleusis ever ceased to exist. But non-initiates who entered the sanctuary would be instantly put to death.

As we crunched over the old stones and the shattered fragments of marble and wondered just what *really* happened here all those thousands of years ago, over the hot air came a two-note '*whoop-whoop.*' On the edge of the site, on the other side of the fence, a police car had pulled up, its lights flashing.

"*Ti kanete ekee?*" – what are you doing there? – one of the cops shouted over at us.

"We're searching for happiness!" I shouted back, thinking it all a bit of a joke.

"*Tin patisate!*" – You've stepped on her!

I felt a little puzzled at this, but nodded and smiled anyway. "Yes, I suppose so..."

"*Tin ehete vapsi poli ashima!*" they shouted again.

I translated this in my head - You've painted it very badly... I turned in confusion to Giristroula and squinted at her for clarification.

"They're Greek idioms…" she said.
"Oh I see."
"They're telling us we're in big trouble."
"Oh… I see."

And so shamefacedly, we had to climb back over the fence and stand, heads bowed, next to the policemen in front of the curious eyes and craning necks of the patrons sat outside the tacky cafés. The policemen enjoyed the lecture, pretending they might even take us back to the police station before finally letting us go. Telling us to leave and head back towards the Sacred Way. They watched as we walked off, making sure we left, while they took a seat at a café next to a large cheaply decorated nightclub – 'Club Opa'. The club looked a terrible place: dark glass windows, illustrated with silhouettes of dancing girls. A club for the industrial workers. So I guessed happiness could still be found in Eleusis, then. Just in different ways these days…

Petroupoli – afternoon

Athens covers the entirety of the Attica valley. It has groped its way up the sides of all the surrounding mountains. Five million people living in this hothouse, this ancient dust bowl, which less than a hundred years ago held barely 500,000. A blanket of pollution sitting over everything. But in Petroupoli, a suburb in the northwest of the city, as I walked down its fairly clean, fairly modern high street, the city just runs out. There was no warning. I didn't feel an end coming, but just as I noticed the street starting to climb, suddenly I was alone. The city had vanished and nothing was around me and I found myself standing on one of the quiet violet-coloured hills that are the backdrop to Athens. The city sprawled out in front of me. Breathtaking in its size. Breathtaking its beauty and in its ugliness. The Attic light above, and the dull haze below that the city seems to bathe in.

My stomach pulled me out of my reverie. Made me forget the strange magic of Athens and instead I found myself on the hunt for gyros. In Athens they confusingly call a gyros a souvlaki, and they call what everyone else in Greece calls a souvlaki a *kalamaki*, which is the same word as a drinking straw. It's confusing, but what was certain was that in the very centre of Athens, next to Agia Irini church, the old, very first cathedral of the city, 'Kostas' was the best place to get a souvlaki, a kalamaki, or whatever you want to call it. Established in 1946, so the sign read, and just as important and venerable as its neighbouring church. The tiny narrow shop, wedged in between the hefty downtown buildings, always had wildly erratic opening hours, all chalked up on a board outside in the morning and then rubbed out during the course of the day as old man Kostas had various changes of heart. New times chalked on, then rubbed out again. The queues were long and they only sold pork souvlakis – kalamakis, as the Athenian would call them – but they were good. Really good. I seemed to spend all my hours in Athens either eating here or waiting outside for Kostas to open up.

The Grande Bretagne hotel sits imposingly over Syntagma Square. The best view of Athens is from the top of this hotel, down onto the square below, black with people moving about, flowing out of the metro, past the parliament building. If you're rich enough to stay there that is. But who is? Not me. I used to enter the dark foyer of the grubby-looking National Bank next door instead, take the lift to the top and there, weirdly, high on top of the bank building was a classic old fashioned kafeneo, with old style Athenians hunched over their coffees, peering down on the square.

The Grande Bretagne hotel has an important place in Athens history though. It was the British HQ during the Greek civil war, and it was where the British army turned their guns on the unarmed pro-communist demonstrating Athenians in Syntagma Square in December 1944, killing 28. A shameful moment in British history. The British turned on those who had been fighting by their side only weeks earlier as the Greeks and the Allied Forces together had forced the Germans out of the country. The RAF bombed areas around the city, including the houses right under the Acropolis, the houses of Anafiotika. All because of a maniacal fear of a communist takeover in post-war Greece. There was a counter-plot by the communists that saw tons of dynamite placed under the Grande Bretagne by the extraordinary figure of Manos Glezos – still living somewhere in this same city as I was today – the man who heroically climbed the Acropolis in 1941 to rip down the swastika flag that had been put up by the conquering Nazis. Churchill was staying at the Grande Bretagne as the dynamite was laid in the cellars. The fuse was never lit though. A fug of confusion and dithering meant the communists missed their chance. How world history could have changed in this handsome bulk of a 19th century building.

I found my favourite place in Athens to sit, to do nothing, to sup Greek coffee, to think, was 'Panellinion' on Mavromichali street. An old quiet kafeneo, a little dirty and ragged at the seams, where every table always had an intense game of chess going on. Scraggy old men with half chewed cigarettes dangling from their mouths took on long lengthy matches against smart brief-cased workers stopping off on their way to the Archaeological Museum. The air was always heavy, the coffee strong, the silence in the city a relief. The nearby Archaeological Museum that the workers were heading to, after their protracted games, was just a short walk away. Past the classical-looking Polytechneio University building where, back in 1973, students – my father-in-law included – protested against the vicious military dictatorship that had stricken the country for seven years. They faced off the tanks, daubing slogans in their own blood on the walls. Twenty-four students' lives taken. It seemed incredible to think my father-in-law had helped rid the country of a dictator. Incredible, when now he struggled to even find his reading glasses.

The Archaeological museum is, of course, the indubitable star of Athens. The dazzling golden death mask of Agamemnon; the carved Kores and statues of Zeus; the bronze statue of the child jockey, looking alive on his horse which had been found and incredibly pulled intact from the sea; the philosopher's head 300 years older than Christ still with his piercing gemmed eyes; a seductive Athena clobbering a randy Pan with her sandal. Thousands of artefacts that soothed my soul. But then, in its own way, so did the old Panellinion café. I would while away hot afternoons in the dark, dusty rooms under the black and white pictures of old chess Grand Masters on the wall, faded pictures of great rebetiko players, photos of past Panathinaikos players grainily captured out on the pitch. I would sit and watch the Athenians walking past the window in the hot sun outside.

As one very tall man and his very short wife walked past, awkwardly arm-in-arm, one of the old men of the café crept up behind me and said in my ear "As my grandmother used to say: like Metropolis and Agios Eleftherios."

He nudged me. "Eh? Eh?"

Chuckling, he turned round to his friend "I just told him: like Metropolis and Agios Eleftherios!"

He nudged me again. I had no idea what he meant, but agreed "Yes, just like Metropolis and Agios Eleftherios…"

Later I was walking through the tangle of streets that run from Syntagma Square to the antique flea markets of Monastiraki to head up towards Athinas Street and the old covered food market of Athens. In the public market, amongst all the chaos and theatre of the sellers and their barrels of olives overflowing, rolling on the ground under your feet, and the huge fish that are proffered under your nose as you walk along, like a magician with a conjuring trick, and the live chickens that have escaped the coup and are making a mad bobbing run for it, are the *very best* places to eat. Cheap, making no play to the tourists in design or atmosphere, just good honest cooking. There's one taverna where you enter by an un-signed wooden green door, leave by another, having sat in the basement by vast barrels of wine and eaten and drunk whatever it is the owner wants to bring you, you don't actually get to order anything. As I walked on my way to the market, I passed the square of the huge central Metropolis church and I spotted for the first time the tiny Byzantine church nuzzled down next to it: Agios Eleftherios. Made of crumbling brick, much older and sweetly small sitting down next to its clumsily tall, lugubrious, partner. It now became clear to me what the old Athenian saying the old man nudged me and repeated again and again in Panellinion meant. I looked at the two comically mismatching churches in the dying Athens evening light.

"Just like Metropolis and Agios Eleftherios," I said to myself, and smiled as I walked on.

53 Chiou, near Larisa Station, 5pm

This seemed a strange part of town. Everything was dedicated to different areas of Greece. There were bakeries from Epirus, Macedonian tavernas, hotels celebrating the island of Corfu. Perhaps it had something to do with the two Athens stations that once used to operate here and served all parts of the country. Now there's only one station, with a fairly meagre and miserable service up through central Greece towards Thessaloniki. The impressive old Peloponnisou Station that used to serve southern Greece lies forlorn, derelict and forgotten, like a decaying Christmas cake sitting on its own over on the other side of the tracks. I was walking through Chiou to search for something else though. Another building. One that also looked as if it had seen better days. And it had. Between 1943 and 1977, one hundred and eighty-five different films were produced, some even filmed, at the sturdy old residential villa. Number 53 Chiou.

The great 'Finos Films'. A cultural beacon of Greece. From the black and white comedies to later colour dramas and musicals, *everybody* in Greece knows and watches 'Finos Films'. You can usually find a 'Finos Film' being shown somewhere on a Greek tv channel most days. The best are easily the comedies. Even someone with a regularly error-strewn grasp of Greek as me, despite the years I'd now been in Greece, can easily understand what's going on, although sometimes the stark street-colloquialisms had to be explained to me. I enjoyed how these 'Finos Films' were always populated by the same characters. They reminded me of the 'Carry On' films back in the UK. The actors who turned up in the 'Finos Films' each had their own idiosyncrasies and bizarre characteristics, just like the old 'Carry On' team. It was all run like a sort of family and, just like the 'Carry On' films, they were churned out on a tight budget under an astringent guiding eye of the patriarchal owner, Filopimin Finos. And all coming from this building, graffitied and a little uncared for now.

Wise-cracks, put-downs, sexual innuendo, meddling mothers, incompetent men reduced to impotent humiliation by hard faced wives. Humour doesn't change much throughout the world. Although the old Greek films, of course, are often rooted in poverty and struggle and strife. A bit less camp too. Here in Greece, the omnipresent good old fashioned British V sign is replaced, but used just as constantly, by the open-hand Greek insult of the muja.

A classic of 'Finos Films' is 'O Bakalogatos.' It tells the tale of Zikos, the small-statured ridiculous-faced corner-shop worker who endlessly argues with his boss, needles his customers, chases women. You often see black and white printed pictures of Zikos loafing and lounging, scheming and arguing, behind the counters of real *bakalikos* – corner shops – around Greece. He seems a sort of hero for corner shop workers, a patron saint hanging on the wall next to their ikons and Madonnas.

My personal favourite actor in the Finos Films was Veggos. Plump, kind-faced, bald-headed, Veggos would always be let down by his hopeless bad luck. Always trying his best to make something of his life, always thwarted by the outside world. Pratfalls and clowning, hollering his catchphrase *"Kali mou anthropi!"* – my good people! He was like a Karagiozis brought to life with his destitution and toil. But sadly, Veggos was born without the guile and cunning of a Karagiozis. Veggos was also famous for his running. Running to try and catch some offer, some tantalising reward, that always seemed to disappear as fast as he ran towards it. Even today people say, when someone is busy rushing about: *"Halara! Trehees san ton Veggo!"* – Calm down! You're running around like Veggos! This being Greece, Thanasis Veggos, the actor behind the character, had an interesting back story. He was a far Left supporter and was exiled during the Civil War, where he first discovered he could act by entertaining the other prisoners. Later in life, after fame, and always overly generous, he lost all his money. Giristroula's godfather, growing up in the suburbs of Athens, told me he remembers a down-on-his-luck Veggos living nearby. The old star was very humble and he would still always give the most when Giristroula's godfather was a child and went with his friends around the streets to sing the *kalanda* carols at Christmas.

Other faces appeared regularly throughout the 'Finos Films' series. The hysterical Rena Vlahopoulou, the ballsy battle-axe matriarch, shouting and ranting and gesticulating at everyone; Lambros Konstadaras, a Sid James-type dominant male figure; the Charles Hawtrey-esque nervous bespectacled Dinos Iliopoulos; the ludicrously eyebrowed, bald-eagle looking, Dionysis Papagiannopoulos, who always played the fathers in these films, who was actually a trained Shakespearean actor with a complex life, but clowned on screen for Finos with the best of them. The most famous of all the Finos actors though must be Aliki Vougiouklaki. A huge star and Greece's blonde bombshell and national sweetheart, their Monroe or Diana Dors. Everyone knows Aliki and her films and the trademark straw hat that she flounced around in, singing and dancing in big hit films like 'Madalena' back in 1960.

Giristroula was working with young children in primary schools in Athens. The kids sang a song in the playground...

"I saw a girl walking by... her name is Aliki Vougiouklaki... and here is Karamanlis... he woke up at three..."

She asked them if they knew who they were singing about. Karamanlis? The four-time prime minister of Greece, a towering figure of Greek history... They stared up at her, blank faced. No? Well, do you know who Aliki was? "Of course!" they all shouted "We love her!"

I personally found Aliki a bit Barbie-ish, a bit too sugary and twee for me. I much preferred her 'rival', Tzeni Karezi. Dark haired, funny, a little cynical and sarcastic, Tzeni was the negative to Aliki's blonde simpering. Tzeni Karezi once spent time in prison for starring in a play which insulted the military dictatorship. Aliki on the other hand was famous for her singing kitten routine. Giristroula had a friend whose grandmother altered clothes in a back-street of central Athens. Aliki used to come in with her dresses to be fixed all the time. The grandmother was never paid once.

Cinema is still a big thing in Greece. A pure Athenian experience is taking in a film at one of the open air cinemas on a hot summer night, alongside all the locals who had tried sleeping in their oven-hot bedrooms, given up, and gone out to see a film. The whir of the old clunky projector, the chatter of the cicadas, the smell of jasmine in the air as you take your seat in rows of chairs on the rooftops set back behind shops or bars, high above the streets. Classical old films flicker at the Cine Vox or Cine Zéphyros or the Cine Thision which was built back in the 1930s overlooking the Acropolis. Watching a 'Finos Films' you can still see a Greece that existed not so long ago. I saw how the *laos* – the poor folk – of Greece lived. I saw many of the streets and areas of Athens that had now altered dramatically and forever. The humour of Greece, the adages and sayings. And all made in this falling-apart house at number 53.

Pagrati, a little after 10pm

The 'Magemenos Avlos' restaurant was full of dark reds, wooden tables, wine glasses, old framed photos yellowing theatre programmes and newspaper cuttings on the walls. It was pointed out to me that on the secluded table next to ours, a New Democracy minister was eating an intimate dinner with an attractive young lady who was certainly not his wife. An old singer, who had seen better, more celebrated days, walked the room singing Greek torch songs, her mascara smudged, telling dirty jokes between numbers. The mood was debauched, but civilised. The food was average, the wine very good. Just off the wide Vasileos Konstantinou Avenue, with the traffic flying out of central Athens, the restaurant was set in a quiet square in the suburb of Pagrati.

Pagrati has many dark, aged old cafés dotted around, old cinemas, a community, and more charm than the wealthy, hoity-toity, Kolonaki suburb across the road where the monied folk of Athens live... '*Laos and Kolonaki*' the old song goes – the poor and the rich living side-by-side in Athens.

The 'Magemenos Avlos' restaurant was also where Manos Hadjidakis came every day. Starting with his early morning coffee, I was told Hadjidakis would stay here all day until long intemperate dinners ended sometime well after midnight. Manos Hadjidakis is Greece's greatest modern composer. He wrote Oscar winning soundtracks and grand orchestral pieces. Even his ditties, like 'Never On A Sunday', which you will hear piped over cheap taverna speakers the length of Greece, have become modern staples. But other, lesser-known, pieces like the heartbreakingly sad 'Waltz Of Lost Dreams' are where his real genius lies. I was a huge fan. I had made a point of walking past the house Hadjidakis was born in, up in Xanthi, every day when Giristroula and I lived there. Hadjidakis's father had died in Xanthi, leaving the family in poverty and so they moved to Athens where Manos later worked in the Piraeus docks and the Fix brewery factory on Syngrou Avenue to support his family. But in between, he taught himself music.

Two side notes at this point: Fix beer is another classic symbol of Greece. Going back to the 19th century, it's by far Greece's best beer. The bottle's label is a work of modernist art in itself, and the factory on Syngrou Avenue is a modern icon of architecture.

Syngrou Avenue is one of the wide, funnelling streets that take you out of Athens, heading down towards the port. It is lined on either side by gaudy sex shops and has always been a seedy place down through the years: prostitutes and pimps. The street's become part of a common idiom now in Greece and you often hear some of the most unlikely figures, priests or old women, a bit hard-up for cash, say "Tha vgo stin Syngrou!" – Right, that's it, I'm going to work on Syngrou!

Hadjidakis eventually moved into the musical world, received formal training and soon became, along with Mikis Theodorakis, Greece's best known modern composer. Unlike Theodorakis though, politics wasn't a strong issue with Hadjidakis. He even said, with comically bizarre Greek logic, he voted for the conservative New Democracy party because at least it allowed him to hate the government. His music isn't as strident as Theodorakis's. There is always a great undercurrent of melancholy. Even Hadjidakis's most jubilant pieces are tinged with a sense of longing and sorrow and poignancy. His concept collection 'Odos Oniron' – The Street of Dreams – is set in Athens, in "a street that doesn't stand out; just a street like all the others." It's a collection full of nostalgia and sad humour. Hadjidakis was also a great champion of the newly re-emerging rebetiko scene, he composed music for 'Finos Films' and he was a director of ERT radio. At ERT he helped create 'Lilipoupoli', the important late-70s series for children. 'Lilipoupoli' was a brilliant kids' education programme and I hunted down all the old recordings I could find. It was where I'd learnt pretty much most of the Greek I had.

A note on ERT – the Hellenic Broadcasting Corporation, Greece's state broadcaster. It started in 1938 and in a sea of rubbish tv and radio it still stands out as a rare mark of quality programming. However, at the height of Greece's financial crisis in 2013, the New Democracy government announced without warning it would be taken off air. With only a few hours' notice, the nation's public service broadcasting media was closed down. A scandalous action. The ERT employees didn't stand for it. For two years they broadcast by guerrilla means, illegally transmitting on stolen airwaves, and kept the institution going. ERT was finally re-installed when the New Democracy government fell. It remains to this day a vital part of Greece's national fabric.

I continued my obsession with Hadjidakis and started visiting the 'Magemenos Avlos' every day. Appearing, just as they opened up, for a morning coffee. Sitting and getting in the way as they cleared up from the previous evening's boisterous revelry. I was fascinated by Hadjidakis's old stand-up piano that he had moved to the restaurant so he could compose if inspiration struck, or to play on during wild nights when surrounded by his crowd of intellectuals and dirty drinkers. It sat in the corner of the restaurant. I chimed a clumsy chord over and over again in reverence to its old owner, driving the waiters mad as they lined up the fresh cutlery and puffed new table cloths into the air to flutter down onto tables.

The maître d', hunched over his newspaper, his cigarette resting in the ashtray, grey smoke spiralling up into the air, had had enough. He looked up and with a sigh said to me "Do you want to see the walk Manos took every day? The walk from his apartment to here?" I nodded eagerly. The maître d' jerked his head towards the door, picked up his jacket and we left and walked out from the dark restaurant quietly preparing itself, getting its breath back from its night's carousing, and into the bright scene of the lively Pagrati streets…

The 1st Cemetery, late afternoon

Behind the stadium of the first modern-day Olympics lies the 1st Cemetery of Athens. Unlike Paris's Pere Lachaise or London's Highgate Cemetery, this is not a real tourists' destination. There are no maps, the plots aren't numbered, the dead are left to lie in their patches of peace here, undisturbed. Or they were until Giristroula and I decided to clamber around the graves to see who from Greece's past was laid here in this rare tract of tranquillity in central Athens.

We found it was a catalogue of some of the greatest names of Greece's history.

Among the quiet lanes, alongside the pines and cypresses and the neo-classical masterpiece graves, away from the city heat, we spotted names. Names such as the formidable Greek poets Elytis and Seferis. The funeral of Seferis attracted thousands lining the streets to this cemetery in 1972, singing his poems which had been banned at the time by the dictator Georgios Papadopoulos. Papadopoulos's rather plain unadorned grave lies nearby. A grave that people danced on after he passed away in prison in 1999. There is a grand tomb for the German Heinrich Schliemann, the man who excavated so many of Greece's archaeological sites. The tomb almost matches his finds in magnificence: a frieze along the bottom, running through the ages, from chariots in Ancient Troy to men with wheelbarrows on Schliemann's own archaeological digs. We passed a grave known as the Sleeping Beauty, sculptured by the master craftsman Yannoulis Chalepas. Chalepas is here too, in a rather dull plot, as after his death, there was no one left to make such a beautiful grave for him.

There was the master rebetiko musician, Vasilis Tsitsanis. Further on my man Veggos, finally able to stop his running and take his deserved rest. Aliki Vougiouklaki and Tzeni Karezi are buried in the actor's corner. Even in death they seemed to oppose each other. Aliki's grave was a burst of colour and girly gaiety, a bright coloured picture of herself, a carving of her famous straw hat, fresh flowers from fans laid on the floor; Tzeni's was hidden away, sombre, just a small monochrome picture and overgrown trees hanging above the grave.

"Is Manos Hadjidakis buried here?" I asked a gardener tending a patch of earth in front of some white gothic grave.

He scratched at his face. "I think so," he said. Up that way…" he flung his head backwards.

I walked around the west part of the graveyard, the area he'd vaguely directed me towards, but could find nothing. I asked another of the ground staff. He directed me to another part of the cemetery. Again, nothing. I asked an old man who had been eyeing me walking around while he sat on a grave, eating olives. He looked as if he came here often.

"Hadjidakis?" he said to me, looking slightly amused. He chewed an olive. Did the Greek trick of rolling the stone round his mouth with his tongue. Made me wait.

"You're miles away," he chewed, spat out the stone. "You'll find him in Paiania…"

Sounio, early evening

The highest cliff on the furthest tip of Greece's mainland. The 'Cape of Athens'. Underneath the cliff, the sweep of the sea murmurs away, but from up here the sound of the waves barely reached us. Set a little way back, on top of the cape is the Temple of Poseidon. Of course the ancients would build a temple to worship the God of the seas on this spot, with the colossal breadth of water spanning away littered with tiny islands. The 15 Doric columns of the temple, sitting regal, surveying the Strait of Makronisos, have been battered by the salt winds since the 5th century BC. They dazzle and glisten when the sunlight hits. The columns also contain, scratched into one of the bases, the graffitied name of Lord Byron, made on his first visit to the country. The first hooligan of Greece.

Two thousand three hundred years before Byron, a thousand of Xerxes's ships had sailed from Persia to conquer the Greek world. In what was perhaps Ancient Greece's most glorious hour, the Persians never made it past this cape at Sounio. The fleets were destroyed off the island of Salamis, defeated by the ever-present Greek courage and an all-too-rare display of unity. The Persians who had fallen into the sea, were left to be speared by the Greeks like fish. In mythology, King Aegeus threw himself to his death from the top of these cliffs and so gave his name to the Aegean Sea. He saw his son Theseus's ship sailing with a black sail on his return from Crete having fought the Minotaur. Aegeus believed the black sail meant tragedy had befallen his son. However it's thought Theseus knew all too well that by not raising the white sail of victory his father would plunge off the cliffs of Sounio in sorrow, leaving Theseus to claim the title of king of this land. Sounio looks onto the island of Makronisos. Uninhabited now, it has a miserable history as a prison and place of exile during the Greek civil war. Veggos's prison in fact. And Giannis Ritsos's.

Giristroula's grandfather's for a while too. The sea at Sounio also holds the wreck of the Britannic, the sister ship of the Titanic, which incredibly also sank with many deaths. This huge expanse of water seems a desolate spot. One that has born witness to many a grim fate. Giristroula and I had timed it perfectly though, with absolute luck, just as the sun was setting and we gazed out on one of the greatest of Greek sights. The sun hissed and crackled and gave off great flares of colours as it dipped into the sea.

We hadn't actually come for the sunset though. Giristroula and I had set off on the road southeast out of Athens to find Paiania. A tiny town underneath the gaze of Mount Hymettus, known round these parts as *trello vouno*, crazy mountain, with its peaks full of bees and honey. Ten kilometres out of Athens, we had found Paiania but there hadn't been very much to it. Vineyards lay on the surrounding hill; Panathinaikos's old training ground, deserted and forlorn with the gates hanging off their hinges, the pitches overgrown. But sitting quietly in a well-tended graveyard, away from everything, under the mountain's shadowed protection, there was Hadjidakis's grave.

At the end of his life, Hadjidakis had told his friend "I'm very happy... I've found a nice grave for you to bury me in..."

Hadjidakis had arranged everything for his burial here. His final peaceful spot, so far away from the bustle and chatter and ego and ostentation of Athenian life. He had demanded no fanfare, no speeches, no crowds. It seemed the humblest of final moves. So I started to feel a little ashamed at being here and hoped we hadn't disturbed any longed-for peace. We soon took ourselves off towards Sounio as if actually this had always been our goal, and the sun chased us away to the end of Attica.

Pagrati, 12 noon

The head waiter had left me on the street corner. "There. That was Manos's flat," he had said, walking away, shaking head, as he turned back towards the 'Magemenos Avlos' restaurant.

I stared up at the white Athenian block of 1960s balconied apartments. It felt just as significant to me as the Parthenon or the Temple of the Olympian Zeus – the broken temple that sits next to Athens's National Gardens, with its tumbled columns, domino-ed down onto the floor hundreds of years ago, caught, suspended in time, so that you can almost hear the booming collapse and feel the reverberations on the ground.

I walked to the door and saw, with a shock, that Hadjidakis's name was still on one of the doorbells. I stood looking at it, dumbly. Someone came up behind me, leaned over and pressed the Hadjidakis bell. I looked up at the man.

"Do... do you know Hadjidakis?" I asked. A little confused.

"His son," the man replied.

His son? He lives here? "Do you think I could meet him?" I asked.

The man looked a little taken aback. "Well… I can ask him. But yes, I'm sure he'll come down and see you."

So I stood on the street. Thinking of how I would get to see the great man's home, where some of the most moving musical pieces of Greece were born. I stood and watched Athenian life going on around me: the deliveries; the hawkers; the lottery card sellers with their cages of tickets around them; the rugs being beaten over the side of the balconies; the sponge sellers; the old women on their way to prepare for services at the small Byzantine Athenian churches that sit round the city, almost crushed between the modern blocks. I stood and waited. And waited. Twenty minutes went by, half an hour. It was clear no one was coming down.

I turned and gave a last look at the building and then started off on the slow walk back into the centre of the city. Down the road, heading towards Athens's bustling pandemonium of life. Where I would soon be swallowed whole.

Here, in this street, the dreams of so many children are born, and die...

Chapter 7
Crete

Rethymno

    We landed at Heraklion sometime in early April. The ferry gliding in, like a vast white seabird, to rest next to the red-brick arches of the city's Venetian arsenal. We left Heraklion though, straight away, for Rethymno, 80 kilometres to the west. Heraklion's charms, and its shabbiness, would have to wait for us. We would meet again.

    In Rethymno, we had barely got our bearings when Greek Easter crashed down on us. Dutifully Giristroula and I took a place with all the Rethymniotes outside the city's proud, looming Four Martyrs church on Easter Saturday, just before midnight. A candle held in my hand, lighting up my face in a sickly yellow glow, so I fitted in with the hundreds of other people milling around with their glowing candles, all taking a light off each other. The light had been flown from Jerusalem to Athens and then carried in a special aeroplane so every church in Greece can receive it. The flame comes from the Holy Light which miraculously appears every year at the Church of the Holy Sepulchre. Everyone believes that their candle holds the very light from the flame from Jesus's tomb in Jerusalem. Everyone ignoring the sound of flicking lighters every time the wind snuffs out a candle. I had stood at this church the day before, on Good Friday, as large decorated floats, which had been passing round the streets with their ornate imitation coffins for Jesus, all started to gather outside the church. Like buses banking up at a city terminus at the end of the day. On the balcony of the church this Saturday evening, the great and the good of Rethymno, those higher up the social order than us on the ground below anyway, stared down at us. They were happy to be seen, wrapped in expensive coats, snapping into action at certain points as the priest droned his incantations into a microphone, frantically crossing themselves again and again as if desperately trying to scratch an itch.

After the bells and fireworks of midnight, as Greek tradition states, we all set off with our candles to get them back home without the flame going out – a sign of huge bad luck – and to burn a thick black, charred, smoke cross on the door frame above our front doors – a sign for good luck, to last you through the year. I was passing one house, crouching low and shielding my flame with a cupped hand, stupidly desperate to get it home without it going out, when a man came out of his doorway and, in celebration, fired a gun rapidly, *bam bam bam bam*, into the sky, a few feet from where I shuffled. The shots' sounds ricocheted around the close old buildings of the town. My hearing became a shriek of white noise. The man grinned at me and went back inside. I was a little shaken and still deaf as we made it back to the village where we had found a house to live in, up the hillside above Rethymno town. Outside the small local church was a colossal bonfire with a representation of Judas on top, set alight, flames streaking from the top of his head, and yet more men stood outside shooting guns into the air. Well, this was Crete, where everyone seemingly has a gun and everyone is happy to use them: in celebration, in theatrical boast, or through some long-held, ancestral, blood-feud grudge. The street signs of every town or village were pitted with gunshot holes. Crete is a proud, wild island.

A friend of mine back in Corfu had warned me before we came here of the guns, and the fiery rankling that lies deep within the Cretans. He had been holidaying here once, driving round the island, when someone on the road had cut his car up. Instinctively he threw his hand forward with the muja gesture of the open splayed palm, as all Greeks do when annoyed. The car ahead screeched to a halt. The driver's door opened. The Cretan got out and walked purposefully back towards my friend's car. Next thing he knew, my Corfiot friend's head was down on the dashboard and a gun planted at his temple... We would have to tread carefully through Crete over the next few months.

"*Christos anesti!*" – Christ has risen – we all said to each other outside the church.

"*Alithos!*" – he really has – we all replied. As everyone must. Sheep's innards soup was eaten. Whole lambs were put on the spit for tomorrow. Dyed red hard-boiled eggs were cracked together like conkers. The winner's egg is the one that doesn't break and gives its owner further good luck for the year. The gunshots of Crete carried on long into the night.

I had lived on the Ionian islands with their Venetian architecture. I had spent my time in the far northeast of Greece, in Thrace, with its old Muslim communities. Rethymno was the perfect combination of both. The grand Venetian citadel; the squat, domed mosque plus, as everywhere, old ancient Byzantine remains sitting next to the modern boxy flats of the city. Rethymno is a microcosm of Greece. As is the whole of Crete, with its beaches, its mountains towering beyond, the gorges, the olives, the vineyards... I chose, however, to sit my Rethymno days in a dark café populated only by the cantankerous old men of the city. Littered with hundreds of old black and white photos on the walls, bottles and pots, Greek bric-a-brac, like a junk shop with the old men reading newspapers, playing cards or just sat staring at nothing in the hot air, looking like dusty curios themselves. In the evenings the raki would come out. Raki is the spirit of the island. Strong and pure and, on Crete, never giving you a headache. Nikos, the barkeeper would give us bottle after bottle for free. "I don't want your money," he would say. "I like you. I look at people, if I don't like them, I don't serve them." But Nikos often drank your drink as he came to the table to serve you. He would then look surprised at the empty tray in his hand and turn round and get another. Usually that had gone by the time he came back too. Tall, wiry, beak-nosed and bearded, both eyes crossed, Nikos roughly kissed and slapped my face, and everyone else's who came through the door of the bar each night, in happy greeting. He was always the drunkest man in Crete by closing time. Souvlaki or gyros pitas were always necessary to line the stomach. Taken from the centre of town and eaten on the palm-lined beach looking out at the sea. The pitas in Crete served with just yogurt, never tzatziki.

I was sitting outside having a raki one night when I met Constandinos. He was dressed as a tsolias Greek soldier, in the costume they fought the Ottomans in: foustanella skirt, scarlet fez, stockings and garters. Constandinos told me he roams all over Greece, walking from town to town, through the tiny villages, posing as a tsolias and asking people to give money for a photo with him. This had been his life for years and years, as long as he could remember, but he'd settled in Rethymno for a while now. He liked it here, he told me. He had a good pitch by the huge doors of the vast Venetian fort above the town. Although it wasn't really, I told Constandinos his English was good, and suddenly this large man who had looked a sad dejected clown in his ludicrous costume hunched over his drink on his small table, was up on his feet. Excited he rushed to tell people in the bar, and passers-by of this compliment. He grew in stature. Started boasting and strutting.

"Can I ask you a question?" he asked quickly, spinning round and pointing a finger at me. "Does God exist?"

I was taken a little aback. "Well, I hope so," I said. "But I think, in my heart, I'd say no."

"He does! He does!" Constandinos was full of animation now. His pom-pom slippers slapping on the smooth cobble stone Rethymno pavement, the oversized sleeves of his frilly bright white shirt billowing in the night.

"He drove away Zeus! You don't know this? Yes! Zeus was powerful but he got too tired to fight. It's true! Zeus and his gods on Olympus they all had too much sex! Jesus knew what to do," Constandinos lent his face close to me, "No sex!" he clapped his hands on his stocking-ed knees wheezing with laughter like a dog chewing a rubber ball.

Constandinos sat back at his table, wiping at his eyes. He fixed the sign he had hanging around his neck: 'Photo with me – only 1 euro'.

Pavlos ran a tavern in our village above the city. He was a weather-beaten old man, with a moustache you could almost hide in. A sailor back in his day, he had travelled the world many times over, picking up hardly one word of English. His skin was burnt deep with sun and salt and he now spent his time up here on dry land being henpecked by his fearsome wife, who wouldn't allow him to set a price for whatever you ate in his taverna. Whatever he charged was always half what she thought you should pay. Pavlos told us about a club he was in. They walked the mountains and gorges of Crete – and there are many, many mountains and gorges of Crete. We told him, vaguely, we might be interested in coming on one of these walks one day, and then, not thinking any more on it, settled down to our *dakos* salad – particular to Crete: tomatoes and feta laid on *paximathi* rock hard bricks of bread that can only be eaten when soaked in the olive oil that's oozed to the bottom of the bowl. Rakis were sunk.

Next morning, at 5am, there was a hammering on our front door. Unrelenting. It was Pavlos. I peered out into the darkness, his almost-black face beamed a smile back.

"We go now. *Ela ela.* Come, come…" Before we really knew what was happening Giristroula and I were bundled into the back of an old military coach with a collection of Greek faces and beards staring up at us. We were driven out of Rethymno, on the north coast, down through the island towards the south.

As the light outside started to strengthen, I could see the pale-pink mountains of the centre of Crete surrounding us. The ravines, like a cemetery of huge boulders; rocks scarred through a million years of wind and rain and heat. The other members of the club were waking up on the coach and talking to each other, each using the prominent '*ch*' sound only found here in Crete. A sound where the everyday '*keh*' – the word for 'and' – becomes '*Ch*eh', where 'raki' becomes 'ra*chi*'. By the time we reached the village of Vasiliki and poured off the coach, there was a great wing of sun high in the sky and a blinding bright morning scene had laid itself out. A lined old shepherd sat at a deserted café pointed us the way to walk with his stick and we set off. I still didn't really know where. We started over the ridges and down into the canyons. Crete has deeper canyons, sharper mountains and a hotter sun than anywhere else I'd previously found in Greece.

We trekked downwards, knees straining at the decent, stepping on dry hardy plants amongst the baked stones, crushing them under foot and setting off an overpowering smell of oregano that came flowing out over us all. One of our party, an older man, fell badly. Scree and rocks came raining down as he passed me, scudding along fast on his back. I stood and watched Pavlos and some of the other strong Cretan men in the group fashion a sort of human stretcher and carry him back to the top. I noticed that I was standing next to the half-perished carcass of a dead goat slowly decaying into the hot ground. This wasn't going to be a light stroll through the island. Perhaps it was going to be one as hard as Crete itself.

At the bottom of the canyon we were marched on, still without any real clarity to me as to where we were heading. Our trail of 20 or so Cretan men and women with rucksacks, boots, handkerchiefs over their heads. We were route-marched onwards. Forcing our way on through the sun-lashed canyon bottom, mountains high above, through the tight gaps between rocks, and finally wedging ourselves out to find a deserted beach and a clear, polished, blue-green sea. I was told that this beach, in Minoan times, was the King's personal beach. I couldn't resist it and tore off my clothes and dived in and swam in the water. The rest of the group sat on the beach, rested aching legs or prowled around smoking deeply.

I wondered what was going to happen now we were so far away from anywhere. Then I heard the faint buzz of a boat. I turned as it appeared on the horizon, getting closer, an old man at the prow. He was a friend of the group and was here to take us round the promontory of rocks to another beach. Trafoulas was where the Minoan Queen's party would bathe. In the surrounding cliffs there were deep natural caves with people, quite extraordinarily, living in the hollows. People had lived for years and years up in these caves: laundry hanging outside, the squeak of a pump inside generating power or water. I couldn't believe it. But then one of our group told me that this was no hippy utopia and that these cave-dwellers had disputes with each other. Often these neighbours would set fire to each other's caves. I stared up, desperate to get a glimpse of one of these rock people, but I was soon being bundled away with the group strapping on rucksacks, off the beach and into another canyon.

We were walked through two close towering points of rock, known round here as the Gate of Hercules, along the coast, in and out of the village Lentas and up and over soaring cliffs looking out to sea. Then, at last, we reached the end. The place we had always been heading to, if only I'd known... At the end of every trek it was a rule that one of the group had to host a gathering for all the walkers, today it was Lambros's turn. At his house, hidden away on its own at the foot of the mountains, as the sun set and the sky faded with streaking golds and faint blues, Lambros took his task of looking after us in the most ridiculously overblown style: killing two sheep on his farm and rolling out barrels of wine that never ended throughout the night. So this was what we had been walking for. It all made sense now.

Giristroula was conducting her research in schools in Crete. This was the reason why we found ourselves on the island. She had been in the schools of Rethymno town but was now based at a school in Agouseliana, in a small village sat alone in the hilly wilds outside the city. One day I went with her and spent most of the morning walking around the small tight paths of the village. I ducked into an old dark kafeneo for a Greek coffee and sat down and ordered. The old woman owner and the only other man in the place, playing cards, raised their eyebrows in response to my few words of introduction but they didn't speak. The old man, in his raggedy old clothes and cap, then remembered he needed to get back to his farm and gathered up his things. He paid for his raki and I heard him say "*Oriste. Kerase ton oti theli...*" – Here, take this for whatever he wants too. He nodded over at me. This man who hadn't spoken, had only sat a few minutes in the same café as me, and who looked as if he had hardly enough money even for himself, had paid for my coffee, and anything else I wanted. This was the Cretan hospitality I'd heard so much about, in pure form. He made a final, almost imperceptible bow of his thickly haired head as he left. I thanked him, and he was gone.

Sotiria, the owner, was over 80 years old, still with long dark hair and a thin, strong face. She had been running this kafcneo for 59 years. Her husband had died nearly 40 years ago and she dressed head to foot in black ever since, as so many Greek widows do. She left me briefly to go and tend her animals at the back, to chase chickens and wrestle with pigs, so I studied the decorations of the café for a while. There were maps on the walls, newspapers, portraits of Nikos Kazantzakis and Crete's other famous sons... and then I spotted a picture of Sotiria herself. Some years ago now, but it was definitely her. Stood, huddled, in an old-fashioned coat, on a wharf under tall buildings, underneath Liverpool's Liver Birds.

Sotiria came back in, brushing a muddy hand over her headscarfed forehead, her knees filthy with fresh dirt. I asked her about the picture. She sighed, sat, and slowly started to tell me the story...

When the British were in Crete during the war, fighting alongside the Cretans, trying to resist the sweeping roll of Germans taking control of the island, Sotiria's older sister had fallen in love with one of the British soldiers posted here. As the Germans brought more and more enforcements onto the island, the British, losing the battle, had to retreat. Helped by Cretans, who risked their lives to assist the withdrawing British fighters, the British were hidden and spirited away down south to the monastery in Preveli. The monks, with guns hidden under their cassocks and as keen to fight the enemy as anyone, helped the soldiers catch boats waiting there to take them away to Egypt. Sotiria's sister had followed her new love down through the island, hiding in barns and strangers' attics as the Germans hammered on village doors. She made it down to Moni Preveli and onto the boat, and finally, with her soldier, back to his Lancashire city and then marriage and children and a life in northern England. Later, a lost and cold Sotiria visited her sister in her small Liverpool home. It was still the only time Sotiria had ever been out of Crete.

Another of Sotiria's sisters, however, had a less happy outcome.

Crete, and the small islet off its northeastern shoulder, Spinalonga, was the place where the lepers of Greece had been sent for the first 50 years or so of the last century. Away from the mainland, infected people had been carted away, sent out of sight, to this rocky hulk just off Crete. A sad chapter of Greece's history. It was especially tough in Crete where there was anger and worry and suspicion of the disease and of people carrying it. Sotiria's sister, though young, had arthritis in her hands. It caused them to bend and twist. The islanders believed it was leprosy. She was chased round the island by self-appointed gangs of vigilantes. Three times they sent her to Spinalonga on the boat, across the small channel of water from the town of Plaka. Sent away from everyday life on mainland Crete onto the island with the genuine cases of horrifying leprosy. Three times she came back, when the doctors confirmed her crippled hands were nothing more than arthritis.

Sotiria's sister had a daughter. As she grew up and started to fall in love with the local boys and told her mother how one day she wanted to get married, Sotiria's sister knew the mistrust about her still existed around the island. She didn't want the stigma to affect her daughter's chances of happiness, so Sotiria's sister left Crete, never to return. She went to Athens, and by chance, feeling she should do something to help those troubled by the disease, she found work in the leprosy hospital in the capital. But she never saw her family again.

Sotiria sat her chair close to me as she told me these stories. She talked with no self-pity for herself or for her sister. She spoke and waited with patience, as I strained and faltered and checked with my ponderous Greek. Then Giristroula turned up after her lessons at the school, and now all could be translated fully. But Sotiria jumped up from her seat, panicked. She rushed out the back and started fussing around. She must find something to offer the new visitor. Finally Sotiria came out with few chocolates and a small bottle raki on a tray. She put them down and looked a little shamefaced. No one can visit someone's home in Crete and not be offered something. If she couldn't have found something to offer, it would almost feel like the very worst thing had happened to Sotiria. Stood here in her widow's black, in her empty kafeneo, with her sisters missing from her long island life.

Giristroula and I set out to explore the surrounding lands around Rethymno, driving out on the roads, over the lit highlands and down towards Arkadi monastery: a 16th century monastery with touches of the Italian renaissance about it. A place of studying and science in the otherwise unenlightened days of the Ottoman Empire here in Crete. We passed through the gate...

"Hi! Hullo! *Guten Tag...*" the guard called out, running after us. Trying every variation he could think of.

I cursed that we'd been caught and would have to pay, but Giristroula answered back in Greek.

"Oh, you're Greek!" the guard suddenly stopped short. "Then you must enter here for *free*. It is a very important place for us... Very important..."

He waved us in with a flourish of his hand. Eyeing me suspiciously at my clunky Greek thanking as we passed.

Arkadi Monastery has a sad and terrible history. In 1866 the Cretans in the surrounding area rose up against the Ottoman rule. Around 1,000 men, women and children revolted against the Turkish, fighting for three days as the Ottoman Army called over 15,000 men to push them back. The Cretans took refuge in the monastery. A large copper bullet still lodged in a giant plane tree in the monastery's courtyard bears testament to the fighting. Tables lie in the halls where deep sword marks show where men had been beheaded. And then you reach the basement. The powder room in the basement was where the women and children were hiding and into where the fighting men were pushed back. With the Turkish at the doors, and the ammunition running out, all hope lost, the head abbot of the monastery gave the command and the remaining gunpowder was lit. All lives sacrificed rather than be caught. Taking many Turkish with them.

'Nothing is more noble or glorious than dying for one's country' runs the inscription in the monastery.

The man at the gate kept eye contact and nodded slowly and thoughtfully at us as we left. He clearly wanted us to know how hugely symbolic what we had just experienced was.

The car took us down under the brightly lit mountains towards Spili, a village in the hills with its centre square ringed by row after row of Venetian lion heads spitting out fountains of water. I walked around Spili, with the waters murmuring all around me, when just for the briefest moment, I looked through the door of an old blue wooden, tattered, kafeneo...

"Come in, come in! Raki!"

I told the old man that I was just passing, I didn't really have the time. But he'd already poured us both a glass and was holding one out for me. We drained them, and he instantly poured me another. He sat me down, got out some *meze*, told me he wasn't looking for any payment. He poured us another couple of rakis and told me his name was Giorgos. Small statured, white haired, moustached, the wrinkled face of an amused brown mouse. Giorgos was once a tailor. His kafeneo was called 'Rafteo' – simply meaning 'Sewing'. He even had his old ancient sewing machine in the corner. Giorgos was well into his 90s but looked strong as a ram. He told me he drank 40 glasses of raki a day. I guessed this must have been the secret. A coach pulled up in front of the kafeneo. None of the tourists had any interest in this little old bar whatsoever. All were heading for the shops of tourist tat and the bottles of bad, expensive, olive oil. One fat German stepped off the bus and with an audible tear, his shorts ripped right up the back of his buttocks. Giorgos was straight out to help, beavering around, batting away the German's protests, wrestling him out of his shorts, getting them up on his old machine, stitching and repairing. I left the bar as the German was falteringly thanking Giorgos, wobbling on one leg pulling his shorts back on, looking a little desperately to see where the rest of his party had gone on their pursuit of carved wooden trinkets. The last thing I heard as I walked away down the street was Giorgos telling the newly trousered German "And now, of course, we must have a raki…"

Heraklion

It was time to leave Rethymno. We set off to see what the rest of the island had to offer. Planning to follow, from our starting point which was just a little bit before 12 the whole way round the clock face of Crete. Travelling east, the first stop was Knossos. The great palace, set out like the cells of a giant beehive, which was the centre of Minoan civilisation. One of the very first places of culture and advancement on earth. There's something you just *feel* in the smooth contorted hills as you approach, something in the very air. It wasn't just by chance that the Minoans set up stall here. Theseus slayed the Minotaur in this palace. The Minotaur that had been fed every nine years with the seven youths and seven virgins that were sent to be eaten alive. Theseus made it out of the Knossos labyrinth, following a thread left by the Minoan king's daughter, Ariadne, who Theseus had seduced but later abandoned as soon as he got out of Crete. I remembered how Giristroula and I had stood at the spot on the cape of Athens, where Theseus had tricked his father to leap to his death and inherited the kingdom of Athens. Theseus sounded a bit of a bastard, to be fair.

The palace of Knossos dates back to 1900BC. In 1900AD, however, that mad British Victorian determination to civilise everything they came across meant that this perfect Minoan monument was beset by renovations and revisions. The excavations and remodelling was made by English archaeologist, Sir Arthur Evans. Concrete and colour were added to the broken stones, the halls, the aqueducts, the potteries. It's hard to say if Evans improved or ruined the place. We can now see the frescoes as they were meant to have been seen; we can picture how life was lived in this nursery of all human civilisation. The central courtyard and passages link many hundreds of rooms, although the walls are now filled with concrete. Staircases exist where previously there had been just bent stones. But was it for Evans to do? Was it for him to tamper with time like this?

Nearby is Villa Ariadni, built by Evans to live in while he conducted his work at Knossos. It was later the villa of General Kreipe. Kreipe was the German commander in Crete during the Second World War. In April 1944 the General was kidnapped by a team of Cretans and British soldiers led by Patrick Leigh Fermor. A famously daring raid... Leigh Fermor stepped out in front of the General's car with his hand raised, halting the car. A joint British and Cretan gang then emerged, coshed the driver, bundled Kreipe into the back and then, with Leigh Fermor impersonating Kreipe, passed several road blocks and drove into the high mountain villages. They were hidden there while the Germans hunted for them, before they marched the General for many days over the vast Cretan mountain ranges down to the south of the island to ferry him away. As Giristroula and I headed from Knossos towards Arhanes, we found the very spot where the abduction took place. Now just a short distance away from a large flyover, but still a quiet road with the bushes for the captors to hide in and the old church which had witnessed the proceedings unfold back then. There was also a bizarre, tall, brutalist monument that had been put up to commemorate this foolhardy yet brave action. We drove on. Following the route Leigh Fermor's team took towards Anogia.

Anogia is a tough village clinging hard onto the side of the Cretan mountains. The villagers here, perhaps more than anyone else on the island, personify the unique traits of Crete. Giristroula and I walked down the streets and saw a few men in the traditional Cretan dress that I didn't believe people still wore for real: black shirt, tall black boots, khaki trousers that ballooned out above the knee, and the *sarik* – a black lattice woven headscarf. There were no women anywhere. Above us, bearded men came out onto their balconies and watched us like hawks as we pottered by. I noticed some had brought their guns out and had started cleaning them pointedly.

Giristroula and I sat down in a café in the village square and we talked to some of the men there. When they realised that I was not from another village in Crete but just a visitor, and there was nothing to prove, they were open, friendly, insisted on getting us a raki. Of course. We clinked glasses and I absentmindedly touched the base of my glass on the rim of another man's. Straightaway all the men put their drinks down on the table. I'd made a terrible error. They told me that I mustn't touch my glass any higher or any lower than theirs; the glasses must be at the exact same level. To do otherwise is a great insult in Crete. Having cleared this piece of etiquette up, we resumed our toast. They then brought up the subject of "Patrick." The villages here, particularly Anogia, had suffered terrible reprisals for their help in hiding the British and Cretan kidnappers, with houses burnt to the ground and mass executions. I wondered if Leigh Fermor would be an unpopular figure, wise not to mention him. But these men talked in admiration for the man who explored and lived and wrote extensively about Greece.

"You see this statue," one pointed to the head and shoulders on the plinth behind him "That's Giannis Dramountanis. Do you know him?"

I didn't.

"He was the leader of the resistance here... Do you know who the godfather was to his daughter?"

I didn't.

"Patrick!" The man looked at his drink and gave a slow shake of the head. "He was a great man." There was a pause. "For an English."

The talk moved on to the time of the Germans coming into the village, exacting their revenge.

"My father had to leave when the Germans came," said one man, a great flame of white hair and a great white bushy beard meeting round his grizzled face, like an albino lion's mane.

"He would have been tortured to death, so he hid in the mountains. When he came back, my mother didn't recognise him. He'd aged years. He had a long thin beard, scars all over his face. She made him sleep in the garden for a week before she believed it was him."

One man had been drinking at a nearby table. He pulled a chair over, joined in the conversation. I was told this was Yalaftis. A one-time shepherd, with a moustache he could have sheltered his flock under, Yalaftis was renown throughout the island and beyond for his *mantinades*. Almost like limericks, mantinades are Cretan 15-syllable poems, most famously coming from Anogia. They are not written down, usually they are just improvised, live, on the spot. Sometimes they are musically accompanied by a lyra. Typically they are about love, sorrow, pain. Yalaftis was famous for sprinkling his with a bit of humour, a bit of satire. It is a great skill to be able to conjure up these mantinades, like wise and moving folk songs, from nothing and usually never to be repeated. As we left, the men of this kafeneo said to us we must come to a wedding that was to happen in the village in a few days' time. I had heard much about weddings in Crete, and Anogia in particular.

"Ah yes," one man replied sadly. "But this one won't be so big. Only last week there was a shooting in the village here. One of the family that is getting married was killed. It will be a very sad wedding now, a very small gathering."

"How many?" I asked.

"Oh, nothing. Maybe no more than a thousand. Nothing…" he said, pulling a disappointed, apologetic face.

Cretan weddings are extraordinary events. Huge gatherings. Cars drive round the villages with a loudhailer inviting everyone to come and the family has to pay for it all: the gledi, the food, the drinks, the music. But the guests all give money as they turn up. It's a sign of honour to be seen to give as much as you can. The married couple end up with more than they ever spend on these lavish affairs. Land is bought and architects employed only on promises made before the wedding, when the couple have no money. The marriage house will be built ready for the wedding night, on just the recognition that the architect knows the couple will have bundles of cash after the event.

We left the men of Anogia in their kafeneo in this pretty square in this hard village: colourful flowers in boxes round the old plane tree and old men as hard as the rocks that surround the village sitting and drinking. We thanked them for the hospitality, hoping we could come back for the wedding, but sadly aware we wouldn't.

The streets were deserted in Zoniana. Just one man outside a café. "The owner will be back in a minute," he said. "Come. Have a raki."

It no longer came as a surprise.

We sat down and had a drink. The café had black and white photos all over the walls and an over-dramatic, portrait painted of the owner as a Cretan hero stood imperiously on the mountainside. The wife of the owner turned up, fussed about to give us more raki and mezes. She told me the old photos were of her and her husband. They had been taken by a professional photographer in the city of Chania.

"That was the day that we left the village," she said, as if it had only been a one-time event. Perhaps it had.

She told me they had just got married in these photos. She was 14. They travelled to Chania for the photos on the very same day as Venizelos's funeral. The Cretan Eleftherios Venizelos is the father of modern Greece, leading the country in its first bold new steps after it had twisted and struggled from under the boot of Ottoman control. He must have died in the 1930s though. I guessed this lady meant his son, another politician: politicians and leaders in Greece flowing down through the great families like regal inheritance. You are often just born into governance in Greece. The leaders of the latter-day right-of-centre New Democracy party – the Mitsotakis family – are descendants of Venizelos. The patriarch of the Mitsotakis family – Konstantinos – died at the age of 98 while we were in Crete and, due to his Cretan roots, the whole of the island lowered flags in commemoration and, of course, fired guns in the air. It is odd that such a wild, rebellious island that only votes for the left also has this history of conservative politics.

More of the villagers appeared in the kafeneo. Some of them did remember the original Venizelos. And more still remembered when the Second World War had invaded these villages. One old man talked about how, as a boy, he would hear the women of the village shouting

"The goats are coming!" – code for the Germans – and the men would have to flee, to hide.

The bar owner, Georgios, who actually did resemble his preposterous portrait on the wall, turned up and took a seat. The men all called him Karagiorgas, a nickname meaning Black Georgios in Turkish. Karagiorgas pulled his chair close to me.

"You're interested in the English here I bet, eh? You know Patrick was here?" he told me this, in a conspiratorial whisper. "With his German general. We kept them in the houses..." he pointed his hand forward at the jumble of small homes running away down the main road of the village. "Every night we would switch and a neighbour would have to take their turn to hide them."

The old man who had first invited us to have a raki in this café but who hadn't said anything, had just gazed into the distance, turned to us.

"He stayed with us. I remember. I had just turned 15."

His piece said, he went back to his contemplation of the road in front of him.

"The Germans shot many of the men here," Karagiorgas said. "They would have killed us all, would have burnt the village to the ground... but we had helped a German you see. A German parachutist had fallen to the ground in the fields over there." Karagiorgas waved his hand back behind him in the opposite direction. "His parachute hadn't opened. We helped him, fixed him up, sent him on his way. Then, when the German army came, looking for Patrick and the General, they took 18 of our men. Lined them up against the wall there. They were ready to shoot, when a man came running. He had a letter from the German command. The parachutist, who was a captain, he told the army not to shoot. It was good luck for those men." Karagiorgas looked sadly at his drink. "Not everyone was so lucky though..."

"And, you know, Patrick came back..." Karagiorgas said, getting even closer to me, shifting his chair round. "Years later. He came to see the village and when I told him I was the son of Konstantinos Parasiris, his face went white. He grabbed me. He hugged me. He said my father was a great friend and had helped him very much. He said he would never forget Zoniana."

It's an unforgettable place, that much is obvious. The defiance, the sense of grand lawlessness, the bonds between men, the sense of honour – which the islanders here even have a special word for: *levedia*. These characteristics had been indispensable when driving out the Turks, or standing up to the Germans. Now the proud insubordination still existed, but in slightly less illustrious circumstances. The Zoniana fields I saw rolling away around me are the key provider for Cretan marijuana: infamously good, grown and protected with an ugly ferocity up here in these Zoniana peaks.

It took some time to adjust to being back in the capital of Crete, Heraklion. Men, hot and harassed in suits and sweat-stained shirts, pacing out of banks and offices and up the main street, past the Venetian Doge's palace and the fountains. The 'Street of Deceit' – so called by the residents of Heraklion, as one told me "If you thought that the whole of Heraklion looked this good... well, you'll soon be very disappointed..." Cretan men seem to *strut* everywhere. A practice worn in over centuries, I guessed. They proudly strutted through Heraklion, with its ugly buildings sprawling in the dusty outskirts. It is not a beautiful city. I remembered the men back in the Rethymno cafés were very keen to tell me "The best thing about Heraklion... is the sign pointing towards Rethymno!"

But I liked it. We spent our nights at a dilapidated kafeneo '*Saradavga*' – Forty Eggs – where a heavy-built patron, Chronis, insisted on teaching me how to dance the *hasapiko*. "Front!" he would shout, as we lurched forward, his powerful hand clasped over my shoulder. "Now to the side!" as we kicked our legs leftwards. "Back!" On and on it went in the heat of this old drinking joint, the music going round and round in circles, the wine and beads of sweat pulling down the edges of his heavy tobacco-stained moustache.

Old friends of Giristroula's family, who lived in the city, invited us to their house. Over dinner, Panayiotis told me more about the island. He had grown up in the small village of Lyttos, southwest of Heraklion. Homer wrote of this village when it was once a great city, famed throughout the Greek world for a golden statue: the Lyttos Boy. Panayiotis spent every weekend going back to his home village and digging in his garden hoping to find this lost solid gold antiquity of unimaginable riches. I laughed out loud at this. Panayiotis didn't take the mocking well.

"Everybody does it," he said, a little wounded. "In my village, on the main road, every night you'll see men digging. One man up; one down, watching. If he sees a car coming, he blows a whistle and all the diggers will stop and hide. It's illegal to look for the old Minoan treasures you see..."

We sat and ate snails – a delicacy here too in Crete, not just in France, but these ones were small and worryingly like the snails you find in your garden. We drank with Panayiotis's family and friends who had turned up. A good raucous Greek scene. I made the mistake at some point of labelling the lady next to me as a Greek, a fairly understandable assumption really, given her country of birth.

"I'm not a Greek," she snapped. "I'm from Crete!" She twisted her chair away from me so as not to look at me for the rest of the meal.

The glasses of raki were filled before you could finish them.

"Some people do find jewels you know," said Panayiotis. "In my village, people who have lived there for years, who you've known all your life, one day they suddenly just disappear, and you know they've dug something up that'll be worth thousands. Or sometimes you see women coming into the tavern *wearing* the jewellery. Actually wearing the earrings, dug up by their husbands! Thousands of years old, cleaned and sparkling Minoan perfection..."

We saw Minoan perfection ourselves the next day, at the Heraklion Archaeological museum. Hundreds of artefacts taken from the Minoan palaces – Knossos, Phaistos, Malia, Zakros – and the archaeological sites around Crete. Incredible treasures. The paint, made so many thousands of years ago just from beetroot and walnuts, is still vivid on the huge vases and sarcophaguses. I asked why it didn't fade and disappear, like the bright paint we are told once covered the Acropolis in Athens, now all gone. No one seemed to be able to tell me. It did make me think, though, that when ancient Athens *was* decorated like this – the Parthenon, the Agora, the temples – the city must have shone as gaudily as Disney Land.

The Minoan Lady – *La Parisienne* – fragments of a fresco from Knossos, shows how the Minoans had sensuality and a sexual freedom and clearly valued beauty: red lips and dark painted rings around her eyes. She seemed to know very well that she was being looked at, as I stood and ogled. But she didn't break. Continuing her 3000-year sultry stare forward. No such coyness from the Snake Goddess statue though, brandishing her wild snakes, her breasts bare above her long layered skirt. Cretan pride and temerity right there in the small, intricate figure, whose lure and witchery pulls you through the museum rooms towards her.

Mount Ida – or Psiloritis as it is also known – stands 8,000 feet tall, southwest of Heraklion. Giristroula and I climbed its slopes one summer day, stopping at the stone-built *mitato* – the shepherd huts. Dark and cool and deserted as we poked our noses in, but each one with the overpoweringly rich smell of the large round dusty sheep's cheeses left there fermenting on the stone shelves. We climbed on and up and over the mountain passes slipping into stone, to the cave where Zeus was born. A vast, deep, cold cave in the scraped rock looking out onto the valley of Nida. The immense plain that lies flat below is spread like a magic carpet of green. The mountains all around are sat like floating turtles on the top of this pea-green sea of grass. To hide the infant Zeus's cries in the cave, so his father, Kronos, wouldn't eat him, Zeus's mother summoned the mythical *korybantes*: dancing soldiers who would drum and clash their spears and drown out the wails of the new-born God. In silence now, Giristroula and I stood at the cave's mouth, the only people here. A few large death-black crows cawed nearby. I watched as one crow calmly and slowly started drumming its wings in the air and then took off, flying east. High over the land, in the direction we were to travel too.

Lasithi and tracking back westwards

Lasithi, the eastern state of Crete. Its capital, Agios Nikolaos, is all large villas and streets of shopping. A huge statue on the sea front celebrates Zeus's metamorphism into a bull to catch the eye of the beautiful Europa, with her odd kink for bovids, and his carrying her away to this spot in Crete to have his mismatched bestial way with her. The act that gave us the name of the continent that sits like a heavy beast above Crete across the water. Giristroula and I drove on from Agios Nikolaos, towards the peninsular towns of Elounda and Plaka. From the pretty blue tableclothed tavern by Plaka's beach we took a small boat in bright sunshine over the water to the blighted island of Spinalonga.

As we landed, we could see people were arranging festivities amongst the broken down Turkish houses and along the lanes with the dilapidated school building, stone washhouses, hospital and the preserved old shops that were opened and run by the lepers cast away from normal life here on the island. They were getting ready to celebrate the day, exactly 60 years ago, when the very last patient left Spinalonga. We weren't meant to be here, they told us. The place was closed. But as we all stood on the quayside and watched the boat that had brought us here putter away back to the mainland, they hadn't really any other option than to reluctantly allow us walk around the empty lanes, past the silent cemetery and over the rocks to the other side. When we left Spinalonga's sad spectral town it was out via the long dark tunnel that opened up into the bright light reflected up from the sea on the jetty, just as the very last patient must have left. The boatman had re-appeared, as if by magic, and it was a relief to leave the empty island really. It didn't seem the right place for celebrations. There was an unsettling feeling left in the very bricks of the place. I felt even sorrier for Sotiria's sister as we sailed back to Crete's mainland.

The grossly obese olive tree at Kavousi watched us drive past. The most ancient olive tree in the world, planted 1,300 years before Christ was born. We headed down the east coast of Crete, stopping and climbing over the trails of the remains of an ancient town, Itanos, that had slipped down its hill so now half of the houses and paths are under the sea. Giristroula and I swam in the clear water, following the roads and routes of the ruins of a lost world sunk below us. Back in the car we wheeled round the bottom right-hand corner of Crete, onto the south side of the island and hit the gorge of Zakros – the gorge of the dead. A few people had left their cars to walk it. Evil-eyed goats were up on the bonnets and the roofs, stretching for the thin leaves on the trees above, their hooves making deep scratches in the paintwork, nibbling jaws bending the aerials. Giristroula and I walked down into the gorge. Flowering trees with deep pinks and whites on the riverbed of the gorge, sheer cliffs of red rock rose over us. In these receded cliff-caves the bodies of the great and good of Minoan society had been laid to rest. We twisted our heads to take in all these dark silent hollows high above us, where now the crows nested amongst the fossiled bones.

Hametoulo was completely empty. We wandered the dead alleyways of the village and were frightened out of our wits by one old lady who appeared from nowhere. She still lived in this ghost village. She was born here and wouldn't leave, even though every other resident had. The old woman offered us grapes that were hot from the sun as we placed them in our mouths. She brought out two chairs and obviously wanted to sit and chat. Who knows when she had last seen a living soul? So we sat on the wooden kitchen chairs, the white walls around us sizzling with heat, the sun in total charge of the day and listened to her memories, as I thought of all these Greek villages being left for dead by the call of the cities and the mainland.

Later, Giristroula and I puttered on along the southern road to Ierapetra. I was told this town is the hottest in Europe. It doesn't necessarily have the highest temperatures, but the temperature never really falls, so over the course of a year the town has soaked up the most heat on the whole of the continent. Every man, from the loafers on the street to the businessmen clutching briefcases on their way to some important meeting, walked around bare-chested and shirtless. Even the local priest, who passed us slowly down the street, was wearing a green plastic eye shade which made him look like some card dealer in a drinking saloon.

Travelling west along the southern coast of Crete, we had crossed back into the state of Heraklion. We took a route through the Asterousia mountain villages. The Cretan accent was so heavy and thick here that even Giristroula couldn't understand what was being said when we wound down the window and asked for directions. The old men sat on benches by the side of the road were in their heavy clothes in the roasting heat. One man pulled what looked like an endless clown's handkerchief from his pocket to wipe at his seamy face.

The road rose dramatically. We were lost, but carried on as there was really no other alternative. The dirt track gave no space to turn around, we just had to keep going forward. The dust road turned this way and that, violently. We climbed so high we could see great swathes of Crete's southern coast flowing away from us below, with huge hungry bites taken out of it by the African sea.

The dust flew from the wheels, covering the whole car. Mile after mile, we swung round the curves, nothing but the deep blue sky swaying in and out our windscreen.

Suddenly we were freewheeling down an angled track towards a monastery. Our blackened car squeaked up to the gate. Moni Koudouma. A monk, up a ladder, pruning a tree, descended quickly. I was expecting the worst, shooed away as we were when we asked to stay at the Meteora monasteries in northern Greece.

"You'll stay won't you?" said the monk before we had the chance to say anything to him. "Please. Stay. You must be lost. It's getting late." He swung open the gates.

I thanked the monk for taking us in. Told him he'd saved our skin, we had nowhere else to go.

"Well we can't turn anyone away. It's not our house of course. It's the Madonna's house. But..." he added, leaning closer to me, "She would always show us a sign if you were not good people..."

We stood for a while here in the flowering gardens, not speaking, the late sun triggering huge flares of orange and purples in the sky above the dormitories and the chapel. The monk appeared to be waiting for a sign, any sort of sign. Eventually, satisfied, he waved us forward and we were taken into the dining room. It was just us, the monks and the monastery's workmen sat on the benches for dinner. And two shifty looking men, one short and cunning with darting eyes, the other tall and idiotic looking. The dinner was overflowing plates of fish and baskets of bread, nothing else. Simple and perfect. Eaten in complete silence.

Afterwards Giristroula and I took a stroll in the grounds of the monastery and I saw, on the far side, the two criminal looking men walking the head monk around and around in the garden. The short shrewd looking man had his arm round the monk's shoulders and was talking closely into his ear, talking him into something. The lunk behind followed, tripping over his feet. At night we were put in one of the small cell-like rooms, with only a hard bed, one table, a jug and bowl, and 20 or 30 golden ikons hanging on the white-washed walls. Our stone room was just outside the great walls of the monastery. The monastery itself was shrouded in darkness, only one light shining in a room at the very top. The workmen, who had spent all day repairing bits of the old church, sat outside the walls and, like some medieval scene outside the city gates, they drank and smoked and talked loudly and sang songs through the dead of night. It was almost as if they were sitting out in a village square, right under the monk's windows. The small crafty-looking man was leading the carousing.

Over dinner the previous evening, the monks had asked us to come to the service the next morning. "From 5am to 7am," they told us "Come at any time..." I set the alarm to go off at shortly before seven. I opened an eye and saw a golden morning sun pushing its beams through the metal grate of our tiny window, and turned the phone off again and rolled back to sleep. Suddenly the wind blew open the iron door, which we had locked and barred, with a crash on the hard stone walls. Startled, we fled the beds, scurrying outside to the church in the monastery grounds, eyes raised to the heavens, touching foreheads in apology. We arrived at the service. The scene was full of smoke and chanting. Monks on their knees, noses to the ground. We were the only two to have come, the two shifty men hadn't made it. One monk, who wasn't wearing completely the correct clothes, not the exact flowing black robes of the other monks, had tattoos running up his arms under his loose sleeves. He stood at the back, behind me, his head lolling, battling not to fall asleep.

After the service the monks invited us into their quarters and offered us a small, plain, breakfast. We sat and talked. The head monk told me he had been here 23 years. He rarely, if ever, left the monasteries' grounds. Another told me that all monks change their names when they come here and talked vaguely about his life before, some business he had run. It seemed quite clear he had racked up large debts that he had to get away from. I wasn't sure *what* the tattooed-armed monk had done in a previous life to have had to run away and to be here, miles from anywhere, dishing out the sacraments, cleaning the toilets, hiding in the mountains with the monks. I didn't like to guess.

I had read that criminals left their old lives to join the monastery set, but kept reminders: a photo of the old gang, posing after some raid, some successful robbery, pinned to their monastery room wall. Like a photo souvenir of an old football team – the good old days. When I took a photo of all the monks sat here beaming like a group of little old ladies on a day out to the sea, the tattooed monk covered his face, not wanting to be recognised. The head monk told me you don't have to have walked a religious path in your previous life to come here, to become a monk, you just turn up, and work, and study, and pray. He will tell you when you are ready.

We were taken down to the beach behind the monastery, completely private, though, of course, none of the monks go swimming themselves. It could be the most fantastic beach in the whole of Crete. A perfect semi-circled shore, the clear emerald water becoming sudden-deep, caves lying under the sea to explore. Giristroula and I swam and dived for hours as the sun climbed, throwing out a blinding light over the sea and rocks. Back on the beach, a little tubby black figure of a small monk stood on the shingle, hands locked over this round belly, rocking up and down happily on his heels watching us.

Later, having hauled ourselves out of the sea and dried off, we packed up the car. I saw the small trickster man still trying to talk the head monk into some plan. He offered us a diabolical leer as we passed. I felt sad that some come and take advantage of the monks here. The monks say they can never turn anyone away and so, word having got around, some people come and stay for weeks. Crowding the monk's tranquil beach during the day, hoovering up their free fish and loaves in the evenings.

A couple of monks stood and waved from behind the gate as we left and our car drove off down the dirt road. They were waving until we disappeared over the brim of the mountain.

Matala was once the prime site for hippies back in the '60s. They turned up at this undeveloped fishing village, living in the caves in the cliff which are crazily set out like an apartment block: ground floor, mezzanines, upper stories of caves. To begin with, they lived harmoniously with the locals of Matala. However, they were slowly joined by increasing numbers of beatniks and fashionable freaks as Matala became well-known and trendy. Eventually the hippies would walk to the bakery and lounge in the café brazenly naked, shocking the redoubtable headscarfed old Greek women, the old priest, the goats and the donkeys. Giorgios Papadopoulos – the terrible dictator of Greece from 1967 to 1974 – sent in the troops to remove the hippies. Harsh vibes remain. The white-sand beach was packed with people as Giristroula and I took a walk to see the old caves. Games of rackets and screaming kids. There was a charge to look at the caves and they were being poked about by bored holiday makers in bright red shorts and caps. 'Zorbas' snack bar was doing a roaring trade. We left quickly. To the Minoan palace of Phaistos. Excavated but not restored, the stones and blocks of Phaistos, lying scattered over the ground, are larger than at Knossos. This was more like it: the ground where man and universe are meant to meet.

The next day we passed the Frangokastello fortress. A Venetian castle the Greeks used during the independence struggle against the Turks. In 1828 the Cretans were defeated, but not before they first took down many of the Turkish army with them. At dawn, every anniversary in May, the shadows of the Cretan soldiers are said to appear on the walls of the fortress, marching in file. They have been seen many times, by quite rational lucid people. We stopped off at a threadbare petrol station nearby and I asked the fat assistant in his dirty dungarees if he had seen the shadows of the dead soldiers.

"*Fysika!*" – of course. "Many times! Every year!" he told me.

When the Germans invaded and took the castle in the Second World War, they saw the shadows marching towards them too, and opened fire at the empty wall.

Sfakia was a bustling hub town, boats coming in and out like the London Underground Central Line, taking people to the villages all along the Cretan southern coast. Giristroula and I drove on down the road towards Anopoli, where the road suddenly hit a toweringly high wooden bridge. We crossed over. The loose planks under our wheels creaking, the metal support moaning, the valley below with the distant channel of river and rock waiting open mouthed. The bored adolescents in the café on the other side watched us, heads rested on their hands, seemingly waiting, hoping, something might happen. To their disappointment though, we made it over to the village of Aradena. The village had been abandoned since a blood feud started in the 1950s when two boys argued over a sheep's bell, of all things, resulting in gruesome vendetta murders in the families until the whole village deserted in fear.

And then we could go no further. This was where the road along the south coast ended. An immense combination of mountain and gorge meant we couldn't get to the southwest corner of Crete. This was as far along the southern edge of the island as we could go. We would have to go round the long way. Heading up north and west, towards Chania – the capital of the western state of Crete.

Chania

Twinkling with pleasure at its own beauty, Chania was hopelessly in love with its reflection: the old town, the harbour, the ancient houses, the stone lighthouse.

"There are two types of people," said the waiter in the café next to the seafront that we were sat in. "Those who see Chania as completely magical… and those who haven't been here yet!" he grinned toothily at us.

The Turkish area – the Splantzia – is more interesting. Narrow streets, houses built inside old ruins, the square surrounded by old knife makers and old kafeneos. A tree where the Turks once hung Orthodox followers; a church which was first a monastery, then a mosque, then turned back into an Orthodox church with the minarets still remaining. Neatly summing-up Greece's impossible history. The mountains standing above the church, high above the whole city, are the White Mountains – Lefka Ori. This huge, sky-scraping range always appears to have snow on the top. It's an optical illusion, but very odd when swimming out on the west of Crete in the Mediterranean sea, the raw sun beating down, to look up and see these apparent floating peaks of snow, rock and ice. The largest peak in the White Mountains, Pachnes, is only around three metres lower than Mount Ida, the highest point of the whole of Crete. I was told, with the arch rivalry between the state of Chania and Ida's home, Rethymno, the climbers of Chania always take a pebble when they climb Pachnes to place at the top, hoping one day to claim top spot of the island.

We camped for the night out by the coast in Kedrodasos. The wind was rising. The sky swirled and constantly changed colour. Other people camped under scrubby trees on the sand peered out of tents and groaned and snapped the openings shut again as we passed with our stuff. Before dawn, our tent was blown apart, becoming just a skeleton of sticks as the canvas hurtled down towards the sea. Giristroula and I lay, exposed in our sleeping bags, as straggly campers passed us, grim faced, carrying their rucksacks and tents and clanking billycans, looking like marching war refugees. The far west coast of Crete had become menacing. We followed this early morning procession of people deserting the beach, and headed round the island's western corner, back onto the island's southern edge.

The Samaria Gorge – the largest gorge in Europe. What was once a challenging hike in amongst all the beauty is now attempted daily by hundreds of sweating tourists in unsuitable footwear. They often have to be rescued by the mysterious custodians of the gorge, turning up out of nowhere, often on mules, to take the twisted-ankle brigade down the long way out to the exit. Giristroula and I decided to avoid the crowds and started our trek down the gorge late. Too late. The sun had already shifted up on its shelf and had climbed far down the sky as we entered the gorge. We descended, along the dried riverbeds, through the forests of scented pines, over the sun-cooked rocks. Time was getting on.

We came across the broken-down remnants of the old village of Samaria, where people once lived, having to make the trek up the gorge for daily provisions rather than for an exacting day of holiday fun.

As we passed, the door of an old building opened.

"Hey, what are you doing there? It's late. You're very late. You might not make it to the end of the gorge now you know... Where have you come from?"

"Amaliada," said Giristroula, referring to her home town, truthfully if a little unnecessarily pedantic.

"Amaliada?" said the camouflaged stranger, emerging out of the dark in his sturdy boots and cap. "*Amaliada?* My wife's family are from Amaliada! You must stay!" he opened the door wide, pushed his cap back on his head. "Stay..." he flung his arms backwards "We have good wine..."

From the backrooms of this building came out other figures, in fatigues and boots, and I realised these were the protectors of the gorge. We were with the wardens of Samaria. As darkness started to drip down and the heat-drenched day was becoming a heat-drenched evening, the five men and two women stationed here this night in the old huts and ruined buildings, invited us in, chatted to us while the walkie-talkie radios buzzed with news of a Belgian man who'd fallen somewhere along the route. And then the tables came out. When everyone has gone and the gates at either end are locked at the end of the day and silence reigns here in the middle of quite-the-most-beautiful nowhere, the workers of the gorge sit down to an incredible meal. I don't know how they make it, but the trestle tables groaned under the plates of grilled meat, salads, barrels of wine. Glasses were all clanked together, laughter rode over the empty gorge.

A very tall man arrived on a very small donkey. Red shirt, beanpole thin, slim neat moustache, long serious face. This was the fire warden of the gorge. He had been trotting his mule over the rocks and ridges all day, scanning the horizons for any problems here in the cinder-box dry ravine. He now toasted his arrival back at base by balancing a long glass of wine on his nose, not smiling, giving me a look out of the corner of his eye, and then in one move, not touching the glass with his hands, he dropped it to his mouth to drain it dry. Everybody cheered. It was his first of many.

As we ate, Sifis turned up. Sifis was the chief of the gorge. Fierce-faced, strong greying beard, shirt unbuttoned to his stomach, robust and capable. He'd been up the top of the cliffs dealing with stray wild animals. He'd been walking the 16 kilometres of this gorge every day, sternly patrolling this land, his patch, since 1974. Sifis had been born at the very tip of the gorge in the village of Omalos. He greeted us with some chariness and looked at Thodoros, the rather meek man who had first invited us in, as if he was some gullible simpleton.

We all carried on with this banquet and, as Sifis sank some of the wine, I felt maybe he had relaxed, not as annoyed at having these strangers in his midst. I tried some conversation.

"This is great meat," I said gnawing on a plump bone. "What is it?"

"The last Englishman who came through here," grunted Sifis, not looking up. His face not showing the slightest trace of humour.

Eventually however, as the food disappeared, and the tall fire warden drained more and more glasses of wine, balancing them on his elbow, drinking from the tip of his toe, the others laughing and gossiping, Sifis mellowed.

This sanctuary in the middle of the gorge was surrounded by the feral animal particular to Crete – the *kri-kri* – a wild goat that can only be found on this island.

"It's not a kri-kri," said Sifis.

"Oh, I'm sorry," I said. "I thought I'd read somewhere..."

"It's called an *agrimi*."

Sifis drained his drink, wiped the edges of his beard, sighed, looked sadly at the empty glass, and turned to me.

"There was a man from Crete," he said. "He wanted to show one of these goats to Harry Truman. You know Harry Truman, yes? The president of America?"

I told Sifis that, yes, I'd heard of him.

"He put the goat on an airplane," Sifis continued. "Took him to America. But he was stopped. They wouldn't let him bring the goat into the country. The man argued and argued but it was no good. So he just left the animal there, in the airport. Left it there until he was allowed to take it to Truman."

Typical Greek thinking.

"They gave in of course. Of course they did, there was a goat walking around, eating the airport. So he took it to the White House. Showed it to Truman. Truman loved it. But he couldn't pronounce the name. Couldn't say 'agrimi'. So, because it came from Crete, he called it a cre-cre." Or kri-kri.

"Truman was touched by this Cretan man bringing his goat all that way to show him," said Sifis. "He told him he could give the man anything he wants in return. Anything. 'You can bring your family here. We can give you a good life.' Do you know what the man asked for? What the only thing he wanted was? He asked for an American gun. That's all he wanted. A gun. So Truman gave him a big American pistol and the Cretan man was happy. He went on his way, back to Greece with his goat and his new gun…"

"Here! Give the Englishman some more of the wine..!" Sifis roared, story over, snatching a glass off the fire warden's forehead and pouring me a great slug of wine.

Sifis stared at me. "I guess you're not so bad for an English," he said. "They usually mess everything up here."

He looked out at the black gorge. A young agrimi, trotted freely over the walled terrace. The fire warden slapped at his legs in his shorts, started a drinking song as the others of the group clapped and stomped.

"The British helped kill men here," said Sifis. "Helped the government in the civil war. And this after we'd helped them fight the Germans… During the war against the Germans, the English didn't understand the Cretans. Didn't understand how we can fight. We told them we could fight for them, we just need the weapons. They gave us a handful of bullets. Nothing. And they said 'Remember when you are captured, the last bullet is for you.' They thought we would all fall. They thought nothing of us. They were amazed when they saw 70-year-old men, Cretan grandfathers, fighting with their teeth against the Germans. And then, after all that, they turned against us. An Englishman stood right where you are. A soldier who'd fought with us, and then turned to fight against us in the civil war. He didn't realise that we'd learnt to hunt the agrimi though. Very difficult to hunt. Good training. One of the men here was able to hit the Englishman right between the eyes. They soon got the message… "

"More wine for us!" Sifis shouted.

The fire warden had slumped under the table. The other wardens were still helping themselves to plates of food over his prone body. Sifis poured two huge glasses for us himself.

"The British took the king of Greece all the way down this gorge," Sifis said. "To escape, during the war. They had to get him out of the country. He slept his very last night in Greece in the surgery right over there," Sifis pointed over to an old block of buildings.

"He wrote his last announcement to be broadcast to Greece, and then left." Sifis lifted his glass, mumbling into his drink, "The scumbag…"

"The King's donkey," Sifis continued, pointing out towards the trees. "His donkey with the gold of Greece in the saddle bags, it fell into the canyon right here. You English, you were very quick. You collected up all that you could. Kept our gold." Sifis sniffed deeply, took another deep swig. "We still search for any gold around here now, while we work. Never found any yet…"

The fire warden was snoring under the table now. It was gone 2am. Fat and drunk, Giristroula and I were shown to a room, just next to King George II's. It smelt terribly of horse manure and I realised as we slept under the rough blankets that this must have served, maybe it still did, as the stables.

I woke up to a face-full of bugs. Pushing the door open, the scene outside was utterly unrecognisable from last night. In the new hot bright day, walkers were swarming all over the old broken-down site of old Samaria village, asking the gorge workers, as if concierges, for snacks and drinks and being wafted away by the black vested, thick-biceped guard on walkie-talkie duty that morning. The fire warden had slept the night out in the open under the table. He smiled a little sheepishly at us before climbing back on his mule and trotting off into the dark green paths to look for fires in the new day.

We said our goodbyes to the group. They didn't have to let us into their world, they could have shouted at us to leave the gorge last night. It was very kind of them. Sifis even said to Giristroula: "Did you try and cheat us? Did you plan to stay here? We don't let people stay you know. One man once told us he had fallen, said he was in agony, so we let him stay, let him eat and drink with us. The next week, he turns up with his whole family… Malaka! After that, we don't want anyone to stay…"

Sifis had long gone this morning. Up at dawn to patrol his kingdom. Giristroula and I set off and walked the rest of the gorge, pushing through the Iron Gates, the colossal pillars of rock, just four metres apart from each other but rising upwards over 300 metres high.

We trekked on to the end of the Samaria Gorge. Like all the walkers, once they have got through, we sat on the white-hot sand at Agia Roumeli and waited for the boat to arrive to take us away. No roads, only a sea exit from here.

The boat chugged in, picked us up, and chugged away again, cutting us through the pure turquoise blue to the village of Sougia.

The temperature at this low southern point of Crete had pushed over 45 degrees. The hot desert air was dense and heavy. A strong wind blew from Africa, whipping and tearing at everything. To stand outside felt like being hit round the head by a thick middle-eastern carpet. We rented a cheap hotel room and sat for days, sweating inside this white box, the blinds drawn down. We were prisoners, the weather our jailor. Like Odysseus kept captive by Calypso. Strangely enough, the people of Sougia actually swear that Calypso's cave was here. I knew from our other previous journeying that her cave was in Othonoi, in the small scattering of islands north of Corfu.

"No, no. The cave was *here*. I tell you her cave was *here*..."

"Well, where exactly?" I asked.

"Well you can't see it *now*," said the old, deep-lined Sougian man, annoyed at this suggestion of doubt. "There was a great earthquake. It covered all the caves. But it *was* here. It was. What, you don't believe me?" He turned his back to me, an open hand thrown in the air back towards me, outraged and insulted.

Giristroula and I only left our hotel cell in the evenings to eat at a nearby tavern. The men talked of the wind, the *meltemi* as we were buffeted outside on the tavern's tables. Wind is a constant companion in Crete, something to always recognise and occasionally fear. One man pinched his fingers and thumb together and wagged them up and down in the air, pursing his lips in respectful approval as he spoke.

"If the wind is coming from the south… Oh-ho! *Then* you're in trouble! Swimmers get taken straight out to sea, pulled out beyond the tide. *Roufihtra* we call it – like the sucking up of a piece of spaghetti."

All Giristroula and I wanted to do was to catch a boat. The wind had cancelled all services for days now to Gavdos, a tiny island off this southwest coast of Crete. A mystical place that we were desperate to see. A land where usual rules do not apply.

We turned up at the jetty in the early morning light, as we had been doing for day after day… and finally it was there. Like a shining mirage, the boat to Gavdos was running at last. I had thought the people who live on the island, and there are only around 50 official residents all year round on Gavdos, would be furious, having been stranded for days on this quayside, sleeping in the heat, renting rooms, being put up by friends. They needed to get to their homes to see families, transfer provisions, food, medicine. I'd imagined this delay would have frayed nerves and tempers, but everyone was sanguine, unfussed, chatting to the boatmen, used to these delays. Gavdos people don't stick to everyday habits. The boat chugged out of Sougia and along the coast. We saw a man all alone on a deserted beach shouting and hollering at us as we sailed by and, quite astonishingly, the big boat put on the brakes, turned in the water and picked him up. Like a hitch-hiker.

For around 20 minutes, when the boat docked, Gavdos exploded into life. The tiny island went from a sleeping cat, legs sprawled out hanging over a wall, to a chaos of broken down vans belching smoke, crowds pushing, tourists stood looking confused in the dust, men carrying heavy thick sacks on their heads. The harbour a sudden riot of life, before just as quickly falling quiet again. The cat rearranged itself out of the blistering sun back in the shade of the old café. Giristroula and I were the last people to leave the quayside, lugging bags onto our backs. A solitary man looked up from his tinkering under the bonnet of his old truck.

"Where are you going?" he asked. "Do you want me to take you?"

Well, we didn't know where we were going. But a lift there would be perfect. So the man took us to Korfos beach, where we pitched a tent in the trees next to old forgotten Minoan walls. Through the next days we hitched lifts in other broken-down cars around this tiny island. There were just a handful of tavernas, no real hotels, no electricity, everything running off generators for a few hours each day.

Ai Giannis beach was full though. Full of people with wild hair. Full of bongos, cross-leggedness, joint smoking. No one big on clothes. A dark haired girl walked over the hot sand completely naked, sunburnt breasts, thick pubic hair, her eyes closed, a beatific smile spread on her face. She moved her hands over the faces of everybody she passed. People danced around her on the beach to sounds inside their heads. The living was free and quite fantastically out-of-it. The sea water was warm as a pan on the stove and the wind now calm. Mainland Crete brooded at us over the water. Gavdos is a land away from all normal expectation of time and place. It didn't take much to find ourselves lost in this untouched land away from people and habitat. In fact it was harder *not* to find yourself on your own, among all the outrageous terrain – mysterious plants; wild birds pausing for breath on their migratory runs; sandy slopes plunging down to pure blue seas.

We sat for long afternoons at a tavern with an old fisherman owner, and his daughter Eva fixing us food – Gavdos goat with onions. Eva told us about the island, and about the one policeman based here. I had seen him at the harbourside, leaning on a wall, smiling, doing very little, contentedly waving at the chaos of newcomers coming off the boat. Tall, a little dim-witted-looking, khaki uniform, very short shorts. Eva told me he happily walks around the island, smoking joints, chatting to the locals, but whenever there is trouble he makes a point of not getting involved, fleeing the scene. When a huge trance party took place on one of the beaches for several days and nights, the locals complained and finally formed a group and broke up the party, scattering the revellers.

The policeman was found in the middle, passed out. He was face-down in the sand, grinning blissfully to himself.

As I spoke to Eva, I recalled the stories I'd heard about how Greece was terrorised for over 25 years from the 1970s by the feared revolutionary anarchist group 'The 17th of November'. Over 100 attacks on Greek, Turkish, UK and US targets. Many killed, brutally assassinated. The leader of this terror group was finally tracked down to Gavdos. He lived all alone here, keeping bees.

The boat back to Crete had been delayed for day after day. No reason given. Even more than getting here, leaving Gavdos seemed an impossible task. But I wasn't sure it was something we really wanted to achieve anyway. One day we set off walking towards the south of the island, into the valleys. The sun beating down, unwilling to hide, even this late in the day. We carried on through rocky pathways, the birds flying madly around us in the sky, intoxicated by the light of the falling dusk. Eventually, on a high coastal cliff, we could see Triopetra beach. Unlike the other beaches of Gavdos, Triopetra looked almost lunar, other worldly. A vast rockiness opening out to the water as we climbed down. The Libyan Sea, flooded blue, flowing out of the very most southern point of the continent. Nowhere further to go. We waded into the sea and then walked up onto the final rocks. A large wooden chair had been placed by somebody on the perfectly alone rock promontory to mark this end of Europe. If you could call it Europe, of course. Could you even really say it was Greece? Here it felt something totally different. Here was Crete.

Chapter 8
Travels in Southern Greece

We had returned from Crete, but just couldn't seem to settle back in Athens. The rented world of streets and offices and cars and shops just didn't feel right. The Attic light was just a dull glow. The Greek gods first give you the journey, then the nostalgia. So we decided to take another tour. Like we had in northern Greece, but this time heading south. Onto the Peloponnese peninsula. Drawn over by the names of legend: Argos, Mycenae, Sparta... We travelled down through the green Arcadian landscape, over the towering Taygetos mountain range and into the three rocky prongs of the Peloponnese at the southern point of mainland Greece.

Part 1
Under The Ditch

We sailed right through the streets of Poros. I had taken up position on top of the bridge of the ship as we chugged along the roadside, keeping pace with the walkers below, the old men on their mopeds, a dog trotting alongside our huge boat. The cafés were just opening up, a woman sluiced water over the street outside her shop. I raised a hand in morning greeting as we soundlessly drifted by, as if the ship was trundling down the road. Poros's clocktower sat high above us, the hulk of the Peloponnese mainland was a short distance away on the other side of the boat. The tiny distance between the coast and island made it feel as if this was just a wide river we were on, not the open sea. The people of Poros claim that at one time you could even wade to the Greek mainland. We didn't disembark in Poros. We stayed on to the next island, Hydra.

"Eh, Giorgos," called the captain down to the man on the quayside tying up the ropes as we landed in Hydra town. "No packages for you from Athens… and…" he looked us up and down. "Just these two today…" He shrugged and pulled an apologetic face.

Hydra expects people, expects tourists. But not now. Not the day after Christmas. The whole place felt quiet, like a theatre stage left empty with rising spirals of houses climbing up the backcloth. Despite its name suggesting water, it doesn't look like there's a single drop on the island. Hydra is a rock. The town the boat draws in at is the only thing here. Giristroula and I walked through the streets: writhing cats in the early morning sun, donkeys waiting on every corner. No cars are allowed on the island and donkeys are the only way to travel. They stood around, idling, like taxis with their engines running. I felt sorry for these donkeys, imagining them sweating in the heat of the summer with the fat tourists on their back. Hundreds of stone steps climb through the town and we walked up and down, up and down, to find somewhere to stay. Most of the houses and shops were shut. The owners, having made their summer money, had all gone back to the capital for the winter. Clean curtains of canvas covered the doorways of the closed houses, like sheets placed over the faces of incredibly attractive corpses.

Giristroula and I had left a deafening Athens at Christmas. Kids in the streets, outside every shop, coming to our door, singing their *kalanda* – the tuneless Christmas songs that are always accompanied by a metal triangle being manically rattled, usually by the smallest member of the group, with expectant hands stretched out for a coin.

A mother and a daughter had passed us, doing their Christmas shopping on Aiolou Street. The daughter stopped dead, looking panicked. "*Mana mou, mana mou*… Have we got the new *kazamias*?" she asked her mother. The mother reassured her, pulling out the magazine almanac that have all the horoscopes, stories and predictions for the year ahead. These periodicals are also full of bizarre dream interpretations that many of the quixotic Greeks live their life by:

'If you have untidy hair in your dream, someone cares about you…' 'If you see cutlery in your dream, you will have family problems…' 'If you dream that you are drinking milk, you're going to have an accident…'

We had left Athens before New Year's Eve too, where we would have been sat indoors playing cards as tradition dictates. Cutting the Vasilopita cake at midnight, hoping to get the money secreted in there for good luck. St Vasilios started all this, back when the Greeks were being overtaxed by the Turks. He worked one of those useful miracles that stopped the taxation robberies and then, to avoid any embarrassment, the saint made sure all the money was returned to the Greeks hidden in their New Year cakes on his name day. I would rake through my slice every year. Not once had I ever found the lucky coin.

Greek Christmas is decorated not by the tree or the angel or any of those western emblems, the Greek Christmas symbol is always a boat. Agios Nikolaos is the saint of Christmas and of sailors. So Giristroula and I were on the right island. Hydra is inordinately proud of its naval history and the island is famed for having the most skilled captains. They say the Ottoman Empire was defeated by these sea dogs and now their statues litter the island, with puffed-chested men up on their plinths. Model boats covered in winking Christmas lights were hanging off the ship's masts, decorating every window we walked past. We called in at an old bar on the deserted seafront for a glass of Metaxa. It was overly expensive. The men in the bar were unfriendly. Photos of Leonard Cohen, famously resident on the island in the '60s, sat drinking in the bar hung on the walls. A dirty man in a long raincoat came in, selling mushrooms from an old bag.

"*Ah... stin iyia sas hartopektes!*" – health to the card players! – he said cheerfully as he entered. The men of the bar soon chased him out again.

"*Katarameni na eeste hartokleftes!*" – a curse to the card cheats! – he spat as he was pushed out of the door.

He clutched at the door frame with his fingernails and leant his dirty face back in towards me as he was pushed by the men.

"You know, when God made Greece, he knew he'd made a terrible mistake. 'I've made this too beautiful', God said to himself. 'What can I do? It's too beautiful!'"

The old man surveyed the Hydra card players in the bar with a leer.

"I know... I'll put *Greek people* here!"

With a final shove, the man was out again on the cobbled harbour side.

Giristroula and I went back to the room we'd found to rent and sat in bed with the moon outside bright enough to read by. We fell asleep to the sound of donkeys' hoofs clopping by on the stones.

Hydra town looks like brightly coloured children's bricks have been pushed into a huge lump of brown plasticine. Greece's great artist, Nikos Ghikas, had lived on the island. His art *is* Hydra: circling cubist buildings, climbing up and round and round in dizzying fractured colours. We walked along the high lanes that Ghikas had painted, above the roofs of the town, to his house. A grand acropolis of a place. With forty rooms or more, built on several levels on the rocky hillside. However, it is just ruins now. Ghikas's Greek housemaid set fire to the house when Ghikas left his first wife for the divorcee Lady Rothschild as the maid was so disgusted at all the bohemian shenanigans going on. Artists and writers had all stayed here: Hydra's lascivious libertine world rests like a sad old spectre on the island. Just as with the later '60s beatniks with their inherited money, waiting for creative inspiration to strike while their muses, the womenfolk, did the daily grind. All a little dismal and ridiculous. As Giristroula and I gazed at the charred white stone walls of this gutted mansion, an owl sitting in an empty hole of a window frame, an old man approached.

"You're interested in Ghikas's house eh? Ah, it was like the jewellery of Hydra…" he looked up at the wreck and smiled at the thought.

"You're English?" he said to me. "I remember your Paddy being here…"

Paddy? I guessed he meant Paddy Leigh Fermor. The man whose legacy had loomed large while we were in Crete.

"Yes, yes, I remember him. We all laughed at him in his English khaki shorts. Oh, they had such parties here…"

We left the man to his memories and started on the path up the long climb to the very top tip of Hydra, Mount Elias. There is a dedication to Saint Elias at the top of pretty much every high point in Greece. He was the saint who had been sailor and had almost drowned so many times he eventually moved to spend his days on the furthest point from the sea that he could find. Giristroula and I looked down on the island from the top, with the town spread below us like a contented submissive cat. The white houses and blue window frames and the outside tables and the donkeys and the sunlit paths. It looked more Greek than anywhere else I could picture. But is any of it real these days? Is any of it true? Or is it all just make-believe postcard stuff?

The boat was soon to leave Hydra for the mainland.

The thick, green, peaceful hills of northeastern Peloponnese passed by slowly. We were heading towards Epidaurus. The old rattling bus juddered us along the road with people piled in the seats around us and the cargo nothing but pure confusion. A woman over the aisle was cutting and stripping cabbages, a towering pile of them by her feet and up on the seat. She handed a few of them over for me to hold for her, so I sat happily for the few hours on the chuntering bus as it passed through the county of Argolida, looking out the window with a heap of cabbages on my lap. The bus stopped at points all along the road, at every small collection of houses, as people ran out of their homes with a tin of olive oil, a headless chicken, to pass onto someone in the next village. An old man walking along the side of a field decided very late that he wanted a ride and jutted out his stick. The driver slammed on the brakes of the bus. A cabbage rolled down the aisle and out the door as the old man climbed on board.

The great amphitheatre of Epidaurus was bathed in a smooth stone light as Giristroula and I approached on foot. It opened up from the stage in a huge curve in front of us, like a great sigh from antiquity. For 2,500 years the ancient theatre has sat in this place of peace and healing, with the encircling hills beyond. The theatre looks like it has curled into the hillside itself, like an enormous fossil. There were a few splattered clouds above, the sun's beam forcing through like a spotlight. We sat up on the stepped stones – 55 long rows of toppling seats – high in the auditorium and looked down into the theatre's bowl. People were stood on the sandy stone stage and spoke to each other in this place of utter acoustic perfection, where even a whisper can be heard in the very furthest seats. I could hear all the conversations from up here, clear as a pin. Although what was being said by the families down on the stage was a long way from Sophocles, Aeschylus and Euripides and their actors in white robes and sandals.

"Gianni! Come here Gianni. *Ela tho, agapi mou.* Eat something, my love. Gianni! Eat something *agapi mou…*"

The sounds rose and flowed over the seats, over us and out, disappearing somewhere over the hills behind. Like all of man's architectural feats – the pyramids or the great cathedrals – Epidaurus is about mathematical perfection as well as aesthetic beauty. Knowledge once just as great a virtue as beauty.

Heading further into the Peloponnese we reached Nafplio. Giristroula and I walked through the town of tight lanes and stone buildings, under the imposing pink Palamidi fortress on the hill above. After the revolution against Ottoman rule, when Greece became a free land, Nafplio was chosen as the first capital of the country. It seemed a strange choice as we walked through this small town of traditional architecture, pretty roofs of round tiles and the quiet main square with its sleeping churches. A reminder of the modest origins of modern Greece. It wasn't until the mid-1830s that nostalgia for Athens's place in ancient history took the capital away from this small but powerfully fortified town. Every café we passed had the sound of the clack of worry beads being spun and caught by old men. This is *the* town of the koboloi. There is a museum dedicated to the loop of cord with the threaded row of beads, always an odd number, that are whirled around fingers throughout Greece. The ancient eastern practice: koboloi hanging from the hand, turned like a clock, ticking off the long hours, whiling away the day; or used like a rosary, flicking the beads nervously, one by one, counting out each of life's problems.

A few kilometres north of Nafplio is Mycenae. It was once the very centre of civilization. For 500 years from around 1600BC, Greek pre-eminence and prestige was collected here. The seed of civilization having been blown from Crete and the Minoan empire to this palace on its rock under the sharp pyramid-shaped mountain behind. Agamemnon had sat in the throne room here, and terrible Greek tragedy had played out all around the columned palace...

Helen, the wife of Agamemnon's brother, was stolen by Paris of Troy and it was at Mycenae that Agamemnon declared his 10-year war against Troy to get her back. However, because of a lack of good ship-blowing wind, Agamemnon couldn't initially get his ships to sail to war and so a sacrifice was needed to be made to the gods to let them conjure up the winds to set them on their course. Agamemnon sacrificed his own daughter, Iphigenia, on the altar at Mycenae. On Agamemnon's victorious return, he was slain in his bathtub by the new lover of his wife Clytemnestra who had, unsurprisingly, held a bitter hatred of Agamemnon for murdering their daughter. Clytemnestra was later slain by her son, Orestis, to avenge Agamemnon's death. Orestis then become insane for a time, the throne of Mycenae going to Aletes, Orestis's half-brother. But not for long. Recovering, Orestis returned to Mycenae and killed Aletes and took the cursed throne back. Orestis later died from a snake bite and, less than 50 years after the great victory in Troy, the palace of Mycenae fell into ruin.

We turned the last bend and there it was before us, the huge building blocks of Mycenae. Stones so large it was thought they could only have been set down by Cyclopes. We crossed the bridge over Clytemnestra's burial place, through the graveyards and passed the colossal Lion Gate: ten-foot-high, ten-foot-wide, two huge carved lions on top, three and a half thousand years since they first stretched and posed up on their plinth. We walked the rooms of the palace and looked down the slimy well in one of its dark rooms. A couple were stood next to us, peering into the dark crypt.

"Agamemnon...?" the man called into the gloom "Agamemnon... *Ise eki*?" – are you there?

He looked over his shoulder and grinned at his wife with his mouth wide open, pleased with himself. The wife roared with laughter, gripped at her fat belly and thwacked at her husband's shoulder.

Agamemnon's tomb is a short way down the hill. A monumental beehive mausoleum, where his famous golden death mask was recovered. The mask now sits watching the visitors enter the Archaeological Museum in Athens. People were running down the hill to get into the tomb before the dusk closing time. The old guard on the gate was enjoying his power with the barrier, bringing it down slowly, inch by inch, as the crowd sprinted closer. Giristroula and I walked out past the man as he stood arms folded, eyes closed, unmoved by the pleas of those wanting to come in and see Agamemnon's final resting place. Mycenae's palace looked down, unimpressed, on the whole pantomime from up on the sun-lit rocky hill. As we walked away from the chaos, I looked across the fields and saw a shepherd stood still and quiet by his flock, his shadow spreading long in the late sun. This man could have been stood in the very same spot as Homer's heroes passed by on their way to Troy.

The temple columns of ancient Nemea rose up suddenly along the road, as if they'd been surprised, emerging over the fields of wine grapevines. Hercules killed the lion for his very first Labour here, and then wore the lion's pelt to cover him for the rest of his adventures, like a boy in a playground with his anorak dangling from his head as superman's cape.

Round the shoulder of the Peloponnese, Giristroula and I tacked alongside the Corinth Canal, through the city of Corinthos to the mouth of the canal at the Corinth Gulf. At this far end there is an old tired looking submersible bridge, rather than the proud road and rail bridges that sweep over the central span. I walked out onto it and looked down the long straight canal, down the whole length of the ditch.

"Hey!" the bridge master shouted. "Hey!"

That was the warning. There were no sirens or flashing lights. I had to dash to get off the bridge as it started to lower and a large ship cruised up to enter the canal. After plunging to the bottom of the depths, the bridge then came up again slowly, sparking in the sun with hundreds of dancing fish caught on the gangplanks. I watched as the bystanders, who had been waiting to cross, jostled with each other onto the gleaming wet bridge, each one battling to pick up the catch of fish flapping around. One old lady putting a whole silver mullet under her arm and walking off home.

Next to the bridge, hidden in some grass scrubland, I could see a long section of a limestone carriageway scored with deep grooves. I poked around in the grass, inspecting this overgrown bit of old road when the bridge master appeared behind me. He told me this was the Diolkos. These long gouged incisions in the stone road showed how the ancients had got their boats from one side of the Isthmos to the other, thousands of years before the canal: dragging them over the six kilometres of land between the Corinth Gulf in the west to the Saronic Gulf in the east. Parallel grooves, a few metres apart, looked like some kind of trackway. The ancients must have pushed and pulled their ships on wheels, making an ancient predecessor of the railway. The inventions of classical Greece startling me yet again.

Giristroula's great aunt worked on the *modern* railway here in Corinthos. We passed her old house in the centre of town, set right next to the rails. Her job had been to raise the barrier and stop any road traffic whenever a train was due. She was given the house by the Hellenic Railways Organisation under the condition that she would be ready, any time of day or night, to stop the cars when a train was coming. Giristroula remembers her great aunt racing outside in the middle of cooking a dinner or hosing down the balcony to bring down the long wooden bar before the train clattered by. The jars and bottles falling off every shelf in the house. On several occasions Giristroula herself was stationed on barrier duty as a little girl, resentfully sat all day on a bucket by the barrier mechanism waiting for expected locomotives to pass.

The trains are all gone now. Once upon a time the rail network spread across the Peloponnese. Since Greece's financial crisis most of the lines have been abandoned. Forgotten metal tracks running down the side of Greece's coast all covered in wild flowers. The old station houses are rotting, or have been turned into bars or storage rooms. The old station in Corinthos houses a branch of the civil service: office clerks with their desks jammed in the old waiting rooms, the buffets and the Gents.

Slowly, beyond the city, mile by mile, we climbed into the higher ground of the northern Peloponnese. At Stymphalia Lake, we hit marsh land. Threshing forests of tall water reeds. A rippling tide of frogs, like a Mexican wave, leaping from under our feet as we trudged along the swamp.

This was where Hercules shot his deadly birds with their beaks of bronze for another of his Labours. We couldn't go any further though. Two mountains stood in our way.

One of the only railways that *is* left in the Peloponnese – an old rack and pinion track, 125 years old, toiled the 14 miles of deep wooded mountain and rock tunnel and river bridges of the Vouraikos gorge. The train sweated and groaned up the steep gradient climbs, complaining and chuntering to itself. At the top was the village of Kalavryta, where the flag was first raised on the monastery of Agia Lavra in 1821, signalling the start of the Greek War of Independence. In 1943 the Nazis burnt the monastery to the ground. Every man and boy of Kalavryta was taken to the hill above the village and made to watch as the women were led into the local school, locked in, and the building set on fire. All 700 men then gunned down. Giristroula and I stood on the vast monument to the dead and looked out at the Peloponnese rippling away before us.

Part 2
In Arcadia

    Giristroula's grandfather was brought down the outside stone stairs from the first floor. At the bottom, a crowd of mourners stood in the bare garden watching as the coffin was carried along. Men from his local kafeneo in the one old suit they owned, the old women who used to buy their currants and olives from him, Giristroula's family, with Giristroula's father heaving back great gulps of tears. Giorgos had had a long life. He'd outlived his wife by many years. He worked every day on his farm, right up until two days ago when he had come home, drunk the one glass of his own-made retsina he always allowed himself, gone up to his small single bed and fallen asleep. As unobtrusive a routine as his whole life had been. He hadn't woken again the next day. As Giorgos was carried out of the garden gate, his donkey brayed a sad little note. She would miss him most of all.

    Greek tradition states the dead cannot be left alone. Giristroula and I had raced back across the mainland of the Peloponnese as soon as we got the call. From where we were staying, in the southeast, to be back in Amaliada in the northwest of the peninsula. As soon as we arrived, Giristroula had been given the task of sitting with her grandfather, laid out on the dining room table, for the night shift. She sat on the hard chair next to the stiff body through the long hours. Now, in bright sunlight, Giorgos was slowly being driven through the streets of Amaliada. It shocked me that the coffin had been left wide open. The gawpers on the street were all able to peer in and see who was the latest in the town to drop off. The old men turning to look at each other with a sad look of recognition that one of their number had gone, and weighing up who was going to be the next under the slab. Someone told me it was the Turks who insisted the coffin stay open, so the Greeks weren't able to smuggle guns around during the years of their fighting for independence. Someone else, at the graveside edge, said that Giristroula's grandfather should be buried with a coin in his hand.

"How will he pay Charon the ferryman to get over the other side if he doesn't have a coin?"

I looked at the old man standing next to his friend's grave and gave him a smile. But it was no joke; he was completely serious in his panic about this unpaid journey to Hades.

Back at Giorgos's old dark home, the wake was a sombre affair. There is no drinking and carousing and rolling the carpet right back and dancing the old Gay Gordons to celebrate the recently departed in Greece. Nobody spoke in the dark dusty front room. Black bitter coffee was drunk, no sugar allowed. Plates of *koliva* – unappealing dishes of wheat and seeds – were handed out, with each piece needing to be blessed by the priest who was hanging around here in his grand robes. Standing around the room, dotted about in tense awkward silence, were also several of the odd figures of Amaliada.

There was Othonas, the crazy man of the town who walked around every day with a sheep's bell round his neck and cages of colourful birds, shouting out daily advice to every person he passed in the street. In the corner was the small round man who ran the local periptero kiosk with his large black moustache, his white vest and muscular weightlifter's body. He wrote poetry and had a permanent sad demeanour as no one ever took his verse seriously. Kyrios Karaflos – Mr Bald – the electrician and Kyrios Trichas – Mr Hairs – the ironmonger, who, predictably, disliked each other intensely but stood stiffly side by side. And there was Andreas. As a boy Andreas had been hopelessly in love with Giristroula. When they were at school together it was an open secret that he was sick with moon-eyed love for her. I felt very sorry for Andreas. He kept looking over shyly at Giristroula, but didn't seem confident enough to approach her. His father had been the local *Vothratzis* – the Shit Man. Before Amaliada installed a more efficient sewage system, his job had been to do the rounds and clear out the tanks in everyone's garden that connected to their toilets. He was greeted with a series of windows being closed, shutters banged tight and curtains quickly drawn wherever he went. Men would sit at opposite ends of the kafeneo when he came in after work. Andreas suffered a terrible stigma at school for his father's profession. The son of the Shit Man. Even now, 25 years later, he wavered on the edge of the mourner's gathering. And Giristroula looked the other way.

Giorgos was left to lie in the small cemetery of Amaliada. He was one of the lucky ones. People who die in Athens or Thessaloniki or other big urban areas of Greece aren't usually allowed to stay in their patches of peace. Dead city dwellers are temporarily buried in crowded graveyards, but the lack of space means they are exhumed three years later and the bones are given back to the relatives or boxed in an ossuary for a couple of decades before being dissolved in chemicals or tossed into a pit. No long sleeps of hoped-for tranquillity for them. Cremations in Greece are not allowed either. People have to ferry their dead over the border to Bulgaria for cremation if they don't want to be buried. But Giorgos rested now under his white marble gravestone, with the cross and the candle burning. His photo embossed into the headstone, next to his wife's.

We had been in Mistras when we got the call that Giorgos had died. We had travelled through Arcadia to get to Mistra, down the centre of the Peloponnese. Over folded mountains, rocky with a stain of green, tress clinging to the creases; past wide rivers – the Alfeios and the Pineios, which Hercules used in his fifth Labour to clean out the supernatural levels of cow dung in the Augean stables. Once over the mountains, Arcadia was full of fields that looked like rich comfortable beds. Clouds, like sheets, billowing out over the hills. Shepherds stood in these Arcadian fields, timeless and indestructible, like figures out of the bible. The clanging bells of their flock the only sound they had for company. In the villages, which would be teaming with life in summer but were slumbering in boredom now, the kafeneos were settled with the usual heavy smoke, idle bets and heaving lungs. The smack of cards, the clatter of backgammon.

I realised I was seeing the end of a certain Greece. When these old men with their old suits and koboloi die out, when the headscarfed old crones are gone, who is going to replace them? The younger generation with their iced *frappe* coffees? A particular look of Greece that has been around for hundreds of years would soon be gone for good. I sat outside a kafeneo and watched as one man took his donkey with him into the local chemist shop.

The land suddenly became flat. Wide plains, like inland green seas, gathered around the city of Megalopolis right in the middle of the Peloponnese. The bellybutton of the island. Pylons and belching chimneys rose up like columns around the city's edges. We went further along the plains. The patchwork of orchards and mulberry trees of Arcadia don't prepare you at all for the approaching austerity of Laconia. Sparta arrived and we drove through the modern town which is characterless compared to the glory of Sparta's past. Not that you would be able to guess the glories from any museums. The people of Laconia were hostile to wealth and beauty. Tough and militaristic and *laconic*. No pretty artefacts for them.

Giristroula and I stopped at a long thin crack in a rocky hill at Kaiadas. The bones of the children who were not thought tough enough to be Spartans litter the floor of this cave, piled under our feet as we stepped inside. The legend says that children were tossed of the top of Mount Taygetos in Sparta's fascistic eugenic cleansing ideals. Spartans had to be warriors, nothing more. Naked girls and boys competed in ferocious wrestling games; youths were sent to live on their own in the wilds to toughen them up for war. They'd have had more fun drenched in wine at an Athenian symposium, I'd have thought.

Mistras, glimpsed from a distance, looked striking. An abandoned 14th century fortress with the whole town lying around its feet in the cypress trees and the tall overgrown plants. The last great centre of the Byzantine world. It was hard work climbing the lanes. The ruined homes were depressing up close. Mistras was destroyed in the 1770s by the Maniots from further down the Peloponnese, over the Taygetos mountain range. Giristroula and I decided we would have to go and visit these Maniots, if they were even tougher and wilder than the Spartans. However, just as we were making plans, stood by someone's 700-year-old stone outside toilet, Giristroula received the news of her grandfather. Instead of further south, we would have to head back to her family home. The loud peals of the bells of the still-working Pantanassa Monastery rang out as we left. The spirits of the past were saying farewell.

It was clear Giristroula and I wouldn't get away from Amaliada to continue our Peloponnese journey for a while. Her mother had to get back to Athens and her work in the parliament and her father needed help at home. He moved around the house like a long shadow, quiet and sad, with his black arm band and mournful face. I was tasked with pulling the wood from the farm every day to the fill up the fireplace, Giristroula stirred the huge pans of lentils. Winter in Amaliada had properly set in. The cold got into the houses and the streets and infiltrated the trees. The sea along the Peloponnesian coast was a blinding metallic carpet under the winter sun. Sometimes the beach would be littered with the carcasses of sheep and goats that had fallen into the rivers upstream and been washed out to sea when the big storms that hit this side of Greece raged for days.

I sat wrapped up in the house and went through boxes of Giristroula's family old things. Photos and little keepsakes and memories. I let out a cry as I opened a small pill-box and came across a collection of teeth. When children's teeth fall out the tradition is to throw them up on the roof so the new ones will grow strong. Giristroula's mother couldn't bear to be without these mementos of her children and had later scrabbled up on the top of the house to get them back. I was told the roof of the house had at times served as a bedroom for the whole family during the roasting hot nights of summer. All of them lying up there at angles in the stifling heat, the smell of jasmine and the crickets still beating out loudly under the moon. Giristroula and her sister remembered cracking eggs up on the tiles in the afternoons and watching them sizzle and fry. When the house was being built, the priest who lived next door had come and asked to bless each part. He ran into the road with his hands in the air when he saw Giristroula's parents undertaking the other, superstitious, Greek ritual to safeguard a newly constructed house – spreading a freshly slaughtered cockerel's blood over all points of the ground the house was being built on.

I came across some old faded pages in one trunk of the family's things that I could see had been written by Giristroula's other grandfather, Stathis Georgopoulos. A good solid Peloponnese name. People of the northern Peloponnese usually get a '-poulos' at the ending of their surnames, meaning 'the child of.' Further down south you find surnames end in '-eas', and in the wild Mani names will end with an '-akos'. It's '-akis' in Crete and '-oglou' or '-idis' in Thessaloniki. You can accurately pinpoint someone's roots in Greece just by the last syllable of their name.

I tried translating the text that Giristroula's grandfather had written, years ago. As I traced the words it became clear he had been writing about his time as a guerrilla soldier, fighting in the resistance against the Germans as the Nazis swarmed over the Peloponnesian land.

The decision was taken that to beat the Germans, we must ambush them. The right place for this was the location of Pousi near Lala in the Highlands.

After noon, we could see a group of Germans were coming by the dust thrown up by their motorcycles. We were hidden close to the road and after letting them get to about 1,000 metres, we opened fire. This confused the enemy. They stopped and retreated to join the main bulk. We had let them know that it would not be so easy for them to move. That the road was well guarded by the ELAS guerrillas.

We moved again and reached the river Cladeo or Stravokefalo. (The river that runs through Ancient Olympia and flows into the Alfeios river). We started walking in the water. After a few hours it started raining and everybody was soaked. We walked through the darkness and the cold, sometimes tripping and falling into the flooded river. This was a terrifying ordeal, but one that we all endured without any fear because we all believed in the vow we had given for the liberation of our country.

At about midnight we arrived outside of Lala. We did not know if the Germans were ahead of us in the village. Something had to be done to find out. There was a barn near where we stopped. One of our comrades took a shepherd's cap and crook and, with his automatic gun (a Marsip which was looted from Germans we captured a month ago near Mirakas), he walked into the village. The Germans caught up with him. As soon as he arrived near the first houses he heard "Halt!" As the comrade told us later, he let the German think that he was from the village and showed him a house with a light on and indicated that this was where he lived. He entered the house through the door and jumped out of the window and crawled back to reach us.

We headed to Pousi, in the weeds and the stones (The road could not be used in case we were seen by the Germans). At four in the morning we prepared for the ambush. To the left was lower ground and on the right of the road a steep hill downwards, full of bushes. We set ourselves on the left. Standing in the rain and cold, we waited for the enemy. Our bodies were frozen. Our hands were shaking.

At half past seven, our forward guard in Lala notified us that the Germans were coming. 5 motorcycles and 2 trucks full of troops armed with heavy weaponry. As if by magic the cold and the shivering stopped. We were on fire waiting.

The Germans were ambushed...

I was amazed reading this. A narrated history from someone who was actually there when these pockets of shoddily-equipped, untrained, resistance fighters struck back at the occupying German forces. The Greek resistance that had fought so fiercely that Hitler had been forced to send more and more troops to keep Greece down, seriously disrupting his war plans in Europe.

"*I must verify that only the Greeks, of all the adversaries who confronted us, fought with bold courage and highest disregard of death,*" Hitler once said.

"The word heroism I am afraid does not render in the least those acts of self-sacrifice of the Greeks," declared Churchill. *"Greeks don't fight like heroes... heroes fight like Greeks."*

A proud moment from Greece's history.

Shortly after this though, the infighting of the Greeks and the betrayal of Britain brought out more shameful aspects of the country... Accompanying the yellow sheets were old photos. There was one of Stathis stood with a group of other disheartened-looking men in a fortified camp. Stathis had been a communist. He had fought with the communist guerrilla groups, the most effective of all the resistance against the Nazis. After the liberation of Greece, however, Britain and the controlling forces installed a right-wing government in the country. Stathis, along with many others who had fought the Nazis so bravely, was arrested and sent into exile to the islands of Ikaria before he was later moved to Ai Stratis and then Makronisos. He was tortured ruthlessly, like all those who had refused to sign a statement of repentance for their communist views. He was released after six years with serious health problems which plagued him for the rest of his life until, aged only 62, he died. Just a few weeks after Giristroula had been born.

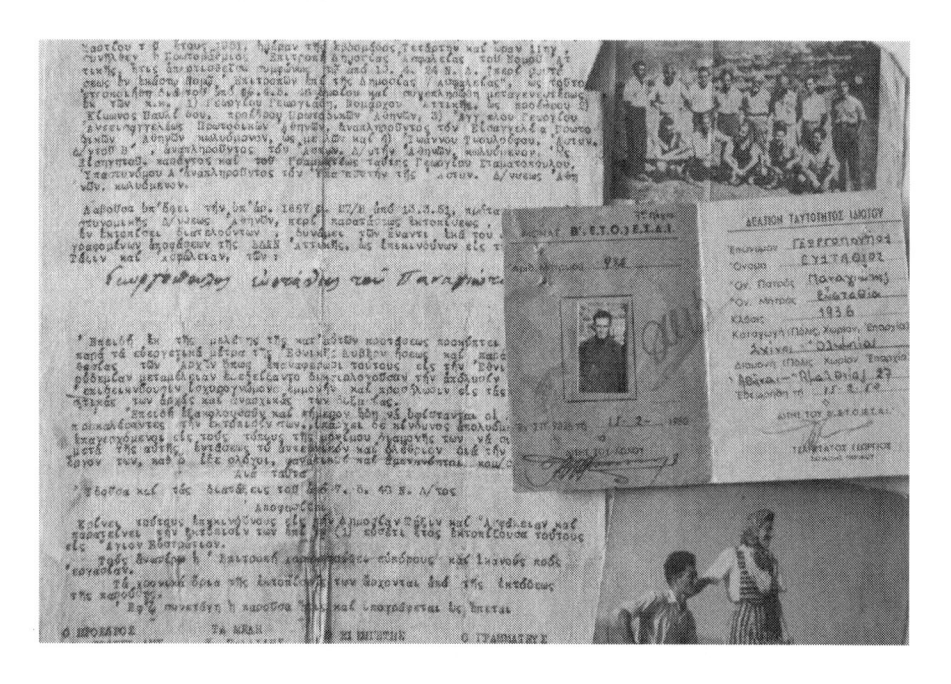

I asked why these scraps of writing and the letters and the photos were here, bundled away, and was told they had been hidden for years in the lining of Giristroula's grandmother's sewing box. After the installation of the right-wing government, and especially in the time of the dictatorship in Greece, the police could invade your house as they pleased. Anything incriminating or linking you to the left movement could lead to serious trouble. Giristroula's mother said that it was often the men working in the periptero kiosks that would grass people up. If you bought any newspaper from them that wasn't the regime's official one, you could be in for the knock on the door in the middle of the night.

Giristroula and I took a drive out to Pousi one cold, wet morning to stand in the spot her grandfather had stood and waited for the Germans to arrive. There is a monument here for what happened on that morning in December 1943. *'Human kind will always fight against slavery'* reads the inscription. Erected on the top of a steep hill, only bushes and silence around. The monument is graffitied over now, uncared for. In the nearby church is another forgotten monument for Theodoros Kolokotronis, the Arcadian general in the War of Independence, who fought a huge battle against the Turkish in, incredibly, the very same spot that Giristroula's grandfather and his comrades had stood, frightened and freezing, over one hundred and twenty years later.

We carried on, over the hills, past the wrinkled olive boughs. Goats stood high in the trees on the terraces of cut soil. We went past the temple at Vasses with its columns and Corinthian capitals hidden away in the deep Peloponnese and so kept from thousands of years of wars and conversions by Christians or Muslims, and kept from the pollution of modern-day Athens's rains.

The Lykaion mountain range looked like it had slipped anchor and drifted dangerously close to the small villages here, crushing them between the slopes and the sea. It was on these mountains, back in 2007, that some of the worst fires of Greece's history raged for several weeks over one long summer. Sixty-three people died. The sky across the whole of the prefecture was thick black, ash falling on the roof all the way back home in Amaliada. People were burnt alive in their cars trying to escape. Whole villages were flame-encircled and houses destroyed. The fires even reached Olympia, passing the ancient running track, scorching the outside of the museum. Giristroula's grandfather had employed an Albanian back on his farm to help him. At the funeral the Albanian had told me how he had been working on different land, up on these mountains when the fire broke out. He had fled through the cinder-dry forests but, knowing he could never outrun the flames, he instead dug himself a hole down in the ground and hid as the fire passed over him. He wore a haunted look as he recounted this.

"I could see no fire. I was looking, but I could see no fire... Then all the air went dry, and suddenly there it was. A wall of fire. Coming towards me..."

The joke in the rest of Greece was that the whole of Peloponnese got high from these fires, as the county of Ilia is well-known for its farms secretly growing marijuana hidden within its fields. But there was nothing to laugh at. This was a devastation for the county. As we drove along the mountains, there were still large areas where trees and crops hadn't grown back. Scalded hills. Black scar-tissue. It is a well-known rumour that the fires were the result of arson. Money-men who wanted to develop the land. The ravenous desire for that golden ticket of tourism... and the ruin it brings.

Down on the sea, past mile after mile of empty beaches, Kaiafas appeared. Plane trees behind the sea and sand dunes. A disused railway station and a dead line. Through the trees though, I could see broken buildings. Once these were hotels. We walked round the grounds with the windows falling out of these buildings, rusting iron beds in rooms left to rot in the open air. Giristroula's two grandmothers used to come here for weekends. They would sit and sew and gossip and at dawn each day they would get up and stand on the pier in the lake and wait for the ferry that appeared through the morning mist to take them away to the natural springs spa. Like an ancient mysterious ritual, they would disappear on the ferry, paying the ferryman not to take them on to Hades and the other world, but instead to somewhere they could try and reverse their aging. To try to find their youth that had long gone. Giristroula remembers how the two old women would come back, smiling and glowing and stinking of sulphur, sure they had taken years off their bodies.

Giristroula and I carried on down through her home county until we hit the Neda River, where Zeus as an infant was bathed and cleansed by the three nymph sisters. This is the border between the state of Ilia and the state of Messinia. The start of the real southern Peloponnese. We didn't dare go further. Not yet. But we would soon.

Spring had arrived, summer was coming; light was ripening over the fields; flowers had started blazing the grass. We stood by Neda's waterfalls, the branches of the trees splitting the sunlight into beams over the pools. The end of the Peloponnese was calling us on.

Part 3
Messenia, Mani & Maleas

Every slipped step set off a small landslide of stones cascading back down the slope behind us as we unsteadily climbed the Taygetos mountain range. Whichever way we looked, the bare empty views trembled in the heat. Just the one lone loyal tree remained on the mountainside. This mountain range runs from the greener easy-going outer Mani to the hard rocky empty inner Mani that has sat resentfully baking in the sun for millennia. The Mani peninsula stretches out at the very bottom of Greece, into the Mediterranean, reaching as far south as the mainland goes, groping down towards Crete and Africa. The middle finger of the Peloponnese fist.

Finally we could carry on travelling after our lay-off in Giristroula's hometown. We had reached the Mani by first coming round the Peloponnese's western digit: the peninsula of Messenia. In Messenia we had seen the great castles of Pylos and Methoni. It was in Pylos that modern Greece was finally set on the road to freedom... The three Great Powers – Britain, France and Russia – had once massed their ships in the very same harbour Giristroula and I had stood looking at. In October 1827, as these ships lay at anchor, facing off the Ottoman Empire's navy, playing a tense game of who-blinks-first, the fate of Greece's independence struggle was decided by one nervy, trigger-happy English sailor who accidentally set fire to his cannon and shot at an Egyptian navy boat fighting for the Turks. Shots were returned and soon battle raged. It was exactly what the British didn't want to happen. All the British had wanted was to *show* their power, not actually use it. Thick acrid smoke descended and filled the whole of the harbour, where now tavernas and cafés sit. When the smoke lifted and cleared, the Ottoman navy was revealed to be completely destroyed. Nothing but floating splinters left on the sea. The end of Turkish rule over the Greeks had started.

Pylos was also the home of Nestor, Homer's old man of endless advice during the Trojan War in the Iliad and Odyssey. His excavated palace sits in the hills above the town. Giristroula and I had stopped at a kafeneo below. A man had approached us, spinning his car keys on his fingers, as all Greeks do, the keys serving as a substitute koboloi: anything that can be used to distract, to entertain, to keep the mind from dwelling on life's problems too much. Just like his town's forefather, the man was keen to give us unsolicited advice.

"Koroni. You should go to Koroni."

We started to ask him why, but his open hand went up, his lips pursed, his eyes closed and his eyebrows rose upwards. He had said his piece. No further explanation would be needed or would be forthcoming.

So, we headed towards Koroni.

I don't know what it is like the rest of the time, we had got there late in the day when the town was at rest, heaving a great sigh to itself, but right there and then Koroni could have been the most tranquil place on earth. On the far tip of the Messenian peninsula, the sea lapping round its edges, the buildings giving back all the heat they had sucked in that day. A lone man walked past the taverns, under the late sun, carrying his shadow behind him. The town's ancient fort throbbed an orange colour high above. From Koroni, we had carried on through this southwestern land, round the groin between two legs of the Peloponnese, from Messenia to Mani. As we passed a village, we asked directions from two women sitting out on their doorsteps in the evening light, peeling beans, both of them singing their heads off.

"You take your *gaitharo* and head this way until you get to the crossing..." one of them said, calling our car a 'donkey' with no hint that she was joking.

We had by-passed the city of Kalamata, in no mood for clogged streets, and then started to climb. The Taygetos range starts straight after Kalamata, and rises rapidly, not waiting for any sort of invitation. Eight thousand feet it soars, throwing pyramid shadows over the Messenian Gulf below. We headed up a winding track and stopped for the night in the cramped village of Kampos next to one of two squat dilapidated Byzantine churches. Artemis, the goddess of hunting, was worshipped around these parts, surrounded by the forests and the streams that she was always getting caught bathing naked in, inflicting horrible retribution to those poor souls who stumbled upon her nude ablutions. After a morning scrub ourselves, Giristroula and I had tried to tackle a slope of the Taygetos range. It was a hard and heat-soaked ascent. Just a short climb and we were regretting our decision, slipping and sliding on the roasting ground. This was unforgiving terrain, not to be trifled with. And we were to go further into this hard-boiled land. There was no turning back now.

The Mani – slate grey and arid in the centre, sea lashed at the edges – runs for a hundred miles down to Cape Tainaron. For now, Giristroula and I were happy just to coast down into the pretty town of Kardamyli, shocked by our initial meeting with the harsh reality of the Mani, pleased for this bit of decorousness. We looked for a place to swim to cool off, away from the tourists in the town, the nice hotels, the trinket shops, the olive-oil boutiques. Down a broken track, off the coastal road heading south, we clambered over a barbed wall of rocks and found an empty, small, perfect beach of smooth stones. We swam out towards an islet and back again and it was only when we were back on the beach that I noticed some stone steps leading up the cliff side.

Wet footed, we padded up to see what was there, as the sun set and a hundred swallows appeared, diving in the sky around us, to catch their dinners. At the top of the stairs we were startled to see there was a villa and grounds laid out. The first reaction was to turn quickly, apologetically, away. But something seemed wrong. It was clear nobody was at home. In fact the whole house seemed wrong. We walked further in. The grounds were marked out with coloured pebbles, heavy stone tables and benches looking towards the wide sea view. An ornate compass carved into the paving stones pointed the radius directions: Βοράς... Ανατολή... Νότος... Δύση... The French windows were decaying and hung open. In the house there were tables, lamps, bookcases covered in dust and grit. The last of the sun flung a flowered pattern through the window onto the fireplace's white wall. On the mantelpiece there was a clutter of cards and notes and pictures and a black and white photo of a uniformed hero. I recognised the man... and suddenly I realised where we were. This was Patrick Leigh Fermor's house. That man again. The 'Paddy' we had run into in Crete and Hydra. I'd read he'd had a house somewhere around Kardamyli. This must have been it. How long had it been deserted? How long had Leigh Fermor been dead? I didn't know. Why had no one wanted to take over this impressive sprawling place?

Why had it been left to fall into semi-ruin? The bedroom was stark and austere as a monk's, the corridors all laid out like a monasteries' too. A separate writing room, a colossal kitchen, all slowly falling apart. There was absolutely nobody about, the sun had died, and so Giristroula and I hunkered down on the old sofa under the dirty window of the living room, cocooned with old books roosting like birds on the shelves.

Next morning we were woken by voices. Workmen. Guiltily nervous at being caught, as the workmen started banging and sawing in another part of the house, we bundled up our clothes and stole away. Down the stone cut steps and out onto the beach. We stalked over the rocks and said a quiet thanks to Leigh Fermor for the night's stay.

Further on down the coast, we found Kalogria beach. I'd read this was where Nikos Kazantzakis had taken a house to live in while he worked in a lignite mine in the hills above. He later wrote about this time living here, on this beach, with his cunning, lusty, zestful engineer friend Zorba – Zorba the Greek. I didn't believe we would find this house, but as we tramped past the sun-soakers on the sand, there, perched on some sharp edged rocks stood a small white one-storey house, all alone. The rocky shore, the sandy stretch of beach for dancing on, the hills above: it all looked exactly as I'd imagined from the book. The door swung open.

"*Eh! Ti girevete!*"

A man in his underpants and a white vest shoved his angry face out.

"Were you going to open my door just then?"

I took a step back. Surprised. He marched forward, grabbed me by the shirt.

"Eh? Were you going to open my door?"

"No…" I said.

"I could have been naked!"

He had a big round red face, perfectly bald head, as if it had been boiled. A gold cross around his neck, glinting and winking in the sun.

"Was this Kazantzakis's house?" I asked. This was a mistake.

"*Ti?*" he put his big red face close to mine. "What did you say?"

"I thought this might have been Kazantzakis's house?" I repeated. He pulled me inside, through the door.

"See this stove?" he banged his hand on his old iron oven. "It's mine. See this table?" he slapped heavily on the wooden table. "Mine." He pulled me through the small kitchen out of the back door. "My fridge... See this well? Mine... Kazantzakis's house?" he spat into my face. "It's *my* house! I'm fed up with you people coming to look every day..."

I made my apologies and he watched us like a hawk all the way back over the beach, glaring at us as we passed the sun-worshippers, up the gentle slope again towards the main road leading away to the south.

Areopoli. A market town. Streets were centred round a decorated Byzantine church: carved flowers, cherubs, sun and moon faces on the buttresses. One man sat at a café table, smiling absent-mindedly at a sleeping dog in the road. Peace rested over everything in the heat. But this is a town named after *war*. Areopoli was the base of Petrobey Mavromichalis, the leader of the Maniots in the fight against the Ottoman Empire. Mavromichalis was such a great warrior that the Mani was never truly run by the Ottomans as the rest of Greece was. A precious independence that the Maniots cling to their psyche to this day. In 1821 Mavromichalis marched north towards central Peloponnese, meeting Kolokotronis, the leader of the Arcadian men, along the way in Kardamyli. A few days ago Giristroula and I had stood in the old church in Kardamyli, the scene of Mavromichalis and Kolokotronis's meeting, where the two men played a giant game of chess in the courtyard using their men as pieces. Together they attacked the Turkish garrison at Kalamata. Then further fierce battles took place, the Ottoman navy was destroyed in Pylos and, by 1830, Greece was an independent state.

The thin, haughty-looking Corfiot, Ioannis Kapodistrias, who I had seen preening in many portraits and statues back when we lived in Corfu, became the first head of the Greek state. This nobleman of distinguished standing, unsurprisingly, didn't see eye-to-eye with the rough, moustachioed *kleftis* Mavromichalis, even though he had done so much to free Greece. Kapodistrias left nothing to chance and soon imprisoned Mavromichalis. The Mavromichalis family had their revenge though. Of course they did, they were Maniots. Kapodistrias was assassinated in cold blood on the steps of the church of Saint Spiridon back in Nafplio town, where Giristroula and I started our journey around these Peloponnese lands. The delicate, mannered world of Kapodistrias's Corfu that I could picture so clearly with the colonnaded Venetian galleries and lanes and the green flowering fields was trounced by this hard world of the Mani, with its own tough codes and laws. Or its lack of them.

Everyone in the Mani called us 'Koroni'. Especially Giristroula.

"*Ya sou Koroni…*" the old men raised a glass at her as we walked past.

"*Efharisto Koroni mou…*" the old ladies said as they gave back her change.

"*Ade Koroni…*" the rough men reluctantly said to me as I lifted a glass of ouzo in their direction in the taverna.

Koroni means crown. I couldn't understand why they kept calling us 'crowns'. It was a very odd sort of greeting. The man who brought us the food at the tavern had an elaborate tattoo of a golden crown, gilded with three arches, around his forearm. As I stared at this, it dawned on me. The people Mani are famous for being great supporters of the old deposed Greek royal family. This love of royalty comes from the time after Kapodistrias's death when the German king, Otto, was installed to rule over a Greece still taking its first teetering new-born steps. Otto attempted to modernise the country. He built grand neo-classical buildings in Athens; he imposed new taxations and spending; he even brought Fix beer with him. But Otto allowed the Mani to keep its singular ways of life, as long as they reined in the bloodbaths and battling – as much amongst themselves as against anyone else. So a passionate pro-monarchy feeling has remained here ever since. The Maniots were dismayed when Otto was deposed. Otto was devastated too, spending the rest of his days back in Bavaria pining for the country he had ruled and he died in Germany in 1867 looking a ridiculous figure, still wearing the Greek national tsolias costume: skirt, fez, stockings, *tsarouhia* pom-pom slippers. There was misery in the Mani when King Alexander of Greece died from a bite from his pet monkey. They enjoyed the reign of the right-wing dictator-supporting King George II and, after the fall of the military junta in 1974 when Greece voted in a referendum as to whether the monarchy should be abolished, the only area in the whole country to vote to keep the King was the Mani.

The man serving us with his crown tattoo around his forearm told me he believed the old King, still living, exiled in London, was the true ruler of Greece. "He's not the ex-King Constantine," he corrected me. "He is *the* King Constantine…"

Giristroula and I left Areopoli and carried on travelling southwards. The road hugged the coastline on our right and I looked down along the sea edge of Mani at cape after cape after cape. On our left, grey mountains and a path that rose up the mountain slope, fell back down again, only to rise up the hard slope once more. A futile route over a devastatingly empty scene. We were definitely now in the inner Mani. The landscape was nothing but huge cactuses, thorns, stones. Inedible prickly pears, a diseased-coloured pink, hung from the huge round paddles of the cactus. It was a shattered looking land. The idea that anyone would fight over this land seemed quite ludicrous, but the Maniots did. Violently.

As Giristroula and I travelled further down into the deep Mani, tall stone buildings rose up each time we met a new village. Every small village had two, three, four high square stone towers dominating the scene. A few new builds had been erected around these hundreds-of-years-old towers, and some of the villages were still inhabited, but many were deserted. There were just the ends of ruined buildings standing like headstones, while the rest of the house had disappeared. Houses like ghosts. But everywhere along the inner Mani route, these towers stood. Towers that were built from the 18th century onwards for status, and to deter unwanted visitors.

During Greece's seemingly endless history of catastrophes, strangers often fled over the Taygetos mountains seeking refuge. These pockets of strangers appearing in the cut-off world of the Maniot villages caused great consternation amongst the Maniots. Towers would be built to ward off the strangers, and the strangers themselves would then build their own towers. Sometimes the towers would be right next to each other, facing off over the thin strip of pathway in the village. Extra floors would be built in the night, building them taller than your neighbour – dick waving. But when the fighting began, then there were no holds barred. Rifles and cannons firing at virtually point-blank range. Anyone walking in the streets when battle was fair game. But not priests or doctors. They were sparred to nervously dance the paths amongst these killing zones. Only the fight against the Turks would eventually unify these warring neighbours against a bigger enemy. And what was the reason behind all this fighting? To gain some sort of small ascendancy in this hard world. To be king of these rock fields. Ruler of a land of bare stone.

Vathia emerged in the distance. The Manhattan Island of these stone flat-top towers. Spike after spike of tower reached up from the village, stretching into the Mani sky. Giristroula and I walked around. It was completely deserted. I climbed into one crumbling tower, up the ladders into different rooms, the decayed wooden floors creaking below my feet. I looked out of the slit windows, across the Mani coast.

I would have had a great shot here at anyone down into the street below. There was no one about though. An abandoned café with a collapsing roof, Loux lemonade dried up and black in the old dirty glass bottles. The village had a *plateia* – the square every village or town in Greece must have for the gossiping of the old woman and the parading of the young girls in the summer evenings. Vathia's square was clean but dated, whitewashed. But it showed there must still be people here, somewhere. We walked around the tight lanes, past the ruins, and there sat on a stool, caught in roasting beam of sun in a derelict alleyway was a woman dressed fully in black. She was sitting, staring at the ground.

"Everyone has gone," she said. "They all left for Athens. They all live in Piraeus. Oh you see a few people come back for the summer, but I'm about the only one who stays here all year… And in the winter, when the wind blows through these mountains, when the cold bites, I'm doubly cursed. The wind is worse than the heat. It shaves you to the bone. *Xirizi*…"

Onwards, downwards. Carrying on through the Mani. The punishing rock landscape didn't change. The Maniots we had sat drinking ouzo with in the tavern all enjoyed telling the old joke that when God had finished making the earth, he found he still had a bag of rocks left over. Not knowing what do with the rocks, they say he just dumped them all over the Mani.

A huge bird flew slowly, soundlessly, high above us out towards the Messenian Gulf like someone in a boat pulling at the oars over the blue sky. The Mani is a thirsty landscape. Despite being surrounded by the sea, and the Maniots being feared pirates, of course, there was a severe lack of fresh water. It used to have to be brought in tankers here. People talk endlessly about water, think about it, dream on it. One of the old tavern men told me that when he wanted to marry, his wife's family only had one question about him: did he drink a lot of water? If he was going to move in to the family home and he was one of those people who liked to drink lots of water, that was it, the marriage was off.

Down on the coast, we passed Gerolimena. Comfortable well-off families sunbathing in front of a golden sea here. Clean tavernas on a road looping round the quay. Nothing to remind you of the villages in the barren mountains just above.   And then we reached the tip of the very southern point of mainland Greece: Tainaron. A long walk over sizzling red, ankle-snapping, rocks took us to the lighthouse at the very edge of Europe. I tried to edge-out as far as I could off the cape. The rocks submerging and then reappearing under the bright turquoise sea. I perched on one rock and turned inland, thinking how, from this point, I could walk back over the whole continent, 5,500 miles to the very furthest northern point, Cape Nord in Norway. I closed my eyes and tried to picture my walk. Poseidon had no time for such trivial nonsense and a large darting wave slapped me on my side, knocking me off my feet, plunging me into the sea. I was buffered back and forth by other whipped-up waves, crunching me into the rocks, dragging me under the surface. I battled to get back to shore, pulling myself up the hard shelf and sat on the dead-grass above, breathing heavily. We would have had a fine grandstand view of the Battle of Matapan here, when, just off the coast in 1941, the Italian and British Navies fought in close battle, littering and deranging this strip of sea. Now the sea is a multi-lane motorway for the great tankers steaming along the edge of Greece's final shoreline.

Below Cape Tainaron is one of the openings down into Hades. A sea cave in the threshing waters and a portal to take the dead down to the underworld, like the River Acheron Giristroula and I had waded in northern Greece. The cave in Tainaron was where Hercules, in the final and most deadly of his 12 Labours, brought back Cerberus, the vicious three-headed guard dog of Hades. It was also where Orpheus had descended into the underworld to bring his wife Eurydice back from the dead. Orpheus sang his way in and Charon the ferryman, the Furies, and all The Shades in Hades wept. No one could refuse Orpheus and his music, so he was told he could take Eurydice back to earth on the one condition that he led the way on the journey and did not look back until they were both back out in the light of the sun. Orpheus was just reaching the end of the long ascent when, eager to see his wife and afraid her strength might be failing, he looked back. At once Eurydice slipped away forever back into the darkness.

Retracing our steps, Giristroula and I found a deserted pebbled beach, near the village of Kyparissos, and a deep cave which was perfect for the night. Later I was told that where we had slung our sleeping bags was the very place where Petros Mavromichalis's father, Giorgos, had met and mated with a mermaid. This remarkable conception was the reason behind his son's later legendary actions. The next morning we travelled round the end of the far point of the Peloponnese again. Over onto the eastern side of the Mani. The distance between the opposite sides of the cape is less than a kilometre here. We passed large graffiti painted on the road leading out to Tainaron. We must have passed this graffiti yesterday too, but I hadn't seen it. Chrysi Avgi – the Golden Dawn fascist party, underlining Maniot reputation for politics of a stronger flavour than mere royalism.

We travelled up the eastern flank of the Mani. With nowhere further south to go in Greece, we were now heading north. We were on the other side of Taygetos mountains. They looked just as hard. No shade from the punishing sun anywhere. For mile after mile the landscape was just naked rock; the buildings sculptured rock, the difference between the two almost imperceptible. Then, at Kotronas, the Mani simply ended. Just like that. There was no warning, there was no expectation. Suddenly the mountains turned thick and green. Areopoli must be on the other side of the Mani, over on the west, 10 or 15 kilometres across.

We hit a big town, which was a shock. Gytheio lay open in the hot sun. Wide seafront roads, pastel-coloured buildings climbing the hills, little fishing boats on the water bobbing a welcome to us like nodding heads. The island moored just off Gytheio was the first stopping off point for Paris and Helen after he'd abducted her from Mycenae, that great coiling palace we had seen on its hill in northern Peloponnese. It was an odd direction for Paris to be travelling. He was making poor tracks towards Troy.

We rounded the curve of the Laconia Gulf, the third leg of the southern coast of Peloponnese, heading down to the Cape of Moreas. The landscape here was mild, compared to all we had seen in the Mani. There were even oranges hanging from the trees. A group of unhappy looking Pakistani men employed as orange pickers, trudged in the fierce open heat along the dusty road.

The landscape may be tame, but the seas around this coast are feared. It was around this cape that Odysseus's boat was blown off course, leaving him hobbled, careering through the Greek seas, unable to get back to his home for those long 10 years. Spirits would feast on the shipwrecks here. More recently an old hermit lived on the tapering final rocks, living off the charity of the sailors as they sailed past.

Giristroula and I pitched up for the night, at the very edge of Greece once again, and watched the huge cargo ships, far too big to get through the Corinth Canal, taking the long journey around the Peloponnese. Bright lights in the dark night gliding by. I called out, but no sailor stopped with any charitable offerings for us.

Next day, we headed up the eastern side of Cape Moreas, with the Aegean Sea now on our right. Monemvasia looked like a Martian rock thrown clean out of the sky, landing on the seashore. The medieval fort town built on its hill, cut off from the mainland by an earthquake, is full of winding alleyways, stone lanes, apricot-coloured Frankish homes. Forty churches. The Byzantines, the Crusaders, the Venetians, the Turks, they've all been here in their time. Monemvasia was now on her back suckling the tourists and day-trippers. Two huge wedding parties were moving around in her narrow streets: one from Britain, one from Sweden. It was busy and expensive and not especially welcoming to two wandering chancers. Everyone was dressed in clean linen suits, we looked like tramps. But we had somewhere to stay.

Just through the huge stone gate into the town, up a flight of stone steps, Giannis Ritsos, the great poet of Greece was born and grew up. The hard southern Peloponnese land around the Maleas and the Mani affected Ritsos deeply in his poetry.

These trees are not happy with less sky
These stones are not happy under foreign boots
These faces are only happy under the sun
These hearts are only happy when there is justice
There is no water! Only light.

Through a family connection of Giristroula's, with her grandfather and Ritsos interned together in a prison camp after the Second World War and Giristroula's mother later becoming firm friends with Ritsos's daughter, we had the key to Ritsos's faded old pink house. The haughty gallery owners and disdainful restaurateurs looked appalled that we had found a right to be here.

I later walked out to the lighthouse on the edge of Monemvasia, onto another jutting piece of Greece. I looked out over the water, and then turned to the lighthouse building. I tried a door, which to my surprise opened. I went in.

The lighthouse master was laid out on the table, surrounded by his radio equipment and maps. He was fast asleep, a cigarette still burning in his mouth. His arm hung down, a koboloi dangled, suspended from his fingers, swaying in the dusty air. I retraced my steps and shut the door. He didn't wake.

Chapter 9
Belogiannis and the Greek Village

The first policeman turned to his colleague.

"We've really lost this, haven't we Gianni?"

Giannis, in his shabby policeman's uniform, looked around at the crowds spilling out over the pavements, gathering around the Prime Minister of Greece, pushing at him, manhandling him, jostling him along the street.

"You know, I think we probably have..."

Giannis took off his peaked police hat, rubbed at his sweat-streaked forehead with the heel of his hand and looked morosely up at the midday sun.

Greece's Prime Minister, Alexis Tsipras, had come to Amaliada to open a museum dedicated to local-born Nikos Belogiannis. The police force of the town had never had to deal with an event of such a magnitude in these sleepy streets before. Tsipras was lurched and shouldered further along the road, past the faded pink building of Belogiannis's old home.

Nikos Belogiannis is a hero of the Greek Left. He was a great figure in the Greek resistance to the Nazi occupation in the country during the Second World War when Belogiannis and his fellow communists had been instrumental in liberating Greece. It looked as if, after the war, the country might have even established itself as a communist-governed country. American and British imperialistic machinations soon put an end to this idea, however, and put Greece on the road to civil war. The Greek Army, backed by the Americans who were desperate to keep a foothold in the Balkans and on the Mediterranean, fought pitched battles with the Greek Communist Army. A vicious and destructive struggle through the country for five long years.

Terrible atrocities carried out on both sides. The country, already ravaged by the years of starvation and hardship of the Nazi rule, was brought to its knees. When the communists were ultimately defeated, Belogiannis was arrested. The trial was a farce. A show trial which Belogiannis knew would always end in his execution.

"We love Greece and its people," Belogiannis said from the stand. "We love them more than our accusers. This is why we struggle – so that our country will see better days, without hunger, without war."

On March 30th 1952, Belogiannis was taken from his cell to Goudi Park. On a scrap of wooded land, under the glare of the truck's headlights, he was shot dead. He was executed quickly, in the middle of the night, to prevent unrest stirring up in Athens. Nevertheless, condemnation rang out around the world. Politicians, prominent figures, celebrities from Sartre to Charlie Chaplin spoke out against the Greek government's brutal actions. Pablo Picasso was so moved at the unjust nature of Belogiannis's fate that he sketched his famous portrait – 'The Man with the Carnation'.

The legend of Belogiannis would last through the years. In the 1960s, Greece was living under harsh military dictatorship. The dictator Georgios Papadopoulos had actually sat on Belogiannis's joke-trial jury. In April 1967 the Rolling Stones played at Panathinaikos's stadium. Mick Jagger, flouncing around in his usual fashion on the stage, threw flowers into the crowd. The police, thinking the flowers were carnations and thinking of Belogiannis and his symbolic flower, believed Jagger was making a gesture of leftist solidarity and stormed the crowd. Rioting, a smashing of the stadium and hundreds of arrests followed.

Greece and its clashing politics: always a storm ready to blow.

Giristroula and I were sat in a silver people carrier with three old ladies and a Hungarian MP. The car swerved onto the pavement in front of Budapest's huge People's Park and another group of old Hungarian ladies, and one solitary, happy-looking, old man joined us in the packed car. They were all speaking Greek. It was the 30th of March. Driving the car was Laokratis, a Hungarian MP who sat in the Greek parliament, representing the over 4,000 Greek descendants living in Hungary today. The old timers in the car were some of these Greek descendants. All of them had been brought to Hungary during the Greek Civil War. Some of them as orphans, some with their families, but all children were initially taken away from their parents.

"We were put up in the old aristocrats' deserted homes to begin with," the white-haired, sturdy old woman told me as we bounced along the wide roads leading out of Budapest. "It was very exciting. The big homes that were taken from their owners by the communists, we had them all to ourselves!"

But in these dilapidated grand old houses, they were given strict psychological testing. Only months later were they finally allowed to join the other Greek refugees in the village we were now heading towards.

South of Budapest, over the beginnings of the Great Hungarian Plains, the land was flat, bare and stark on all sides of the car. After just 40 minutes we pulled off the main road, bumped over a rail track and there, standing proudly, were two town signs in different languages on a post just a few metres before a large Greek Orthodox Church: 'Μπελογιάννης' – 'Beloiannisz'.

Built in the early 1950s, this village was created from nothing to house those who had had to flee from their home country of Greece due to reprisals at the end of the Civil War. Communists, who had fought with the beaten EAM army, experienced vicious retribution. These violently dispossessed Greek families were welcomed in by countries behind the Iron Curtain recently drawn across Europe. But only in Hungary was a complete Greek village built solely for the Greeks who had been made to leave their homeland.

We drove further into Beloiannisz village. It had originally been called Görögfalva – simply meaning 'Greek Village' in Hungarian – but soon it was renamed after the great hero of the communists, the man who had only recently been executed in Goudi park. We were visiting this village on this day as it was the anniversary of Belogiannis's death. As MP for Amaliada, Giristroula's mother had been invited to the village, but at this very moment she was lying desperately ill on the top floor of Athens's Evangelismos hospital. She had begged her daughter to attend this occasion in her place. Giristroula hadn't wanted to leave her mother's bedside, however, her mother had made it very clear how important it was to have someone from the family to represent her. It was not just a political duty, it was something deeper in the blood than that. Giristroula's grandfather had fought alongside Belogiannis up in the mountains of Epirus. It was a family honour to be here. We climbed out of the silver People Carrier into a chilly Hungarian late afternoon. The main square of the village had a sign on the wall – Amaliada Square.

They were setting up speakers on the bright patterned tiles of the main square. Playing Greek music, getting ready for a presentation. I stood next to an old lady, dressed against the chill. She was looking down the arrow straight road. *Odos Athena* the street sign said in Greek, *Athen u* below in Hungarian. She looked upset.

"Are you ok? I asked. Then I realised I should try *"Ola kala?"*

She took my hand. "I helped build this village..."

This old woman had been taken from her family as a teenager in Epirus, in the northern lands of Greece, in 1948. She was one of the Greeks here who, after they had been given this small plot of land by the Hungarians, built the houses, the town hall, the school, the bakery. She came back every year on the day of Belogiannis's death. Every year it upset her.

Giristroula and I took a walk down the roads to see the village. The straight main road led, in both directions, pretty much nowhere. Other roads crossed over, in dull parallel lines. They also led out into just cold bare countryside. Some kids cycled past, the first few talking in Hungarian, those behind talking to each other in Greek. The village hadn't really been built in Greek style. The houses were flat and one-story high and very Hungarian-looking. And, with the best will in the world, it couldn't really be called a beautiful place. We walked along the broken-down fences: junk heaped in the yards, broken down Eastern European cars rotting next to grim houses, livid dogs on chains barking and baring their teeth and singing a horrible tune into the air as we passed. Having exhausted all options in the village, we returned to the main square. The old lady was still there.

"It is a very nice village, no?" she said. "This village has *money*," she puffed-out proudly. "Other villages in Hungary are very poor. Oh, you would be very disappointed if you saw them..."

The crowds were starting to gather in the square. Many of the Greek descendants of the village – over half of the 1,000 or so people who lived here still called themselves Greeks – plus other Greeks from all over Hungary. They milled in front of the town hall, waiting for things to happen. Giristroula and I had a look inside the town hall. It was as cold as a freezer. Along the walls were framed black and white photos of the village being built. Greeks set down here, a thousand miles away from their homes, with shirts off, rudimentary tools in hand, laying bricks, digging trenches. All of them seemed to have a look of apprehension, of loss, but also of a fierce determination. Upstairs we went through a door and found a room bursting full with racks and racks of Greek traditional costumes: elaborate *karagouna* dresses, fluttering down from their hangers and as colourful as the Queen of Hearts; foustanella men's skirts; embroidered jackets; Greek tasselled caps on shelves; bright red fezzes. It was a vivid, bizarre sight to see them here, with the grey-twilight Hungarian sky and fields lying through the windows beyond.

We left the town hall building and, stepping back onto the square, walked straight into an old tall Hungarian-looking peasant. A long, holey coat, straw beard streaked with tobacco stains, mad hair under a Russian hat with ear flaps. He stared at us with wild eyes.

"*Szia*," I said – hello – one of only the few words of Hungarian I'd picked up since we'd been there.

"*Ya sas*," he said back, in a perfect Greek accent.

The presentation on this day of Belogiannis's death was about to begin. Speeches of his heroism, the struggle of the Communist fighters in Greece, the burdens they had suffered building this town, the pain of being banished so far from their homelands. Garlands were placed at the memorial for Nikos Belogiannis.

"And we have two people from Belogiannis's town of Amaliada here today," the mayor of Beloiannisz said into the microphone. "They should come and speak to us..."

Giristroula and I were pushed to the front. We weren't prepared for this. Giristroula apologised for her mother's absence. She talked of the museum in Nikos Belogiannis's old house, and how Beloiannisz village and Amaliada were sister towns and that Amaliada will always be there to help them if they can. The crowd seemed touched at the connection between the two nations, linked by this one man. Then they all looked towards me. It was clear they expected me to say something. There was a long drawn-out pause as the villagers of Beloiannisz stared. Children poked heads around parents' legs. A huge waiting silence with a few small coughs from the back. I couldn't think of *what* to say. I looked across the crowd gathered on the square dedicated to the town back in Greece I'd adopted as mine. I stepped forward.

"*Zito o Belogiannis!*" I boomed into the mic.

There was a long howl of silence. A crow cackled somewhere on the cold roofs. And then someone at the front of the crowd slowly started clapping. Another joined in. Then another. The clapping got louder and louder.

"*Zito o Belogiannis!*" the crowd called out. "*Zito!*"

The mayor told me I was the first Englishman to have come to the village. He introduced me to some of the old timers. Men who had been here since the village's conception.

"You would have loved this town," said one. "There were four kafeneo on this square. Four! Ah we had such good *kefi*. Dancing, music..." he shook his head in happy memory. "Now we just have the one kafeneo in the town. You see, now that we have more Hungarians here... well... you know. Hungarians are a bit more closed than us Greeks..."

The Greeks of Beloiannisz were allowed to travel. Unlike the Hungarians in the other towns or villages, or in Budapest, the Greeks were granted greater freedoms. They were also sent money from back home. It seemed that what the old lady told me was true, this village was richer than other Hungarian villages, and the Greeks here still are. I had seen that Laokratis, the MP for these displaced Greeks and Greek descendants, who remarkably is allowed a seat in the Greek parliament in Athens, had brought boxes with him. I had thought perhaps they were for the Greeks, but he'd actually brought them for the Hungarians of the village.

One thing the Greeks weren't allowed though was to practise their religion. Once Communism fell in the early 90s however, the Greeks of Beloiannisz found themselves finally free to embrace a religion that many had forgotten and some hadn't ever known. In 1995 they constructed an Orthodox church here: traditional Byzantine tower, cruciform shaped, iron gates with the two-headed eagle looking east and west. Laokratis and a few of the village elders told us there was to be a service in the church, celebrating the recently passed date of March the 25th – Greece's day of independence from the Turkish Empire.

The church inside, with its newly painted ikons on the walls and the ceiling, was a little tacky. The Orthodox priests had been bussed in from Budapest and didn't speak any Greek, only ancient Greek for the liturgy. I am no expert myself in matters of Orthodox procedure, but I could see the village folk really didn't know much more than me. They mouthed the words, were unsure when to cross themselves and when to stand or sit. But they were utterly earnest in their participation in these fairly recently initiated practices. Perhaps a little over-keen. But they just didn't have the natural, unthinking movements; the religious muscle-memory of those back in Greece. It had all been learned from scratch, and it seemed to take a lot of effort.

After the service, we piled out of the gates. An extraordinarily Hungarian-looking man was standing on the path. Tall, upright, flattop haircut, sad eyes and a huge dropping Magyar moustache; this man had been waiting, a little stiffly, outside the church for the service to end, not daring to go inside. He was the local MP for the area, but unlike Laokratis, this man represented all the citizens, not just the Greeks, and sat in the Hungarian parliament not the Greek. There was an election coming up in Hungary, so the MP had made an appearance today to curry favour with the Greek community. He came back with us to a building next to the town hall, on one of the sides of Amaliada Square which a sign told me was the Greek Cultural Centre.

Inside it was impressive: a long hall with a lit-up stage at one end and rows and rows of seats. The hall was decorated with large portraits of Greek heroes – Kolokotronis and Bouboulina – those who had driven the Turks out of Greece two centuries ago. The children of the village were going to put on a performance to celebrate the March 25th Revolution. I took a seat and nodded to the old man next to me. He told me his name was Zisis, and he was originally from Kastoria in northern Greece. He was the old mayor of this town and was one of the very first to come and build the village as a young man.

The lights went down and we all stood up as the national anthems were sung. First was the Hungarian one. It was mumbled through without much effort. Then the Greek anthem struck up and everyone stood upright and sang hard and loud with patriotic gusto: fists clenched, chest flung forward. The curtains opened and the village school teacher was surrounded by her youngest children. All dressed in the karagouna costumes. These five or six-year-old kids were word perfect, telling us the story of the Greek fight for independence. They were followed by students performing dance after dance. All brilliantly dressed, all the moves carried off expertly. The girls dancing *syrtaki* and *kalamatiano*. The older boys, with red sashes round their shoulders and billowing white shirts, leaping head-high in the air, brushing imaginary dust contemptuously off their pom-pomed shoes as they fell, landing lightly on the stage. Jumping up onto their partners and hanging suspended with their legs wrapped around the other's waists.

All these Greek dances, all these Greek stories. Could these kids – three generations, at least, away from Greece – really understand what it all meant? They had obviously been raised on a strict diet of Greek culture, that much was obvious, and the amount of practice they must have put in for these dances meant they clearly had a passion for it, but could it really *mean* anything to them?

Zisis leaned in close to me and told me something.

"Most of them up there are Hungarians you know…"

I was amazed by this. I had understood that the Greek decedents would want to follow the culture, keep a link to their history, but the Hungarians who moved into this village later as well? They seemed keener, more intense on celebrating March 25th than many of those back in Greece. It was very strange.

As the dances and songs continued, I made my way outside for a breather. Rain splattered the square. The light from the cultural centre door threw itself over the wet black paving stones. I noted that the only people outside now in the dark, milling around in the rain, were Hungarians. Drinking dripping cans of beer, looking in enviously and listening to the music coming from the well-lit warm building. In the hallway I talked to one of the teachers from the local school. She told me that, originally, all lessons were in Greek, and in the afternoon the students learnt Hungarian privately. As the dynamics started to change and more Hungarians came to live in the village, it was reversed and lessons were conducted in Hungarian and later Greek would be taught in private lessons.

"Now, thanks to him," the school teacher said, nodding over at Laokratis "the school teaches both Greek and Hungarian equally."

"Why would the Hungarians want that?" I asked. I was genuinely curious as to why they would learn a whole new language in their own country.

"We tell them 'If you learn the language and if you can learn the culture, this is all you need. You will become a Greek. And they love it! They love the idea of becoming Greeks."

I talked to Laokratis after the performance, as we walked over to a reception where a Greek feast had been laid out in another large building off the square.

"Most people I talk to in Hungary realise I'm not quite a Hungarian," he said. "After all this time, nearly my whole life here, when I've spoken to them for a while people will look at me, a little confused, and say '...and so where are you from?' I have to tell them 'Ah... it's a very long story...'"

One old man and his wife were sat at the dinner. The way people talked to them, gathered around them, fetched them food and drinks and made sure they were happy, it was clear they were respected people in this village. I went over to say hello and, as we spoke, I found this man was the very last survivor in the village of those who had actually fought in the Greek civil war. Both this old man and his wife were a sweet couple in their late 80s or early 90s, still looking completely in love with each other. They sat and chatted to me, even though I was an outsider with slow, ponderous, Greek. They looked at me with patient, kind faces as I spoke. But when I asked them about the war back in Greece, they didn't really want to talk about this at all.

"Ah, our eyes have seen such things..." said the old woman. And she held my hand tight and kissed it, as if to say 'that's enough. No more.'

In the 1980s Greece experienced great changes in their society. The socialist Prime Minister Andreas Papandreou came into power and the country altered radically. One of the changes was that those who had fought for the Communists in the civil war were finally pardoned and were allowed to come back into Greece. It was then that the Beloiannisz village really changed. Hundreds of Greeks left the village, their empty houses taken by the Hungarians.

We headed back towards Budapest in the dark that had settled down over the Plains. One of the old women being ferried back to the capital told me that in for many of those who went back to Greece, it wasn't the dream return to their home country they'd always thought of.

"Hungary was not so bad in communist times," she said. "We could buy food, we had a good education, good health. But Greece… Greece was different in the '80s. Greece was in love with money then. Many of those who left Beloiannisz found it very hard to cope in Greece. Many came back. Disillusioned, disappointed. Beloiannisz was a good place to have lived…"

The old woman looked out of the car window. She breathed out and smiled sadly to herself in the reflection. Budapest started to emerge around us. The lights and the buildings of the city lay in shattered forms all along the wet pavements.

Back in Amaliada, down in the Peloponnese in Greece, Giannis the policeman had given up. He was sitting on the kerb watching the mob shout and push at the prime minister of the country. Giannis's officers' cap lay abandoned on the pavement next to him. He lit a cigarette and watched, defeated, smiling ruefully to himself, as the people in the crowd shouted out to Tsipras. One man lifted a thin-looking goat high in the air above the heads for Greece's premiere to inspect. Some in the crowd wanted photos, others wanted to curse and swear as loudly as they could. Two old men sat on an outside table and refused to acknowledge the commotion at all. They plopped olives into their mouths without a care as the crowds surged around them. Not allowing anything to ruin their midday ouzos.

Few here in Amaliada really know much about Nikos Belogiannis and his place in history. Fewer still know of Beloiannisz village back in Hungary. But the people of Beloiannisz village think of them often. And they think of Greece. For them it stays like a dream that they can almost hold.

Chapter 10
Here is Greece

"*Domates, patates, karekles...*"

The man's voice, thick with dust and heat and cigarettes, plagued me every morning. "Tomatoes, potatoes, chairs..." A bizarre collection of things to sell, but wherever you go in Greece there will be a broken-down old van, slowly doing the rounds on the tight Greek streets with this foul voice coming through a cheap tannoy wanting to sell you "*Domates, patates, karekles...*"

Greece is a country of sounds. All of them loud. Crossing Filellinon Street in Athens, the men driving their beaten-up cars that look like boxers' face, with the fronts like busted noses, thump at their horns. The car's horns are dead though, due to overuse, and emit just a wheezing squeak like an old dog whose voice has become a croak.

The real dogs, still with their voices very much intact, won't let you take a walk anywhere in Greece. Just come up with the idea of taking a stroll and they'll bark their livid complaints, sprinting out from alleyways with slavering jaws, comically rebounding at the end of their chains and barking even louder at the injustice. Howling dogs up on balconies, bad-tempered men down on the streets below shouting from the periptero kiosks. People gather together, talking loudly, just to reassure themselves, just to be sure that there's someone there. Greeks often seem to me like children afraid of the dark, always needing company. Old men with nothing left to say must sit side-by-side with their friend in the cafés every day.

Giristroula left me once for the weekend and I was enjoying the idea of a little time on my own. My mother-in-law called everyone she knew in Athens to come round to see me, fearful I would get lonely. Visitor after visitor. People I had never met before in my life, sitting on and on.

The idea of being on your own in Greece is a madness, almost a sin.

My mother-in-law had been released from Evangelismos hospital. For a long time it had been touch and go as she had lain there on the top floor, overlooking Athens at night with the national gardens plunged in darkness, the Parthenon lit-up but alone. The family kept vigil day after day, smoking furiously, faces haggard and grim. She was out now, and we were to take her to recuperate on the island of Lesbos.

The boat from Piraeus approached Lesbos in the early dawn light. The island on the horizon emerged and then changed shape as we got nearer, stretching and shifting like a cat waking itself up. We were heading to Lesbos as my parents-in-law's koubara from their wedding long ago, lived on the island in a red tower set all on its own on the Aegean seashore. Before we even got off the boat, we could hear the trees full of *tzitzikia*. The insects filling the air with their clicking songs, sounding like a thousand guiro instruments rubbed with two thousand sticks. They say that if the tzitzikia ever go quiet, Greece will fall. But then they also say that if you take Greece apart and all you are left with is just an olive tree, a vineyard and a boat, you can rebuild it again.

My mother-in-law spent her days slowly repairing herself on the veranda looking out to where the sea and sky met, towards the edge of Turkey's mainland and the Greek island of Chios. As she stirred her huge pans of food on the outside fire, Mirsini, the koubara, talked to me about how she was related to the great Greek poet Elytis, from this island. Lesbos was once prosperous but when the Turkish were routed in Greece, the trading markets and the money was cut off. Just like her island, Mirsini's family also lost their prestige and money along the way, and she now lived in this one timbered-room Ottoman tower. Her husband, Paraskevas, set off swimming into the sea every morning with his long hand-held trident to hunt for octopus. I watched him as he returned, flinging the octopus against the rocks in the shallows again and again to soften it for our lunch. We would sit on the terrace and drink ouzo – famous from this island, the very best you can find. Glass after glass would be drunk. *"To proto!"* Paraskevas would toast with each new glassful – "The first!" – as you are really not meant to count how many you sink.

Giristroula and I left her mother sat in her chair looking out at the water one hot afternoon as the wind got up and created a racing sea with hundreds of white waves breaking out beyond – *provatakia* the Greeks call these waves: little sheep. We went to explore the island. Lesbos is not built-up. From Olympus, its highest mountain, you can see only green hills. We walked through the smattering of villages, past a bus stop where no bus looked as if it had ever arrived and a goat was standing tied to the pole chewing at overgrowing weeds. A man with a taxi suddenly appeared and we flagged him down. The man drove us manically through the roads past the hills carpeted in olive trees, throwing the car through the bends. I reached for the sea belt.

"You don't have to do that," he chuckled. "Here is Greece! We do what we want… Do whatever you like!"

"Well, I would like to wear a seat belt…" I said.

"No," he snapped, putting his hand across my chest.

We got to the village of Eressos – Sappho's home. Sappho was the formidable poetess of ancient times, and supposed heroine of homosexual desire. Sapphic, Lesbian, words that come directly from this island. Women still gravitate to Eressos to be free in their sexuality. Open displays of lesbianism and the freedom to celebrate individuality are quite rare in Greece, but here the women all sat cross-armed, legs astride the chair, next to the old men in the cafés. I watched the men with their big yellowing moustaches playing backgammon, having escaped their wives for the afternoon, happily sitting side-by-side with the lesbians smoking cigars.

Giristroula and I swam out from the long stretch of sandy, orange-coloured, beach as the sun set. We were still swimming as the stars rose in the sky. As the moon started to shine brightly and the stars got shy, we hitched a lift in the back of an old pick-up van and made our slow way back home, round the huge bay of Kaloni that has eaten a deep eclipse into the island, giving Lesbos its odd shape. The island looking like an artist's palette.

There was a piled-up collection of life jackets on the beach in front of the old red tower. Mirsini told me how she would see the boats from Turkey, carrying refugees, out on the sea at night sailing towards Lesbos. They would land here, on her beach. Up on the road there would be men shining lights shouting for the boats to come their way. They would then take the motors off to sell. The refugees, staggered to be on land would rip off their life jackets, making their way up the pebbled shore, throwing them to the ground in relief to have made it. There hadn't been a landing for a few months on Mirsini's beach, but the jackets lay as reminders. Hundreds of red and yellow markers.

Giristroula and I travelled further down to the south of the island. Skala Sykamias is a pretty little fishing village, known first for its oddly named church Panagia Gorgona – the Virgin Mary As A Mermaid; then known for the tree that the famous author Myrivilis would sit and write underneath. Later the village gained notoriety for Demetra, an old gruff fisherman who found her real self later in life as she promenaded up and down the small fishing boat harbour in stockings and suspenders and full make-up. Again, rare to see in Greece. Newspaper men were even sent to report. More dramatically though, Skala Sykamias had recently become known throughout the world as one of the main landing places for the migrants fleeing Syria and the Middle East and Africa. Two thousand refugees landing every day. The lucky ones.

I went for a swim just outside the village. As I dried myself on the beach one resident walking past turned to talk to me.

"You know you've been swimming *stin thalassa me tis nekres psihes*?"

It took me a moment to translate this in my head – the sea of dead souls.

There was a chill feeling hanging over this village. The Greeks, being Greek, had many theories as to why the refugees kept coming. Turkey, Germany, the EU, they were sure *someone* was behind it.

"Tsipras came here," one man told me. "In the days before he came there were hundreds of boats. When he was here, not a single boat came across. Then, after he left, I counted 48 boats coming over. How did they know? You tell me that…"

The island was suffering. The camp at the small village of Moria outside Mytilene was at bursting point. We had driven past the camp the night before and seen the refugees spilling outside, walking in bunches down the unlit roads, sat listlessly on the grass. Boredom, frustration. Tents pitched beyond the camp walls as there was no more room inside. Men praying towards Mecca in the olive trees. The refugees were penned in these camps in Greece as Europe waited to decide what to do. Who to let through, who to send back. Which borders should be shut. Which, if any, countries will take some of these migrants. The residents of Lesbos couldn't work out what was happening, and couldn't understand what had happened to their island. But still this confusion and the sense of grievance that their lives here had been altered by uncaring outside world didn't stop them from helping – the hearts of Greeks often as open as the sea itself. The people of Lesbos were even nominated for the Nobel Peace Prize for their efforts rescuing the collapsed boats, pulling people out of the Aegean to safety, helping the weary female refugees and their children make their way up onto the shores and into Europe. But when three old ladies of Lesbos were told of their nomination, they had little time for it.

"What special am I doing? Wouldn't you do the same?" said the 86-year-old Maritsa Mavrapidou.

Fisherman Stratis Valiamos seemed stunned to be approached by reporters. "I'm out fishing, I can see people shouting for help. What should I do? Pretend I can't see? Pretend I can't hear?"

The whole of Greece had been affected by the migrants that had come to the country. There were many stories. The baker of Kos who woke up early every morning to make 200 extra pounds of bread to give away to the migrants. The men with less good intentions, circling Victoria Square in Athens with specious offers to smuggle the desperate away over the borders for cash. Men and money that will never be seen again.

A few years ago I stayed with Giristroula's cousin in Thessaloniki. Vasiliki went every day to the Lagadikia refugee camp outside the city. She played games and entertained the children there. She said it wasn't too bad, the containers where the refugees were housed were heated and the spirits of the people hadn't sunk too low. Now the camp had three times the amount of people as it should. The containers had been overtaken by hundreds and hundreds of rain-soaked tents. Vasiliki had gone every day to the camp full of purpose and hope. I sat with her one day on a bus as she went to work at the camp. We sat amongst the Thessalonikian commuters with Vasiliki dressed as a clown with full make-up and curly red wig. But the last time I spoke to her she had lost her positivity, and her hope.

"I've seen hundreds and hundreds of people arrive. They have nowhere to go, we are their very last resource. Where does the money go for them? *Ta troi i marmaga?* – It falls in the black hole? Between the EU and Greece? Or between Greece and the camp? I don't know. These people have fled war. They just can't believe that this is how Europe is receiving them…"

Arion of Lesbos, the greatest lyra player of classical times, once threw himself from a ship into this sea I looked at from Skala Sykamias. He threw himself into the waters to avoid capture by pirates and is seen as a hero, a great example of the contempt for danger the Greeks have. His courage was rewarded by the gods as he was rescued by a school of dolphins. Arion and the dolphins have now been put in the sky as stars. There are no dolphins for the refugees though.

The people of Skala Sykamias were good, but they were tired. I talked to a woman as I walked on the dusty road just outside the village on the way to Molyvos.

"How would you like it?" she said to me. "How would you like it if a Muslim man gets off the boat and straight away tells your daughter to cover up, to not wear her bikini because he has never seen a girl's skin before..? How would you like it if your son was swimming in the sea and a corpse washed up on the beach..? How would you like to live here?"

I thought of the small village. The church and the tree and Demetra the ex-fisherman sashaying by. The men mending their nets on the harbour wall. The tranquil beauty which was all I had seen. I couldn't answer her.

Theophilos's house is in the port capital of Lesbos, Mytilene. Theophilos Hatzimihail was a primitive painter, from around the end of the 19th century. He travelled around Greece painting themes from ancient Greece, or from the war of independence, or merely from everyday Greek life. Completely unrecognised and unheralded in his lifetime, he lived an itinerant life in poverty painting his scenes on the walls of coffee shops and tavernas for a few scraps of food. I think he was a genius. Giristroula and I walked around his house in solemn silence. His brilliant naïve art paintings and the black and white photographs of Theophilos himself were up on the walls. Pictures of Theophilos in his ancient tsolias soldiers garb of skirt and fez and sword, surrounded by local children half laughing, half in love with this incredible child-like man. A living sculpture. A brilliant symbol of Greece.

Giristroula and I sailed away from Mytilene. Into the sea where Orpheus's head had washed up after his death at the hands of the Thrace women, who had torn him to pieces and thrown him into the River Evros. They say his head was still singing when it landed on the shore. The water was calm as our boat left, just a few dark waves hissing at the keel. There was no sign of Thessalonike, the sister of Alexander the Great. Legend has it that Thessalonike haunts the waters all around Greece as a fearsome mermaid. She is grief stricken at her brother's death, especially as she once carried a cup of water from the Fountain of Immortality but spilt it before she could give Alexander a sip. She appears and shrieks at sailors passing by on the sea. "*Zei o vasilias Alexandros?*" – Is King Alexander alive? To appease the guilt-racked Thessalonike, you *must* reply "*Zei keh vasilevei!*" – He is alive and he reigns! Otherwise she will raise the winds and the waters and your boat will be lost.

We sailed the Aegean. Through the islands, scattered like gems across the sea.

Lemnos to the north. An island of fierce femininity in classical times. The women here massacred all their menfolk out of loyalty to the god Hephaestus. Hephaestus must be my favourite of the gods: lame, clumsy and ugly, mocked by the other gods, frequently picked up by the foot and contemptuously tossed out of Olympus by Zeus, usually landing on the island of Lemnos. Here is a god at last you can identify with. But he was also the god of fire and the forger of metals, making golden palaces and beautiful jewellery. Better than being the god of war, I'd say. He was, quite implausibly, married to Aphrodite the goddess of erotic love and beauty.

"I pray Aphrodite…" begins one of Sappho's poems "…Don't break my spirit with heartache."

Of course Aphrodite was at it like a randy old goat with whoever she could get hold of. She would often take the war-god Ares as her lover. When Hephaestus caught wind of these goings on, he fashioned a gold-spun net above their marriage bed. One day, while Hephaestus pretended to be away on business on his favourite island of Lemnos, Aphrodite took Ares to her bed. During their passions the net descended catching them together. Hephaestus called all the other gods to witness the humiliation of the naked, helpless, pair. The gods gathered around the bed pointing and laughing – though Hermes whispered to Apollo how he'd happily suffer a far greater penalty for just one night with Aphrodite. The women of Lemnos cheered for Hephaestus and so, in retaliation, Aphrodite afflicted them all with a terrible odour. A repugnant smell that meant their husbands wouldn't go near them, only having sex with slave girls brought over from Thrace. So, in return, the Lemnos women slaughtered every man and boy on the island, leaving the land empty aside from the smelly women.

Our landlady back in Athens was from Lemnos. The offensive smell appears to have cleared up.

Giristroula and I sailed past Tinos, with its white-washed villages reflecting the blinding light of the sun. The holiest of Greece's ikons is housed on this island. Visitors climb the long stone hill up from the port to the Church of Panagia Evangelistrias on their knees in veneration. The ikon has great healing powers and women crawl on their grazed hands and raw knees to reach it to pray for a sick husband or a suffering child. You see them climbing inch by painful inch up the road, with impatient husbands standing next to them, pacing alongside, like a farmer taking his donkey out for a walk.

Tinos was the island longest in the Venetians' possession, so it has the largest Catholic population in Greece. The people dividing themselves, even in the present day: this village Orthodox, this village Catholics.

The clash between the logic of ancient Greece and the faith of Greece's Orthodoxy always puzzled me. The ancients believed you should question everything, but doesn't the church say you should only follow? You see it in the buildings too: the lightness and rationality of the ancient temples, the churches dark and smoky and oppressive. These churches have often been built on exactly the same spot where a temple once stood, and Greeks also feel they are made of both these conflicting foundations. They have the blood and spirit of the ancients *and* the Orthodoxy inside them. I can never really see how they square the circle.

Tinos was the home of the god of wind, Aeolus and his father Poseidon. Our ship's captain looked very closely at the waters as we passed by, nervous to detect even the slightest rippling on the waters. Giristroula and I didn't have the money for a cabin. We slept each night out on the deck, the sea running just below us, breeding and breaking in threshing foam. We were woken in the morning by a flare of sun running over our faces. Back in the early 19th century it was Greek travellers out on these waters that first saw how the outer world had a love for ancient Greece. It was only after Greek merchants visited France, Britain, Germany that they became aware, with a shock, of the hold which the language and civilisation of ancient Greece had over the minds of their European contemporaries. How they were the heirs to a heritage that was revered throughout the civilised world. This national consciousness grew quickly, as did the Greek rising resentment of continued Ottoman rule.

Patmos passed on the starboard side, looking as though it didn't have a splash of green on it. God spoke to St John through a hole in a cave on Patmos, with John writing down all the proclamations in his Book of Revelations: the predicted barbarian invasions, the downpours of rocks and blocks of ice, the balls of fire, the explosion of the moon. We chugged on and on over endless sea before we finally put in at Rhodes.

Rhodes Old Town was depressing. A magnificent ensemble of medieval architecture, but spoilt. Spoilt by Mussolini, who thought the fascist Italians were the inheritors to the Knights of Jerusalem, who had reigned this island in the Middle Ages, and so he had reconstructed a film-set Palace of the Grand Masters that now gets touted as the great tourist spot of Rhodes. The old town is spoilt by the businesses hawking for tourist loose change: the tavernas and nauseating gift shops wedged under the Streets of the Knights. The Greeks might have been surprised and suddenly proud of their ancient roots when they were told how much they meant to the outer-world; they might maintain today they have a mistrust of Western ways, but they certainly took Western materialism closely to their hearts. Becoming intoxicated with the tacky trappings of success, it resulted in the terrible buildings from the 1960s onwards; the rich and the middle classes' lack of taste; the bars and the restaurants built since the monied '80s and '90s, all gaudy and grotesque. Greece's recent struggles meant that some of the vulgar displays have been arrested – you don't see as much the men who used to pay a fortune for endless flowers to throw in great piles at warbling torch singers up on the tables every night, the terrible plate smashing, the braggadocio of showing how little money mattered. But bad taste was still rife in Greece.

Rhodes Old Town heaved, so we crossed over the broad moat surrounding the city walls and hitched a lift around the island. Two thumbed lifts got us to Lindos and we slept the night on the beach under the acropolis perched on the rock cliff. In the morning as the sun left the waters of the east, we swam in St Paul's bay with the ruins high above us: white stone columns, standing like the bleached bones of an ancient empire; blue sea and sky; the day building up with a hammer of heat. We cadged another lift from a young woman with a dark, powerful face. Her name was Sevin. Her family were from Turkey.

"Ah, if you can call them family. They all live over there..." she waved a hand out towards the sea. "In Marmaris. They only come to see me when they want a holiday."

As Rhodes was under control of the Italians when the exchange of population occurred between Greece and Turkey, the ethnic Turks in Rhodes were not affected. So now there are nearly 4,000 people with Turkish roots on the island. Although, who in Greece can say they don't have a heavy Turkish influence in them anyway? After 500 years of Turkish rule, the DNA, the cuisine, the types of entertainments, the look and the dress... Of course, I had learnt quickly not to air my opinions to the people who shout about "pure Greekness." When I travelled in northern Greece I met a man who didn't believe there was *any* Turkish or Slavic influence in Greece at all. Like a dog on a chain, he was spoiling for a fight between the countries.

"We're ready for Turkey this time. Not like what happened in Cyprus... We'll get them this time. Oh-ho, you better believe we're ready..." he clumped his fist into his hand in happy anticipation.

It was that sort of grind of a conversation. The know-all, speaking for Greece as a whole. The prickly sensitivity to any perceived insults, waiting on a hair-trigger for me to suggest I didn't agree. This man also showed the strong regional loyalty I'd noticed many Greeks have. I talked to him about the Peloponnese.

"Bastards," he said before I'd even finished.

"I'm sorry?"

"Peloponnese bastards" he repeated.

I told him my wife was from the Peloponnese.

"All the Peloponnesians were raped by Egyptians." He said this simply, as if it was an unequivocal fact.

The only other place, other than northern Greece, he seemed to like was Italy.

"Ah the Italians," he said. "They are like us. '*Una fatsa, una ratsa!*' – that's what we say: one face, one race!"

I told him I'd only ever heard Greeks say this phrase, never actually the Italians. The man thought about this for a while.

"Bastards," he said.

"Italians love only themselves. Only themselves." He sniffed in the air. "Bastards."

Sevin, back in Rhodes, drove us through the centre of the island over towards the east coast. The car chewing its way along the road, with unnatural-looking trees planted on the hills all around us, as we crossed Rhodes's belly.

"I didn't like the stupid Greek culture when I was young," Sevin said. "I didn't like all the dancing on the tables. I'm shy. I believe in respect."

She told us she wanted to marry a Cretan or someone from Thessaloniki.

"Why's that?" I asked.

"I want to be told what to do. I want a dictator. I want a Hodja…"

Sevin dropped us at the bottom of a hill.

"The Filerimos Cross is up there," she said, nodding up the thick tree-lined climb.

She smiled at us. "You should go… You go up two, you come down three…" she said, cryptically.

Giristroula and I clambered up to the top of the hill, wondering what she meant. A huge cross and a tiny broken church sat at the top. An old woman was at the altar, lighting a candle.

"Ah you've come to the cross, eh? You are looking for the Madonna to help you with a child, eh? Light a candle, she'll help you…"

We fled back down the hillside again. Back down towards Rhodes port.

We should have sailed out between the legs of the Colossus but the great sun-god had a very short life, standing over the sea here for just fifty years. When it crashed to the ground the Rhodites didn't dare touch it so as not to displease the gods. It was a Turk who finally collected all the gold and metal nearly a thousand years later and sold it off. The grim-humour story is that Rhodes got back its Colossus during the attacks by the Ottoman fleets in the form of cannonballs. Giristroula and I sailed even further east. Lumbering underneath the southern coast of Turkey, with its bare tall mountains, past the deserted rocky island of Ro where Despina Achladioti had lived. Despina Achladioti – the Lady of Ro – and her husband moved to this inhospitable rock, just 800 metres off the Turkish coast at around the time of World War One. No one could understand why. Despina's husband died in 1940 and for the next 42 years, the Lady of Ro lived on her own on the island and every day, in every sort of weather, she would raise and lower the Greek flag. While Greece and the neighbouring islands were evacuated and occupied by the Germans, the Lady of Ro continued with her loan ritual of flying the Greek flag on her completely deserted islet. Greek pride and resistance. When she died in 1982, Despina was buried with full military honours. The island is left deserted again.

Giristroula and I landed on the very final flung island of Greece. Kastelorizo. A military gunship sat in the harbour. It rumbled and growled all day and night, like a small wary dog, ready for any sudden movements by Turkey across the water. We walked along the quayside. I'd heard people talk about Kastelorizo and how sorry they were for the people who have to live here. '*Akritiko*' people say of this island – far away and forgotten. But actually Kastelorizo was doing very well for itself. The cafés were prosperous and full, the taverna owners busy and rich. Once upon a time there were 10,000 people living on Kastelorizo, now there are about 400 residents. Many people emigrated to Australia – 'Kazzies' they call themselves over there. Australian accents rang out as we passed tavernas with people who'd come back to visit the island they descend from.

The harbour has big sea turtles that float languidly by, but the tourists have fed them with titbits from their plates and now the turtles have got a taste for meat. A swim across the bay is fraught with danger as you run the gauntlet of a snapper going for you.

Giristroula and I swam nervously around the island, the sea crystal clear, our shadows stalking us far below. Sea caves and grottos bluer and more beautiful than Capri. Back in April 2010, Kastelorizo was chosen by the prime minister Giorgos Papandreou to declare that Greece was bankrupt. He stood by the achingly pretty harbour, next to the sparkling waters and told the nation down the television camera that they had all eaten the money together.

"Giorgos Malaka we call him," said one of the taverna owners as we sat and drank a souma – a tsipouro with a taste of mastiha, popular in the islands in this part of Greece.

"When a prime minister comes to your island, you think he's going to improve the island, not say we've all gone bankrupt... Then the malaka went for a swim!"

Giristroula and I climbed the rock-strewn hills of Kastelorizo. From the high peaks you can see the chain of islets in the sea running from here to Turkey, like a rope barrier saying 'this is the end of the line – no more Greece beyond.' Coming back down the side of the hill above the island's stone police station, I saw a man urinating against the side of the wall. This was Mohammed. I stopped and chatted to him for a while. Mohammed and his friend Ahmed had come from Syria. They had been waiting here for two weeks to be allowed to take a boat to the mainland. The island's policeman had allowed them to sleep in the cell at night. Mohammed told me he had previously walked all the way from Edirne, on the Turkish border, to Thessaloniki. But he had been sent back to Turkey. He didn't know what to do then. He knew Lesbos was a bad place to end up, that the camps were at bursting point. He looked on Google maps and saw how close Kastelorizo was to Greece.

"No one knows this place," Mohammed said to me. "But it looked so much closer."

"How did you get over?" I asked.

"Swam," he said. "It took all night. I had to keep going under the water. Waiting for the police boats to go. I had one bag round my neck."

"You're a good swimmer then?" I said.

"No. I hadn't really swum before! While I was waiting in Turkey I stayed in the town of Demre and every day I went to the sea and I practised swimming. I swam, and the next day I swam a bit further. Then the next day I practised swimming a bit further. I swam for one hour, then the next day two hours, then the next day three hours. When I could do two kilometres, I knew I could swim over the sea to here."

Mohammed and Ahmed wanted to go to Sweden. Ahmed had a brother there. Over the next few days as Giristroula and I sat around Kastelorizo doing nothing, bathing like fat seals in the sun on the harbour front, I saw both of them had managed to get themselves some work while they waited to be told if they could leave this tiny island. An amazingly bad tempered café owner barked orders at Ahmed as he limped with a bad leg, lugging crates of empty bottles. Mohammed would wrestle and fight with the umbrellas on the beachfront, folding them up and putting them away each evening.

On these evenings I would stand on the rocky hills, at the end of Greece, and watch the sun dying into the sea. I would lose myself in thought. My country was leaving Europe. I wondered if I would be allowed to stay here. Nothing was ever said by governments. Politicians had decided it was best just to leave people dangling. Would I need to get citizenship in Greece? And then a nagging thought hit me. Something which had been gnawing inside me for a while but which I had tried to ignore... Was I even really so sure I wanted to stay in Greece anyway? It came as a shock to even allow myself to think it. But I had to wonder where I was going in this world.

I had fallen into the classic Greek mess of living in a house on top of my wife's parents. Trapped in that oppressive, loud, emotional theatre of home life, as all Greek parents seem to want for their children. I tried each day to make my way through Greek life, with its huge capacity for generosity and kindness set against its huge capacity for suspicion and anger. The pride and the reluctance to admit offence or ever apologise. The constant struggle. Men and women wearing faces of either intense bad luck or of greedy pleasure, like masks from some ancient tragedy.

As I watched a sunset like stained glass shattering into the sea, I knew I needed the beauty of Greece, the air and the light that always seems as if it has just been washed clean, but could I ever really be accepted here? But then, did it matter? I was free in Greece. Why would I want to be back in Britain? I knew as soon as I left, I would be desperate to return.

Giristroula walked up the hill and joined me in the last of the day's light. I wanted to tell her I was being stupid, that I knew I should stay. Before I could speak, she looked up at me.

"Well you really *have* to stay," Giristroula said, with a bite of her lip. "The Panayia of Filerimos seems to have worked her magic. *Yiname tris tora…*"

I ran this around my head for a moment and then looked at her quickly.

"There's three of us?"

Giristroula took my hand and smiled at me.

"*Ehis rizosi tora pia stin Ellada…*" – Your roots are deep in Greece now…

We turned and looked out at the sea together. The sky and the water had turned dark, but all I could see was colour. And I realised, inside I was singing.

Printed in Great Britain
by Amazon